THE
ENVIRONMENTAL
CRISIS

Opposing Viewpoints

Additional Books in the Opposing Viewpoints Series:

THE ENVIRONMENTAL CRISIS

Opposing Viewpoints

David L. Bender and Bruno Leone, *Series Editors*

Julie S. Bach & Lynn Hall, *Book Editors*

OPPOSING VIEWPOINTS SERIES ®

Greenhaven Press   577 Shoreview Park Road   St. Paul, Minnesota 55126

Library of Congress Cataloging-in-Publication Data

The Environmental Crisis—opposing viewpoints

(Opposing viewpoints series)
Bibliography: p.
Includes index.
1. Environmental policy—United States. I. Hall, Lynn, 1949- . II. Bach, Julie S., 1963-
III. Series.
HC110.E5E49835 1986 363.7′058′0973 86-19565
ISBN 0-89908-391-8
ISBN 0-89908-366-8 (pbk.)

"Congress shall make no law... abridging the freedom of speech, or of the press."

First Amendment to the US Constitution

The basic foundation of our democracy is the first amendment guarantee of freedom of expression. The *Opposing Viewpoints Series* is dedicated to the concept of this basic freedom and the idea that it is more important to practice it than to enshrine it.

Contents

Why Consider Opposing Viewpoints?

"It is better to debate a question without settling it than to settle a question without debating it."

Joseph Joubert (1754-1824)

The Importance of Examining Opposing Viewpoints

The purpose of the Opposing Viewpoints Series, and this book in particular, is to present balanced, and often difficult to find, opposing points of view on complex and sensitive issues.

Probably the best way to become informed is to analyze the positions of those who are regarded as experts and well studied on issues. It is important to consider every variety of opinion in an attempt to determine the truth. Opinions from the mainstream of society should be examined. But also important are opinions that are considered radical, reactionary, or minority as well as those stigmatized by some other uncomplimentary label. An important lesson of history is the eventual acceptance of many unpopular and even despised opinions. The ideas of Socrates, Jesus, and Galileo are good examples of this.

Readers will approach this book with their own opinions on the issues debated within it. However, to have a good grasp of one's own viewpoint, it is necessary to understand the arguments of those with whom one disagrees. It can be said that those who do not completely understand their adversary's point of view do not fully understand their own.

A persuasive case for considering opposing viewpoints has been presented by John Stuart Mill in his work *On Liberty*. When examining controversial issues it may be helpful to reflect on this suggestion:

> The only way in which a human being can make some approach to knowing the whole of a subject, is by hearing what can be said about it by persons of every variety of opinion, and studying all modes in which it can be looked at by every character of mind. No wise man ever acquired his wisdom in any mode but this.

Analyzing Sources of Information

The Opposing Viewpoints Series includes diverse materials taken from magazines, journals, books, and newspapers, as well as statements and position papers from a wide range of individuals, organizations and governments. This broad spectrum of sources helps to develop patterns of thinking which are open to the consideration of a variety of opinions.

Pitfalls To Avoid

A pitfall to avoid in considering opposing points of view is that of regarding one's own opinion as being common sense and the most rational stance and the point of view of others as being only opinion and naturally wrong. It may be that another's opinion is correct and one's own is in error.

Another pitfall to avoid is that of closing one's mind to the opinions of those with whom one disagrees. The best way to approach a dialogue is to make one's primary purpose that of understanding the mind and arguments of the other person and not that of enlightening him or her with one's own solutions. More can be learned by listening than speaking.

It is my hope that after reading this book the reader will have a deeper understanding of the issues debated and will appreciate the complexity of even seemingly simple issues on which good and honest people disagree. This awareness is particularly important in a democratic society such as ours where people enter into public debate to determine the common good. Those with whom one disagrees should not necessarily be regarded as enemies, but perhaps simply as people who suggest different paths to a common goal.

Developing Basic Reading and Thinking Skills

In this book, carefully edited opposing viewpoints are purposely placed back to back to create a running debate; each viewpoint is preceded by a short quotation that best expresses the author's main argument. This format instantly plunges the reader into the midst of a controversial issue and greatly aids that reader in mastering the basic skill of recognizing an author's point of view.

A number of basic skills for critical thinking are practiced in the activities that appear throughout the books in the series. Some of the skills are:

Evaluating Sources of Information   The ability to choose from among alternative sources the most reliable and accurate source in relation to a given subject.

Separating Fact from Opinion   The ability to make the basic distinction between factual statements (those that can be demonstrated or verified empirically) and statements of opinion (those that are beliefs or attitudes that cannot be proved).

Identifying Stereotypes   The ability to identify oversimplified, exaggerated descriptions (favorable or unfavorable) about people and insulting statements about racial, religious or national groups, based upon misinformation or lack of information.

Recognizing Ethnocentrism   The ability to recognize attitudes or opinions that express the view that one's own race, culture, or group is inherently superior, or those attitudes that judge another culture or group in terms of one's own.

It is important to consider opposing viewpoints and equally important to be able to critically analyze those viewpoints. The activities in this book are designed to help the reader master these thinking skills. Statements are taken from the book's viewpoints and the reader is asked to analyze them. This technique aids the reader in developing skills that not only can be applied to the viewpoints in this book, but also to situations where opinionated spokespersons comment on controversial issues. Although the activities are helpful to the solitary reader, they are most useful when the reader can benefit from the interaction of group discussion.

Using this book and others in the series should help readers develop basic reading and thinking skills. These skills should improve the reader's ability to understand what they read. Readers should be better able to separate fact from opinion, substance from rhetoric and become better consumers of information in our media-centered culture.

This volume of the Opposing Viewpoints Series does not advocate a particular point of view. Quite the contrary! The very nature of the book leaves it to the reader to formulate the opinions he or she finds most suitable. My purpose as publisher is to see that this is made possible by offering a wide range of viewpoints which are fairly presented.

David L. Bender
Publisher

It is important to consider opposing viewpoints and it is important to be able to critically analyze these viewpoints. The features in this book are designed to help readers master these thinking skills. Statements are taken from the books whose point and the reader is asked to analyze them. This technique aids the reader in developing skills that not only can be applied to points in this book, but also to situations where opinionated spokespersons try to convey a biased message. All issues that are presented are helpful to the serious reader; they are more useful if the reader can learn from the experience of many different authors.

Using the basic skills in the series should help students develop basic reading and thinking skills. There is no shortcut to prove the reader's ability to understand what they read. Readers should be able to separate truth from opinion, understand fact and opinion, differentiate original information in order to draw accurate conclusions.

This volume of the Opposing Viewpoints Series does not tackle a particular point of view. Quite the contrary. The very purpose of the book leaves it to the reader to formulate his or her own ideas and opinions. With a representative view that this is made possible by offering a wide range of viewpoints which are being presented.

David L. Bender
Publisher

Introduction

"The existence of technologies that are both useful and potentially harmful raises difficult questions."

Americans are avid consumers. Homes, offices, entertainment complexes, and factories use almost 74 quadrillion British thermal units (*Btu*) of energy a year. An average American home uses a thousand kilowatt hours per month. To satisfy this appetite for energy, power companies produce over 2 trillion kilowatt hours of electricity a year using coal, natural gas, water, and nuclear power. Over 72 million households use motorized vehicles and consume 124 billion gallons of gas a year. More than 5 billion barrels of petroleum are imported daily. Farmers produce millions of metric tons of wheat, corn, and other produce. Much of it is exported for profit; some of it feeds livestock that provides the 143 pounds of meat the average American consumes every year. These astronomical figures indicate an undeniable dependency on modern technology—and indirectly, natural resources.

The Environmental Crisis: Opposing Viewpoints explores the debate over the impact human beings have had on the environment and how to balance present human needs against the environment's future. The debate becomes more than academic as environmental issues figure ever more seriously in the most basic concerns of human beings: jobs, health, family, and life. Public concern runs especially high when the frightening effects of environmental disasters, contaminated water supplies, and rising cancer rates are publicized. While catastrophes like those at Three Mile Island, Love Canal, Bhopal, and Chernobyl are rare, their devastating effects demonstrate how dangerous the advancements of technology can be. In each tragedy entire communities were threatened by an industry that had provided jobs or by a technology that had improved standards of living. The existence of technologies that are both useful and potentially harmful raises difficult questions. Should certain technologies, for example, nuclear power, be abandoned, or should additional dollars be spent to make those technologies safer?

If, indeed, it is possible to make technology safer, then questions of who, how, and when naturally follow. Who should allot funds for environmental safety measures, government or the private sector? When should measures be taken to avoid the greenhouse effect, before or after scientists have proven its inevitability? Which is more important, providing industrial jobs for workers, or regulating pollution?

The issues debated in this volume include: Is There an Environmental Crisis? Should Corporations Be Held Responsible for Environmental Disasters? Have Pollution Regulations Improved the Environment? Is Nuclear Power an Acceptable Risk? How Dangerous Are Toxic Wastes? and How Harmful Is Acid Rain? These questions, hotly contested by policymakers, scientists, corporate executives, leading environmentalists, and researchers, represent some of the most urgent in the environmental debate.

Is There an Environmental Crisis?

**THE
ENVIRONMENTAL
CRISIS**

"The world is confronted by an environmental crisis of global proportions."

There Is an Environmental Crisis

Lynton Keith Caldwell

Lynton Keith Caldwell is the director of the Advanced Studies in Science, Technology, and Public Policy Program; the Arthur F. Bentley Professor of Political Science; and a professor of Public and Environmental Affairs at Indiana University. A consultant to many prominent national and international organizations, Dr. Caldwell is a writer and lecturer on environmental issues. In the following viewpoint he describes a growing worldwide environmental awareness that has raised difficult questions about how to safeguard natural resources. Dr. Caldwell addresses some of those difficult questions. He believes the global environmental crisis should and can be solved by governments willing to cooperate.

As you read, consider the following questions:

1. On what evidence does the author base his conclusion that there is an environmental crisis?
2. Why, according to the author, is the position taken by the United States in world environmental affairs important?
3. What critical environmental issues does the author address?

Excerpted from *US Interests and the Global Environment,* Occasional Paper 35 by Lynton Keith Caldwell, published in February 1985. Complete text available from the Stanley Foundation 420 East Third Street, Muscatine, IA 52761.

Since the mid-1960s public awareness of serious maladjustments between people and their environment has been growing. A worldwide environmental movement has emerged and apprehensions have been aroused—reinforced by studies, conferences, and reports which investigate threatening environmental developments, analyze their causes, and propose remedial action. Scientists have taken leading roles in these inquiries, many of which have been sponsored by governments as well as by nongovernmental and international organizations. This new environmental awareness has posed difficult policy problems. Scientific evidence and public concern have caused governments to address problems for which they have had little previous experience and for which legal and technical solutions have not been readily available. President John F. Kennedy proposed a new course for US policy when he wrote in the introduction to Stewart Udall's book *The Quiet Crisis* (1963):

> The crisis may be quiet, but it is urgent. . . . we must expand the concept of conservation to meet the imperious problems of the new age. We must develop new instruments of foresight and protection and nurture in order to recover the relationship between man and nature and to make sure that the national estate we pass on to our multiplying descendants is green and flourishing. . . .

The Weight of Evidence

The weight of evidence and opinion since the early 1970s has demonstrably grown toward recognition that the world is confronted by an environmental crisis of global proportions. Beginning in the technoscientifically advanced countries and among better informed individuals, awareness of environmental problems has spread throughout the world, gaining an unforeseen strength in many developing or Third World countries. The mutual need of nations for cooperation in environmental protection measures has been affirmed through new international arrangements, organizations, and agreements backed by national statutory law. New nongovernmental environmental organizations have emerged in nearly every country where voluntary citizen action is permitted. . . .

Much has been accomplished within a relatively short time, and yet as more has been learned about the human impact upon the earth, the more critical the circumstances appear to be. Collectively the nations have the knowledge and technical capability needed to overcome their environmental problems. The crisis is one of choice—of timely and appropriate action to be taken before environmental losses become irretrievable or environmental damage irremediable. Because this crisis occurs within a world of independent yet interdependent nations, the role played by the stronger among them inevitably impacts upon the effectiveness

Paul Conrad, © 1986, *Los Angeles Times*. Reprinted with permission Los Angeles Times Syndicate.

of the whole. Thus the position taken by the United States in world environmental affairs assumes an importance transcending its political boundaries. . . .

A Gloomy Picture

Beginning with Jay Forrester's *World Dynamics* (1971), more explicitly in the studies on *The Limits to Growth* (1972) and *Mankind at the Turning Point* (1974) sponsored by the Club of Rome, and followed by at least six additional global systems models leading to the US *Global 2000 Report* (1980), the literate world received a picture of its present ecological circumstances with prognoses of its possible futures. In a letter of transmittal to the president, the *Global 2000 Report* summarized its findings:

> Environmental, resource, and population stresses are intensifying and will increasingly determine the quality of human life on our planet. These stresses are already severe enough to deny many millions of people basic needs for food, shelter, health, and jobs, or any hope for betterment. At the same time, the earth's carrying capacity—the ability of biological systems to provide resources for human needs—is eroding. The trends reflected in the Global 2000 Study suggest strongly a progressive degradation and impoverishment of the earth's natural resource base.

> If these trends are to be altered and the problems diminished, vigorous, determined new initiatives will be required worldwide to meet human needs while protecting and restoring the earth's capacity to support life. Basic natural resources—farmlands, fisheries, forests, minerals, energy, air, and water—must be conserved and better managed. Changes in public policy are needed around the world before problems worsen and options for effective action are reduced.

These conclusions, and those of comparable studies stirred controversy and stimulated conferences and research efforts. Although widely rejected as prophecies of gloom and doom, they have nonetheless changed the thinking of many people regarding the responsibilities of government in relation to the world's environment.

Reports of the Crisis

No less significant have been the reports of scientific investigators regarding specific environmental effects and trends. National and international scientific studies have reported findings regarding sulphur dioxide, carbon dioxide, and particulates (for example, dust) in the atmosphere. Other studies have reported the spread of toxic substances in the environment, especially through water and food chains—ending in humans. Reports on environmental factors in health, disability, and death, especially from the World Health Organization (WHO), have contributed to public apprehension. From these and other publications from many different sources, a growing consensus has emerged regarding the reality of a global environmental crisis. The concept of the biosphere as the sum total of all planetary systems, almost unknown a generation ago, is now commonplace in environment-related international documents and agreements, and is gaining currency among the general public.

A series of global environmental issues have now been identified as critical to human welfare. They are global because their effects, and often their causes, are not contained by national or even continental boundaries. However localized their immediate consequences may be, their effects ramifying in one form or another—economic and demographic as well as ecologic—are ultimately felt, however indirectly, throughout the biosphere. . . .

There are many ways of categorizing environmental problems and the policy issues that follow from them. Any list of critical environmental issues would include the following six. They are widely regarded as critical because the trends which have placed them on the agendas of scientific inquiry and public policy threaten human welfare over all or large areas of the earth and, unless reversed in the very near future, may result in irretrievable damage to planetary life-support systems. They are also critical because, although the need for remedial action is urgent, remedial means are presently either not available (that is, carbon dioxide in the atmosphere) or would require complex socioeconomic changes that even willing governments could not readily bring about (for example, tropical deforestation). Yet none of these trends are today beyond remedy if the will to reverse them can be mobilized.

Vulnerable Beauty

Floating down a portion of Rio Colorado in Utah on a rare month in spring, 22 years ago, a friend and I found ourselves passing through a world so beautiful it seemed and had to be—eternal.

Such perfection of being, we thought, these glens of sandstone could not possibly be changed. The philosopher and the theologians have agreed that the perfect is immutable—that which cannot alter and cannot ever be altered.

They were wrong. We were wrong. Glen Canyon was destroyed. Everything changes, and nothing is more vulnerable than the beautiful.

Edward Abbey, *Environmental Action Visions 1985.*

One further characteristic of these issues requires notice—none are compartmentalized; each issue interrelates with two or more of the others and with still more issues—ecologic and economic—not mentioned here. These interrelationships pose difficulties for policymaking because any solution to an issue-creating problem may have implications for other issues. For example, toxic contamination has become a critical issue throughout the world and its effects are found in air, water, soil, and food chains. Direct, short-range policies to eliminate toxicants in any single medium (that is through air pollution control) may merely drive the toxic material into other media (for example, from landfills to ground water).

What follows is a summary of the salient facts regarding six critical issues. . . . In each of these cases human behavior has disrupted the natural biogeochemical cycles of the biosphere thereby

which met in Rome in April 1981. This issue among others is now on the agendas of the Consultative Group for International Agricultural Research (CGIAR), which is associated with the World Bank, and of the International Board for Plant Genetic Resources on which CGIAR, FAO, and UNEP are represented. . . .

Tropical Deforestation

The rapid reduction of the tropical rain forest appears on every list of critical environmental issues. Its effects are global, first because the forests are believed to be major regenerators of atmospheric oxygen, second because loss of the forests is accompanied by loss of habitats and species with the resulting genetic impoverishments previously noted, and third because resulting damage to tropical soils through erosion, laterization (rock-like hardening), and loss of soil fertility impairs the life support base of people and other living things. . . .

Toxic Contamination/Hazardous Materials

The enormous ingenuity of the chemical industry has produced an unprecedented number of useful compounds during recent decades. This innovation, although widely beneficial, has created serious ecological problems, sometimes resulting from unforeseen side effects (as with DDT and PCBs), and more often from failure to adequately assess the risks involved in releasing new chemicals into the environment and in neglecting to take effective measures for their harmless disposal. Toxic contamination of air, water, soil, and biota was initially believed to be a problem largely confined to developed countries; but international trade, and the atmospheric and oceanic transport of toxicants, has spread the problem around the world. . . .

The foregoing discussion provides a selective sample of the environmental issues that have aroused worldwide concern and have caused governments to institute new forms of international cooperation in defense of their environments and of the biosphere.

"The environmental view is . . . dead wrong and damaging."

There Is Not an Environmental Crisis

Ben J. Wattenberg

Ben J. Wattenberg, a speech writer for former President Lyndon B. Johnson and former Vice President Hubert H. Humphrey, is a Senior Fellow at the American Enterprise Institute in Washington, DC, where he is co-editor of AEI's *Public Opinion* magazine. A nationally syndicated newspaper columnist and a radio commentator for CBS's "Spectrum," he has written several books, including *The Good News Is the Bad News Is Wrong,* from which this viewpoint is taken. Here he examines the environmentalists' argument that the quality of life is deteriorating. He believes that argument is false, saying that in reality the lives of most Americans have never been better. He attributes this higher standard of living to technological advances. The environmentalists, he concludes, are wrong to predict an environmental crisis, and do not understand the benefits of the technology they condemn.

As you read, consider the following questions:

1. Why, according to the author, has the bad news argument grown in popularity?
2. What are the five strands of the environmental argument, according to Mr. Wattenberg?
3. Why does Mr. Wattenberg believe that the environmental argument is "dead wrong and damaging"?

Ben J. Wattenberg, *The Good News Is the Bad News Is Wrong.* Copyright © 1984 by BJW, Inc. Reprinted by permission of Simon & Schuster, Inc.

If you visit American city,
You will find it very pretty.
Just two things of which you must beware:
Don't drink the water and don't breathe the air.

Chorus: Pollution, pollution—you can
use the latest toothpaste,
And then rinse your mouth with
industrial waste.

It may seem like only yesterday to the middle-aged, but that was sung, to a calypso beat, by satirist Tom Lehrer . . . in 1965. By then, the nation had already started grappling afresh with the altogether proper and age-old issue of "the quality of life."

If it seems cavalier to date the advent of a serious movement from a strumming guitar, then perhaps the . . . much publicized wave of concern about environmental degradation can be said to have been well begun with the publication of Rachel Carson's best-selling *Silent Spring* in 1962.

Carson maintained that chemicals, particularly pesticides, particularly DDT, remained in "the food chain," unbalanced the ecosystem, and caused grievous harm to plants, animals, and human beings. She was also making a more general point, which has taken on a life of its own: that modern life could be spinning out of control and that we'd better do something about it, and quickly.

Castle of Ideas

It is upon that central beam—the possibility of runaway modernism—that a great castle of ideas has been constructed during the last generation. It is a castle with many rooms. It is an argument with many strands.

I recall it here because "environmentalism," as the big argument has come to be called, has become one of the potent engines of popular thought and action in the world today. From the Clean Air Act to Love Canal, from Three Mile Island to dioxin at Times Beach, from carcinogens to ozone depletion, much of the argument concerns the sad effects of modern living on our health. But from that starting point it goes almost everywhere. From small Japanese cars in American garages to "Green" political parties in Europe, from OPEC gas lines to saving the whales, from the population explosion to the era of limits, from suburban sprawl to acid rain, the idea of environmentalism is omnipresent. In terms of specifics, the concept often yields programmatic guidance that is both correct and valuable. But as a comprehensive vision of our time—one that says the Quality of Life is eroding—the environmental view is, in my judgment, dead wrong and damaging.

The environmental notion that the Twentieth-Century-May-Be-Bad-For-Your-Health—and just plain bad—is one of the backdrops

25

against which this . . . is written. It is an idea that has grown in importance in large measure because, at its core, it is a bad news argument. Accordingly, it has attracted the red eye of the TV camera: Meltdown at Three Mile Island! Cancer at Love Canal! Mercury in your tuna fish! We're running out of oil!

The Bad News Is the Wrong News

And so, to properly put forth the case that we are moving ahead, not backward, that the bad news is often the wrong news, it is necessary to start out by remembering and recounting the twisting strands of the environmental argument.

First strand: *pollution.* From Carson's account of DDT in the food chain, the general idea of pollution spread broadly to include water pollution, air pollution, radiation (a most malign and insidious kind of pollution), and a host of specific sources such as mercury, toxic waste, oil spills, Kepone, and a list of carcinogens long enough to lead the evening news on any day that nothing else was happening, and even on some days when other things were happening. Indeed, there were some environmentalists who said that our entire economy could be best described as a new kind of GNP—a "Gross National Pollution."

Second strand: *consumerism.* If runaway modernism creates unhealthy pollution, it also creates unhealthy products, such as unsafe drugs and plastic fabrics and stepladders that collapse when you step on them. . . .

No Threat Exists

What if there is evidence that Americans have never been healthier, that with one major exception, the age-adjusted cancer death rate has been *declining* over the past fifty years; that air and water pollution account for not one known death in the United States today; that pesticides, to our best knowledge, are not contributing to ill health, but rather promoting good health; and that nuclear energy is safer than any other kind currently available? . . .

What if, instead of technology *threatening* us, it is offering us an opportunity for even *more* improvements in the quality of life?

Elizabeth Whelan, *Toxic Terror,* 1985.

Third strand of the bad-news quality-of-life argument: *the population explosion.* Unlike pollution and consumerism, this is not directly a proposition about health, although it ultimately leads there. After World War II, population growth rates soared. World population jumped from 2.5 billion in 1945 to 4.7 billion in 1983. Neo-Malthusians shuddered: we were told that famine, pestilence, ecocatastrophe, and war would follow the population explosion. Man the lifeboats! . . .

The idea of a population explosion blended easily with a fourth strand of the quality-of-life argument: *running out of resources.*

More people, obviously, use more resources. In 1972, using computer models, the Club of Rome published "The Limits to Growth." It was a work, seen to be seminal, that declared that the physical world within a hundred years would no longer be able to provide the resources necessary to maintain a high standard of living. (Only years later did the Club publicly retract and disown some of its findings and methodology.)

In 1973, the Arab states of OPEC embargoed oil exports to the United States. The ensuing dislocations caused high prices, spot shortages—and provided a rocketlike boost to the idea that our resources were disappearing. All this was intensified by nightly television news clips of less than even-tempered motorists, with odd-numbered license plates, seeking a fix at the pump.

And soon, also on television, the voice of the environmental pundits could be heard across the land, saying, "We live in an era of limits." Oil was limited, and so were other nonrenewable resources, such as natural gas, coal, strategic metals, and everyday metals too.

It wasn't only the nonrenewables; we were told there were problems with renewables too. There would be shortages of water, of farmland to produce our food—after all, it was said we could see with our own eyes that farmland was being paved over every day into suburban malls for as far as the eye could see.

All this too was laid at the doorstep of runaway, reckless modernism. An underresourced, overcrowded, polluted world would surely be one that imparted less "quality" to its inhabitants. That, of course, reverberated in media land: our echo system covers the ecosystem.

Effluent Americans

There is an aesthetic aspect of the quality-of-life argument as well. Strand five: *gluttony, antinatural materialism, ugliness.* Americans, said many in the environmental movement, consumed too much. They drove big gas-guzzling cars. They lived in big, detached, single-family houses, each with an energy-consuming air-conditioning plant. All this meant a still greater demand upon finite resources and still more pollution, and therefore a worsening quality of life. We were, said Paul Ehrlich, an "effluent society."

Moreover, and more deeply, it was also understood that America's concentration on material values was not just bad in terms of resources or pollution, it was its own punishment. All that materialism not only despoiled the air, it took us far away from nature and defiled our souls. Our children were hooked on quadrophonic rock 'n' roll and fast-food hamburgers. What kind of a

27

could we hope for? . . .

hen, a vast constellation of ideas pointing toward a single
ht: things are in a bad way. Our health is harmed. Our
rces are strained. Our lives are crass and ugly.

Bad news. And all of it reported, directly and indirectly, night
after night in living rooms across the nation as never before.

A Case for the Good News

Such, briefly, is the case. I sketch it here in perhaps harsh
strokes, with too few shades of gray. After all, no sane people are
antienvironmental; we are all for improving the quality of life.
No one proposes to swim in polluted waters; no one gobbles carcinogens just for the hell of it. Wise people know that at some
point, exponential population growth will, and should, stop. And
while there was much exaggeration, surely some of the alarm bells
that have sounded to point to real problems: asbestos can cause
cancer, Kepone did harm people, thalidomide has caused
deformed infants. There is much merit in the old argument, "better
safe than sorry." When dealing with nature, a modern industrial
society must mind its manners.

But that is not the point. The point is that much environmental
thinking in recent years has been directed toward the idea that
the overall quality of our lives was poor or deteriorating, and
would likely get worse.

The World Is Getting Better

If present trends continue, the world in 2000 will be *less crowded*
(though more populated), *less polluted, more stable ecologically,* and
less vulnerable to resource-supply disruption than the world we live
in now. Stresses involving population, resources, and environment
will be less in the future than now . . . The world's people will be *richer*
in most ways than they are today . . . The outlook for food and other
necessities of life will be *better* . . . life for most people on earth
will be *less precarious* economically than it is now.

Julian L. Simon and Herman Kahn, *The Resourceful Earth,* 1984.

Such a view is incorrect. . . . Moreover, such a mind-set is not
only wrong, it is probably harmful in its own right. . . . If we come
to believe the vision put forth by the Quality-of-Life movement
and trumpeted by the media, we may well diminish our quality
of life.

Can it be that environmentalism may be bad for the environment?

28

"There is a great deal wrong with the sort of environmentalism to which our nation has been subjected."

Environmentalists Have Not Improved the Environment

Robert W. Lee

Robert W. Lee, a former corporation president, is a contributing editor for *The Review of the News*, where his "From The Hopper" and "A Capital Report" columns appear regularly. In the following viewpoint he examines the role of environmentalism in America. He expresses doubt that environmentalists have helped improve the quality of the environment at all, saying that most of their energy has been ill spent on ineffective regulations. These regulations, he concludes, have cost the public far more than it has gained in a cleaner environment.

As you read, consider the following questions:

1. The author draws a distinction between two types of environmentalism. What, in his opinion, is wrong with the sort of environmentalism prevalent in the US?
2. What, according to the author, are some of the ways Americans have paid for environmental regulations?

Robert W. Lee, excerpted from, "Conservatives Consider the Crushing Cost of Environmental Extremism," *American Opinion,* October 1983. Reprinted with permission.

There is certainly nothing wrong with environmentalism, but there is a great deal wrong with the sort of "environmentalism" to which our nation has been subjected in recent years. It is one thing to strive to be good stewards of the land, air, and water through the application of sensible, cost-effective policies based on marketplace and common-law incentives for polluters to "clean up their act." It is quite another to impose on industry and individuals the sort of draconian, often counterproductive, schemes which have become a hallmark of federal intervention in the field of environmentalism since 1970.

There is substantial doubt whether federal policies have resulted in a net improvement in the quality of the national environment, but there is no question at all that they have led to a massive increase in the size and expense of government and its control of the private sector, while seriously encroaching on the personal freedom of individual Americans. Some observers believe such results were the primary objectives from the start, with scare stories about environment being cranked up as an excuse to achieve them. . . .

Blaming Private Enterprise

Gary Allen reported in *American Opinion* for May 1970, more than 13 years ago: "Through the use of highly emotional rhetoric, and by playing upon fears of impending social and environmental chaos, the Left is hoping to convert sincere and legitimate concern over the quality of our environment into acceptance of government control of that environment. . . . The objective is federal control of the environment in which we all must live." Which might explain why, no matter what the immediate ecological grievance has been, private property and individual enterprise have always been branded the culprits while more government was offered as the solution. Every new regulation has in some way controlled and manipulated one or more aspects of our social or economic life while decreasing our individual freedom. Gary Allen was, alas, right on target.

The average American has paid for all of this government regulation as a *taxpayer* (to finance the bureaucracy itself) and as a *consumer* (since the cost of regulations imposed by the bureaucracy boosted the price of nearly every commodity). In addition, there have been such less-obvious costs as those suffered when plans to build factories and other important projects were delayed or abandoned, along with the jobs they would have created, after government red tape made such endeavors unbearably frustrating and financially unrewarding.

While it is impossible to settle an exact figure for the total financial burden which American industry has suffered from over-zealous, often malicious, environmentalism during the past decade, the direct cost undoubtedly exceeds half a trillion dollars, while the indirect cost may be three or four times that amount. One study released in the late Seventies concluded that pollution controls alone had already cost our country approximately ten percent of its industrial capacity. Another study by a prominent accounting firm, evaluating the impact of regulation on forty-eight major companies during 1977, had discovered: "The complexities and volume of EPA [*Environmental Protection Agency*] regulations made it necessary for [*the 48*] companies to incur $36 million [*in expenses*] . . . solely to maintain internal environmental programs and to keep current with existing regulations and practices and to prepare for new regulations." Needless to say, those millions of dollars were *not* devoted to increased economic productivity, job creation, new plants and equipment.

A Hatred of Man

The environmental movement has covered itself with a patina of scientific objectivity, yet it acts very much like a secular religion that permits no facts to disturb its accepted dogma. Environmentalists are persistent in their alleged love of animals and nature, but have a corresponding hatred of man and the economic system of private enterprise. They worship not only nature but also the political power of the state which they want to use to control those who do not share their beliefs.

Kathryn Boggs, *The New American*, November 18, 1985.

In 1980, direct environmental controls added approximately $400 to the annual expenses of a family of four. That figure is predicted to reach $638 . . . . The Council on Environmental Quality speculates that the cost of administering the Clean Air Act will total $300 billion for the period 1979 through 1988. And, no less a "Liberal" than the late Nelson Rockefeller estimated the cost of implementing the Water Pollution Control Act at *three trillion dollars.* And each new car is saddled with close to $700 in antipollution paraphernalia, while homes cost two to three thousand dollars more due to direct federal, state, and local environmental regulations. . . .

Keeping Pollution in Perspective

It is important to keep some sort of perspective regarding the extent of man-made pollution. For instance, during all of his earthly existence, man has yet to equal the particulate and noxious-gas levels of the combined volcanic eruptions on Krakatoa, Indonesia (1883), Katmai, Alaska (1912), and Hekla, Iceland (1947). Indeed, nature contributes approximately sixty percent of all particulates in the atmosphere, sixty-five percent of the sulfur dioxide, seventy percent of the hydrocarbons, ninety-three percent of the carbon monoxide, ninety percent of the ozone, and ninety-nine percent of the nitrogen oxides. While environmentalists become frenzied about the ten million tons of man-made pollutants injected into the atmosphere by Americans each year, they largely ignore the 1.6 *billion* tons of methane gas emitted each year by swamps, and the 170 million tons of hydrocarbons released annually by forests and other forms of vegetation. On one occasion, officials of a major city on the West Coast became agitated about the extent to which the disposal of human waste might be "polluting" the Pacific Ocean, oblivious to the fact that similar waste from gray whales, or even schools of anchovies, far exceeds any such contribution which residents of the city could conceivably make.

Attacking the Automobile

Although trees and other greeneries contribute to some 3.5 billion tons of carbon monoxide to the atmosphere each year, compared to mankind's 270 million tons, environmentalists continually attack the automobile as a deadly polluter. Professor E.J. Mishan of the London School of Economics, for instance, once described the private automobile as a disaster for the human race which pollutes air, clogs streets, destroys natural beauty, *etc., etc.* Which is verbal pollution of the worst sort. As Professor Hans Sennholz has noted in rebuttal, "The automobile has meant high standards of living, great individual mobility and productivity, and access to the countryside for recreation and enjoyment. In rural America it is the only means of transportation that assures employment and income. Without it, the countryside would surely be depopulated and our cities far more congested than now." . . .

A balanced perspective of the pollution picture could lead to reasonable, cost-effective programs to moderate man-made pollution. Unfortunately, the environmental field is today dominated by special interests and advocates of big government who willfully distort and exaggerate the problem in order to justify their efforts to undermine the Free Market economic system and increase government control over our lives.

The Santa Barbara Oil Spill

Consider, for instance, the National Environmental Policy Act of 1969, and how it came about. On January 28, 1969, a Union Oil Company well on a lease in the Santa Barbara Channel blew out. Within ten days, it discharged 235,000 gallons of oil into the Pacific Ocean, fouled thirty miles of beach, and damaged some boats and wildlife. Environmentalist organizations and radical politicians, bolstered by the "Liberal" news media, labeled the event an ecological catastrophe. *Life* magazine reported that the Channel was "a sea gone dead." And news commentators routinely referred to the "hundreds of thousands" of birds killed by the blowout. Yet, it was subsequently established [in *Congressional Quarterly*] that only "an estimated 600 birds were affected by the oil." And, when all the facts were in, there had been no increase in mortality among whales or seals and no long-lasting ill effects on other animal or vegetable life. Nature accomplished most of the cleanup (and man the rest) in short order.

Reprinted with permission of *The Union Leader*.

Yet, in the wake of the Santa Barbara oil spill, and the wildly exaggerated reports about the damage it had supposedly inflicted on the environment, our fickle Congress approved the National Environmental Policy Act in December of that year.

The new law contained a number of loosely worded provisions which sounded humanitarian and harmless to most observers. But it gave environmental activists the legal foothold they needed to make court challenges against business activities nationwide. Indeed, this new law defined "environment" in such vague terms that the courts had virtually unlimited authority to nullify or modify at whim various laws passed by Congress, actions by Executive agencies, *etc.* During the previous 182 years of our history (from 1789 to 1971), the Supreme Court had heard only four cases relating to the environment, all of which had been brought by state governments. But, by the end of 1971, more than one hundred sixty cases based on the 1969 Act were pending in federal courts, nearly all of which were filed by activist lawyers representing radical environmentalist groups. As author Dan Smoot noted in his best-selling book *The Business End Of Government:* "Within 18 months that law had been responsible for stopping the building of nuclear power plants; for preventing oil exploration on the outer-continental shelf; for sharply curtailing oil production in off-shore fields already explored and tapped; for prohibiting the building of the Alaska pipeline; for preventing the leasing of oil-shale lands; and for reducing the production of coal." . . .

Earth Day and Lenin

The momentum ignited by the Santa Barbara oil spill eventually led to the first so-called Earth Day, an event organized by the radical and anti-capitalist student activists associated with the ecology movement, as a mass protest against "destruction of the world's life-giving resources." Earth Day, which involved cleanup campaigns, parades, and meetings, was scheduled for April 22, 1970, a date which raised some eyebrows, since it was the one hundredth anniversary of the birth of anti-capitalist ideologue (and first Soviet dictator) V.I. Lenin. Many observers undoubtedly concluded it was merely a coincidence that Earth Day organizers selected that particular April weekend, when workers and young people would not be at work or school so they could participate in the festivities. But April 22nd was a *Wednesday.* Earth Day was purposely scheduled to bolster the worldwide (and highly publicized) celebration by Leftists of the Lenin centenary.

More Harm than Good

It was less than three months after Earth Day that President Richard Nixon transmitted his "reorganization Plan Number 3" to Congress, announcing that he would create the Environmental Protection Agency as an umbrella agency to consolidate and administer federal anti-pollution programs. Congress concurred in the plan on October 2, 1970, and—following a sixty-day planning period—the E.P.A. formally began operating on December 2, 1970, with a Budget of $303 million and staff of 3,860. My how Topsy has grown! For Fiscal Year 1983, the agency's budget was $3.7 *billion* and its staff equivalent to 10,925 full-time employees.

According to the American Legislative Exchange Council, the E.P.A. has spawned an average of ninety regulations each year since its inception. In some instances, the heavy-handed manner in which those edicts have been administered has itself discouraged advances in pollution control.

"*The environmental movement has succeeded in publicizing problems and in securing laws and regulations designed to safeguard our air and water.*"

Environmentalists Have Improved the Environment

Jay D. Hair and Alden Meyer

Part I of the following viewpoint is by Jay D. Hair, the executive vice-president of the National Wildlife Federation, an influential environmental organization based in Washington, DC. Alden Meyer, the director of Environmental Action, a national political lobby organization also based in Washington, is the author of Part II. Mr. Hair begins by enumerating the successes of the National Wildlife Federation and the environmental movement as a whole. He concludes with a mandate to work harder for environmental improvement. Alden Meyer picks up that mandate in Part II, suggesting that continued activism by environmentalists is necessary to protect natural resources from corporate exploitation.

As you read, consider the following questions:

1. What does Mr. Hair list as the environmentalists' successes?
2. What, according to Mr. Meyer, is the fundamental problem with environmental activism to date?

I

As we turn our thoughts toward . . . opportunities and challenges, let's pause for a moment of quiet pride in our conservation achievements.

Despite . . . difficult environmental battles . . . we see emerging an era where cooperation replaces confrontation and old problems are finally reduced to manageable proportions.

Although the road of environmental recovery is long and rugged, it is helpful from time to time to walk in the sunshine of our magnificent achievements. With an ever cautious eye to the future, let's savor a few important conservation accomplishments.

Savoring Our Accomplishments

First, we now know that the Conservative Consensus occupies a central, pivotal position in American life and politics. It cannot be ignored. It is stronger than ever and will not be overcome. It was tested, and it held. Beneath its overarching framework there is still considerable room for flexibility and compromise, but the centrality of its basic principles and responsible direction is beyond question.

We should also take pride in the kindling spirit of cooperation and openness between the conservation and business communities. The National Wildlife Federation has made great strides in establishing a dialogue with business leaders who, in the past, too often have been seen as adversaries.

Our Corporate Conservation Council, composed of representatives of major corporations, has provided a forum through which conservationists and business leaders have been able to establish contact, to break barriers to communication and to work together to achieve mutual goals.

There is growing acceptance of the notion that a healthy economy and productive environment are two sides of the same coin.

Environmental Progress

Symptomatic of the environmental progress that now characterizes many of the earth's resources—water, air, plants and wildlife—is the dramatic return of recreational fishing to downtown America. Urban rivers that caught fire a few years ago now support fishing tournaments. Everywhere—in Grand Rapids, in Memphis, in Minneapolis, in the District of Columbia, in the Great Lakes and in coastal ports—the story is the same: people of good will and character and imagination can overcome even the most intractable environmental problems.

Suddenly, our national goal of having fishable and swimmable waters no longer seems to be an impossible dream. *We can do it!*

With a cleaner environment and stronger protection laws, we have inevitably produced better habitat and healthier populations of plants, fish and wildlife. The American bald eagle, symbol of our nation and symbol of past neglect of our natural endowment, is making a comeback.

Almost 30 states have enacted tax check-offs that fund non-game wildlife programs. The Clean Air Act is working; our air is significantly improved. Acid rain, long ignored in Washington, is viewed by more and more members of Congress as a matter of immediate concern. Now there is talk of acid rain controls rather than more research. Legislators also are focusing attention on non-point water pollution, chiefly runoff from farms and urban streets.

We have much to be proud of, but also much remains to be done. Let's resolve to work in a positive and constructive manner for a better America—one where the quality of the environment is the centerpiece of the quality of life.

II

If we don't act now, Earth Day 2000 could well be brought to us by Mobil Oil, Dow Chemical and IBM—featuring the first genetically-engineered whooping crane and simulated wilderness-on-a-chip. The tragedy would be that we might not even recognize how much we'd lost.

In the . . . years since the first Earth Day on April 22, 1970, the environmental movement has succeeded in publicizing problems and in securing laws and regulations designed to safeguard our air and water, our public lands and public health.

Environmentalism's Goal

We can no longer afford to dissipate and destroy the natural resources that constitute the web of life. Once the threshold of recovery is passed, the loss is irrevocable. What environmentalists are trying to do is to protect the long-range interests of human society on this wasting planet from those who would plunder it now and let the future take care of itself.

John B. Oakes, *Minneapolis Tribune,* January 2, 1980.

Yet, acid rain still ravages our lakes and forests. Our industries generate more and more hazardous waste and continue to dump it in dangerous ways. Widespread deforestation and climate change threaten the entire planet.

How can this be, if we've been so successful? I believe our vision and strategies haven't been radical enough, not radical in the wild-eyed sense, but in its original sense—getting at the root of the problem.

Stronger laws are important: we can't stop fighting for an expanded Superfund, a Clean Air Act that confronts acid rain, a Safe

Drinking Water Act that lives up to its name. But these reforms don't address the root of our problems: That citizens aren't making the key decisions affecting our environment, health and quality of life—nor are our elected representatives. They're being made by the small group of people heading the most powerful institutions in our society—the industrial corporations. They are made largely on the basis of profit and loss. And in many respects, these decision-makers don't pay for the "side effects" of their "business" decisions—pollution, disease and death.

During the last 15 years, we've opened up the government decisionmaking process. Our challenge for the next decade must be to win full corporate accountability.

It's time to:

• Send executives to jail for knowingly poisoning our water and making our children sick, not slap them on the wrist with token fines.

• Make utility executives and investors pay the multi-billion dollar cost overruns on the dozens of nuclear "white elephants" now entering service, instead of *rewarding* their mismanagement by sticking the excess costs on ratepayers.

• Eliminate tax subsidies for nuclear and coal power plant construction, timber overproduction, groundwater depletion and other harmful activities.

As long as we allow corporations to be insulated from the true costs of their practices (or worse, bribe them with tax breaks to do exactly the wrong thing), we shouldn't be surprised when our laws fail.

Even full corporate accountability—internalizing the costs, as economists call it—isn't enough. Some decisions just shouldn't be made on the basis of profit and loss. As organizer Tony Mazzocchi puts it, "We have to have control over our lives, what we breathe and what we ingest."

The Battle Is Underway

The battle is already underway. Toxics activists and union members have won "right-to-know" laws across the country, giving workers and communities access to information on production, transport and disposal of toxic materials. *But knowing what is poisoning us isn't enough.* Citizens must demand the "right to decide" what's produced and what's disposed of in our communities.

Other examples abound of the drive to gain real citizen power;

• Some energy activists advocate giving ratepayers equity shares and board of director seats whenever utility customers must absorb the costs of cancelled nuclear plants.

• Citizen groups are calling for a moratorium on the development and use of genetic engineering until a full public debate has taken place on the environmental and ethical implications of this technology.

• The nuclear-free-zone movement, while largely symbolic, asserts a community's right to be involved in nuclear weapons decisions. It will be more than symbolic when enough cities ban purchases from nuclear weapons companies.

Other activists are using nonviolent direct action to halt such irresponsible corporate activities as dumping radioactive wastes at sea or discharging carcinogenic chemicals into drinking water.

Facing the Challenge

Halfway between the first Earth Day and the second millenium, the task confronting us is daunting: Nothing less than making our society's most powerful institutions, the corporations, accountable.

But then, the challenge that faced those who organized the first Earth Day—raising the nation's consciousness and turning Congress around—must have seemed pretty formidable. Thanks to them, we've learned just how high the stakes are. Now we face a tougher challenge. Besides, cloned whooping cranes just wouldn't be the same.

"The greenhouse effect . . . can't be stopped, or even slowed, without the most drastic measures."

The Greenhouse Effect Is Potentially Disastrous

Lewis M. Steel and *USA Today*

Part I of the following viewpoint was written by Lewis M. Steel, president of the New York City chapter of the National Lawyers Guild. Part II is an editorial from *USA Today*, a daily national newspaper. Both parts discuss the dangers of the greenhouse effect, the theory that burning too much fossil fuel traps carbon dioxide in the ozone layer and causes the earth's temperature to rise. Mr. Steel outlines what might happen if the earth does warm significantly. He expresses concern that so little has been done to counteract the greenhouse effect. *USA Today* imagines a world overcome by excess temperatures and warns that something must be done immediately to avoid the scientifically certain catastrophe of the greenhouse effect.

As you read, consider the following questions:

1. Why, according to Mr. Steel, is the greenhouse effect a different and greater threat than other environmental problems?
2. *USA Today* describes a world changed by the greenhouse effect. Do you find this scenario believable or unbelievable?

Lewis M. Steel, "Fear of Frying," *The Nation,* May 26, 1984. Reprinted with permission, *The Nation* magazine, Nation Associates, Inc. © 1984.

USA Today, "Warming of the Earth is Genuine Threat," June 19, 1986. Copyright, 1986 USA Today. Reprinted with permission.

I

The greenhouse effect, a heating up of the earth mostly as a result of the burning of fossil fuels, may create worldwide disaster. While most environmental problems do not necessarily have the potential to destroy civilizations, and appear to be controllable if political processes work fast enough, this threat is different. The Environmental Protection Agency says that the greenhouse effect—which occurs because a byproduct of combustion, carbon dioxide, allows the sun's rays to penetrate the earth's atmosphere but prevents infrared radiation from escaping it—is just beginning in earnest. And it can't be stopped, or even slowed, without the most drastic measures.

The . . . E.P.A. report "Can We Delay a Greenhouse Warming?" suggests that the phenomenon could raise temperatures worldwide by 2 degrees centigrade (3.6 degrees Fahrenheit) by the year 2040 and 5 degrees centigrade (9 degrees Fahrenheit) by 2100. "Two degrees," the E.P.A. notes, "is significant in comparison with temperature changes that produced ice ages." Before the end of the next century, sea levels could rise from two to twelve feet. "All human activities are likely to be in some way affected," the E.P.A. report continues.

Extraordinarily Pessimistic

The E.P.A. is extraordinarily pessimistic about the situation. Even if the world stopped burning coal by the year 2000, the report says, that would only slow the process, not solve the problem. The use of other fossil fuels will continue to create carbon dioxide, which will cause the earth to heat up.

I am not an expert. I don't know whether the E.P.A. projections are correct, or which people and countries might bear the brunt of the predicted heat-up, or whether there are any remedies. I do know I'm worried. It looks like industrialization is finally catching up with us, perhaps irreparably.

If the greenhouse effect is that serious, why are we doing so little about it? Progressives and environmentalists have raised a cry over acid rain and have put forth various solutions. They have attacked nuclear power and demanded the control of many forms of pollution. Assuming the E.P.A.'s projections are reasonably accurate, and so far even the coal industry has not issued any don't-worry reports, environmental and progressive forces should be spreading the alarm and putting forth proposals to meet the threat. But so far, they are as silent as those of more laissez-faire persuasions.

A Massive Problem

The silence may result from the massiveness of the problem. Regional and even national approaches would be inadequate. Fossil fuel consumption is the key to the economies of all industrialized nations, and it will grow as Third World countries increase their productive capacities.

Moreover, progressives in this country continue to look to coal-fueled industrial production to revitalize depressed regions. . . . Bruce Schmiechen, Lawrence Daressa and Larry Adelman . . . suggested that "100 billion tons of known coal reserves" as well as a skilled labor force and unused plant capacity could be tapped to save the Pittsburgh area's crumbling economy. Responding to plant closings and unemployment, progressives there advocate locally accountable and democratically run regional planning authorities. Perhaps progressives would make their plants as pollution-free as possible, but coal consumption is coal consumption no matter who controls the plants. Although antipollution devices may help reduce acid rain, emissions of massive amounts of carbon dioxide would still continue to the greenhouse effect.

A Serious Problem

The scientific evidence is telling us we have a problem, a serious problem. There is a very real possibility that man—through ignorance or indifference—is irreversibly altering the ability of our atmosphere to perform basic life-support functions for the planet.

John F. Chafee, quoted in *The Christian Science Monitor,* June 12, 1986.

So what can we do? In an industrialized country seeking to maintain its primacy in an increasingly industrialized world, few are willing to advocate any approach that might limit America's growth. Most organizations across the political spectrum push programs that would bring about even more industrialization. Apparently everyone is hoping for a technological fix or is simply unwilling to face the fast-approaching future.

Neither America's private sector nor its political representatives will deal with the greenhouse effect until it is upon us. If one area of the world heats up a little too much for comfort or is flooded, corporations can move to more suitable locations and use their economic muscle and military friends to maintain themselves. Most people, however, don't have that option. Now is the time to begin asking the hard questions: Is the greenhouse effect the threat it appears to be? If so, what, realistically, should progressives be doing in response? Can someone reply?

II

Imagine a world like this:

Omaha, Neb., sweats through the worst drought in its history. In July 2030, the mercury hits 100 on 20 days. Crops are wiped out; the Midwest is a dust bowl.

New Orleans is under water. The French Quarter has shut down; the Superdome holds a small lake. The governor says property damage will be in the billions.

Washington, D.C., suffers through its hottest summer—87 days above 90 degrees. Water is rationed; brownouts are routine because utilities can't meet demand for electricity. Federal employees, working half-days in unbearable heat, report an alarming rise in skin cancer across the USA.

Abroad, floods have inundated Bangladesh and Indonesia. The seas are four feet above 1986 levels. The United Nations reports millions will die in famines; shocking climate changes have ruined agriculture.

Worst Fears May Come True

That sounds far-fetched, but if some scientists' worst fears come true, that could be what our children inherit.

Since the beginning of this century, man has been spewing pollutants into the atmosphere at an ever-increasing rate. Carbon dioxide and chloroflourocarbons—CFCs—are fouling the air, our life support system. Everything that burns releases carbon dioxide. CFCs are used to make refrigerants, Styrofoam, computer chips, and other products.

In the past century, carbon dioxide in the atmosphere has risen 25 percent. The problem is that carbon dioxide holds in heat, just as the roof of a greenhouse does. That's why the Earth's warming is called the greenhouse effect.

CFCs retain heat, too, and break down the atmosphere's protective layer of ozone. If it is damaged, more of the sun's ultraviolet rays will reach Earth, causing skin cancer and damaging sea life.

Combined with the loss of forests that absorb carbon dioxide, the effects of this pollution could be disastrous. By 2030, Earth's temperature could rise 8 degrees, polar ice caps would melt, weather would change, crops would wilt.

There is growing evidence that these pollutants are reaching ominous levels. At the South Pole, the ozone layer has a "hole" in it—it's been depleted by 40 percent. NASA scientist Robert Watson says: "Global warning is inevitable—it's only a question of magnitude and time."

Action Needed Now

Some say don't panic, probably nothing will happen. The trouble with that is that we know these pollutants are building, and by the time we are sure of the worst effects, it may be too late. Action is needed, now. The USA must:

• Recognize that global warming may worsen and begin planning responses; more research is needed, too.

Deja Vu?

• Renew the search for safe, clean alternatives to fossil fuels, nuclear fission and chlorofluorocarbons.

• Report on the extent of the problem to the world and press for international controls on air pollution.

The possible dimensions of this disaster are too big to just "wait and see." If a runaway train heads for a cliff and the engineer does nothing, the passengers are bound to get hurt. Let's check the brakes before it's too late.

"The whole CO$_2$-climate problem is . . . a 'cascade of uncertainty.'"

The Greenhouse Effect Is Exaggerated

H.E. Landsberg

H.E. Landsberg was Professor Emeritus at the Institute for Fluid Dynamics and Applied Mathematics, University of Maryland. He has served as president of the American Geophysical Union and vice-president of the American Meteorological Society. In addition to writing several publications on the climate, he edited *Advances in Geophysics* and the *World Survey of Climatology.* In the following viewpoint he defines climate and explains how the burning of fossil fuels may warm the earth. Mr. Landsberg believes that though carbon dioxide does affect the atmosphere, it is impossible to predict the consequences of a greenhouse effect.

As you read, consider the following questions:

1. What, according to Mr. Landsberg, have been humanity's effects on climate? What does he say is the most troublesome change?
2. In the author's opinion, what is the primary problem with predicting a greenhouse effect?
3. Mr. Landsberg states it is unlikely that clear evidence of a temperature rise will be discovered before 2000. *USA Today* in the previous viewpoint says it would be unwise to "wait and see." Which attitude should be used in environmental decision-making? Why?

H.E. Landsberg, "Global Climatic Trends," from *The Resourceful Earth* edited by Julian L. Simon and Herman Kahn. New York: Basil Blackwell Inc., 1984. Reprinted with permission.

There is little doubt that urbanization and industrialization have affected the climate of fairly substantial areas occupied by man. . . . By far the most troublesome atmospheric alteration has been the steady increase in *carbon dioxide* (CO_2). This and a few other minor gases have been lumped together under the term "greenhouse" gases. Their action is supposed to increase surface temperature, somewhat analogous to the glass panes of a greenhouse (actually an incomplete interpretation of greenhouse action). Undeniably CO_2 has steadily increased on a global basis, probably since the 1860s, and at an accelerated rate since the end of World War II. Systematic global measurements started during the International Geophysical Year 1957/8. Since then it has risen about 7 percent. The total increase since 1860 has been from 280 ppmV (parts per million by volume) to 335 ppmV. These are the established facts. They have prompted a staggering amount of literature pertaining to the climatic consequences of a continuing increase in atmospheric CO_2. The potential of a rising CO_2 level in the atmosphere to raise global temperatures at the surface has been discussed on and off ever since Svante Arrhenius advanced the idea in 1896. There is general agreement that the infrared-absorbing qualities of this gas will reduce the outgoing radiation from earth to space and thus raise the surface temperature. At the same time the radiation from the gas itself would cool the stratosphere.

No Agreement

The question about this temperature rise is how much, how soon, and with what regional distribution. There is no agreement on that. Some of it is a result of the initial uncertainties. These include principally the projections for future CO_2 increases. There had been the contention that this is primarily due to the increases in the use of fossil fuels. The calculations had shown that the past increase of CO_2 corresponded to about one-half of the CO_2 produced by combustion of the reasonably well-known consumption of fossil fuels. This was extrapolated to the future with scenarios of exponential increases in the use of fossil fuels. It must be said here that not all the CO_2 increase is caused by fossil fuel use. There have also been some decreases in uptake of CO_2 by vegetation, caused by deforestation especially in tropical areas. According to some estimates the depletion is presently at the rate of nearly 8 million hectares annually. However, the potential increase of other biomass as a result of additional CO_2 remains to be fully quantified.

The whole carbon cycle and the transfers from the various reservoirs' soil, sea, and plant cover have not been adequately represented in past considerations, as pointed out in an excellent . . . review by [B.] Bolin. He points out that the regional biogeochemical processes are important for climatic models and have so far

46

been inadequately considered: "Important feedback mechanisms may therefore have been overlooked, some of which may possibly cause natural climatic oscillations. Important also are the man-made changes in the surface of the land and the fact that on longer time scales ecosystems are hardly static."

A Cascade of Uncertainty

The whole CO_2-climate problem is, in the words of Kellogg and Schware, a "cascade of uncertainty." There is recognition that the prime problem lies with the scenarios. Kellogg and Schware proceed with the assumption that by the year 2000 atmospheric CO_2 will have risen to 360 ppmV and that it will have doubled from the pre-industrial level by 2035. While they admit the need for research to improve knowledge they proceed to discuss dire consequences. They are quite conservative compared with more alarming views by [H.] Flohn. He writes "the possibility of a drastic rapid climatic modification on a large scale must be envisaged," setting a critical limit at 450 ppmV with "catastrophic" possibilities at higher levels. Without much reference to the uncertainties this is elaborated in a report of the International Institute for Applied Systems Analysis. It is partly based on a paleoclimatic scenario, the hypsithermal of the Holocene, when global temperatures were estimated to have been 1.5°C above the present. CO_2 and the infrared-absorbing trace gases methane, nitrous oxide, and the chlorofluoromethanes are expected to constitute 70 percent and 30 percent, respectively, of the absorbing mixture. By the year 2050 the pre-industrial CO_2 has doubled and a 4°C global temperature rise is projected. Rain belts will be shifted, some areas will have more droughts, the polar ice will melt rapidly, coastal areas will become submerged. Doom will be there.

Nothing To Worry About

Even if the worst of the predicted climate changes show up . . . carbon dioxide isn't going to be on my list of the half-dozen things we need to worry about.

Thomas Schelling, quoted in *Discover*, January 1986.

Such views prompted some scientists to propose policy changes that would postpone the evil day. Many of the scenarios had envisaged an annual use increment for fossil fuel of 4 percent. It was thus natural to urge a "low-risk" energy policy. Actually there had already been a slow-down to an annual increase of 2¾ percent, presumably due to economic factors. Yet the predictions of temperature increases of several degrees in 50-70 years continued with adverse effects on the United States, the Soviet Union, and

China: "It now appears that the possible global climate change may be very disruptive to some societies. It may trigger shifts in agricultural patterns, balances of trade, and habitual ways of life for many people—and eventually, a few centuries from now, may even force abandonment of low-lying land due to a rise in sea level."

With such prospects being bandied about it is not surprising that legislative concern is being aroused. Thus subcommittees of the U.S. House of Representatives held hearings on carbon dioxide research and the greenhouse effect. Fortunately there was very cautious scientific testimony. It brought out that there are widely different results from various models used to simulate the CO_2 effect. It also indicated that it would probably take centuries to melt the Western Antarctic ice sheet. Even though there is a fair amount of consensus that the greenhouse effect is real, there remains a wide range of opinion as to the magnitude and the rate at which climatic change will occur and, in particular, about the changes that will take place on the all-important regional scale.

Deceptive Models

Because so many conclusions are based on the mathematical—numerical modeling of climate, it is imperative to take a critical look at the various models. The fact that they appear in the exact framework of mathematics is deceiving because they can only simulate nature successfully if they represent all variables and their interactions. With the present state of knowledge that is virtually impossible. Hence it is also not surprising that various modelers have used different approaches and parameterizations to achieve approximations. The tests of validity have usually been that they present a fair representation of the current mean value of a climatic element and its annual variation. Yet when they are employed to project, say, the global mean temperature for the case of doubled atmospheric CO_2 the answers vary widely. . . .

Where lie the problems? There are many. The question of the biospheric reservoir has already been pointed out (Bolin, 1982). The study also clearly stated the inadequate consideration of storage and circulation of CO_2 in the ocean. It is quite clear, as others have also pointed out, that the circulation of the deep sea is not well known and the available data are insufficient to verify current theories about that circulation. We know very little about the CO_2 transfer to greater depths in the ocean and the depth of the thermocline and its role in this transfer remains to be explored. In a . . . study of the turn-over of the deep waters of the world oceans it was concluded that their replacement-time is between 200 and 500 years. No such time lag appears in any of the climate models. The question of evaporation from the ocean and its thermal effect, the role of increased water vapor in the atmosphere,

48

the proper cloud cover for a higher-temperature earth and its albedo effect, other surface albedo changes with numerous inter-element feedbacks, both positive and negative, call for intensified efforts for modeling, observations for the verification of models, and a highly conservative attitude with respect to conclusions.

There have been a number of statements that a CO_2-induced warming has already occurred and that there is observational evidence for it. These refer particularly to shrinkage of the Antarctic ice sheets and sea level changes. However, there is no detectable decrease of Antarctic sea ice in 9 years of satellite observations. There are, as in all such elements, notable fluctuations. In satellite observations between 1967 and 1981 there are ice increases of considerable magnitude. These obscure any CO_2-induced trend and the postulate of such a trend is purely speculative. Also calculated temperature rises of 0.14°C because of CO_2 and 0.1°C because of other trace gas increases for the 1970-80 decade simply disappear in the noisy climatic temperature pattern. There has been an estimate of sea-level rises. These amount to about 10 cm in a century and are probably due to some general melting of the earth's ice and snow cover. Natural warming since the last decades of the nineteenth century is probably a major cause. It is unlikely that clear evidence of a CO_2 induced temperature rise, if it occurs, will be discovered before 2000. . . .

Not Absolutely Certain

Carbon dioxide is being measured in lots of places now, and we've found it to be increasing at a rate of one and a half parts per million per year. When the studies began, there were 315 parts per million. Today there are 344 parts per million. That's a nine percent increase since 1957. I estimate that the total increase over the past one hundred years has been about twenty-one percent. But whether the increase will lead to a significant rise in global temperature, we can't absolutely say.

Roger Revelle, interview in *Omni*, March 1984.

The current stand of the CO_2-climate question has been . . . comprehensively discussed. . . . It is worth nothing here that the eminent atmospheric scientist, F.K. Hare, states the only thing agreed upon is the atmosphere CO_2 increase. He then states:

The volume is a long litany of uncertainties—of the internal transport processes in the ocean, of ocean atmosphere interaction, of the magnitude of forest and soil carbon wastage, of the future course of fossil-fuel consumption.

He also notes the many "ifs" that lead to the uncertainties. Were the models right, were CO_2 increase to continue, were the present assumptions of the role of the oceans correct, then an unprecedented post-glacial climatic change in global climate could occur next century.

At the end of this brief review of the CO_2 problem it is perhaps worthwhile to quote the laconic opinion of the members of the Executive Committee of the World Meteorological Organization. . . . This committee noted

> [the] increasing amount of CO_2 released into the atmosphere as a result of human activity may have far-reaching consequences on the global climate, but the present state of knowledge does not permit any reliable prediction to be made of future CO_2 concentrations or their impact on climate.

Distinguishing Bias from Reason

Environmental issues often generate great emotional responses in people. When dealing with such highly controversial subjects, many will allow their feelings to dominate their powers of reason. Thus, one of the most important basic thinking skills is the ability to distinguish between statements based upon emotion and those based upon a rational consideration of the facts.

Many of the following statements are taken from the viewpoints in this chapter. Consider each statement carefully. *Mark R for any statement you believe is based on reason or a rational consideration of the facts. Mark B for any statement you believe is based on bias, prejudice, or emotion. Mark I for any statement you think is impossible to judge.*

If you are doing this activity as a member of a class or group, compare your answers with those of other class or group members. Be able to explain your answers. You may discover that others will come to different conclusions than you. Listening to the reasons others present for their answers may give you valuable insights in distinguishing between bias and reason.

If you are reading this book alone, ask others if they agree with your answers. You will find this interaction valuable also.

> R = *a statement based upon reason*
> B = *a statement based on bias*
> I = *a statement impossible to judge*

1. The increased legislative action on environmental issues may be a result of greater public awareness of environmental problems.

2. The environmental crisis may be quiet, but it is the most urgent crisis facing humankind today.

3. Only US intervention can save the world from ecological disaster.

4. The abundance of nonprofit environmental organizations indicates a voluntary commitment to protecting the environment.

5. The environmental view is dead wrong and damaging.

6. If the world population continues to increase, it will probably place more stress on the environment.

7. The environmental movement, far from increasing our quality of life, will diminish it.

8. There is a great deal wrong with the sort of environmentalism to which our nation has been subjected.

9. Higher taxes due to environmental controls may make it more difficult to pass environmental regulations.

10. Natural atmospheric conditions contribute approximately sixty percent of the pollution in the air. This fact suggests that nature itself is more of a problem than industry or automobiles.

11. Life on earth has never been better or more promising for the human race.

12. The private automobile is a disaster for the atmosphere.

13. Environmentalists may change their political tactics when a new administration comes to office, just as they have done with other new administrations in the past.

14. According to the American Legislative Exchange Council, the EPA has written an average of ninety regulations each year since its inception.

15. People of good will and character and imagination can overcome even the most intractable environmental problems.

16. Based on EPA statistics from 1970 to 1985, freshwater lakes are cleaner now than they were several years ago.

17. Environmentalists have nothing to be proud of.

18. The greenhouse effect will become a major public issue only if it can be proved to be true.

Periodical Bibliography

The following list of periodical articles deals with the subject matter of this chapter.

Sharon Begley — "Silent Spring Revisited?" *Newsweek*, July 14, 1986.

Kathryn Boggs — "Environmentalists Still Carry Clout," *The New American*, November 18, 1985.

James Bovard — "Bankrupt Environmentalism," *The New York Times*, July 10, 1985.

Paul Brand — "A Handful of Mud," *Christianity Today*, April 19, 1985.

Harold Gilliam — "Deep Ecology vs. Environmentalism," *Utne Reader*, October/November 1985.

Neal Karlen with Mary Hager — "Pollution: Now the Bad News," *Newsweek*, April 8, 1985.

Gina Maranto — "Are We Close to the Road's End?" *Discover*, January 1986.

Thomas H. Maugh II — "Studies Renew Anxiety About Fading Ozone," *Los Angeles Times*, February 2, 1986.

Jim O'Brien — "Environmentalism as a Mass Movement: Historical Notes," *Radical America*, March/June 1983.

Donald L. Rheem — "Earth Atmosphere in More Danger than First Thought," *The Christian Science Monitor*, June 12, 1986.

Robert Rodale — "The Earth's Garden Doesn't Have To Burn Up," *Organic Gardening*, March 1984.

Science 86 — January/February 1986. Entire issue on environmental crisis.

Philip Shabecoff — "'Silent Spring' Led to Safer Pesticides, But Use Is Up," *The New York Times*, April 21, 1986.

Ronald A. Taylor — "Pranks and Protests Over Environment Turn Tough," *U.S. News & World Report*, January 13, 1986.

Glenn E. Watts — "Is Office Work Dangerous to Your Health?: The Hazards of High Tech," *USA Today*, January 1986.

Should Corporations Be Held Responsible for Environmental Disasters?

**THE
ENVIRONMENTAL
CRISIS**

"Corporate executives need to hear the slam of the jail door behind them."

Corporations Must Be Held Responsible for Environmental Disasters

Richard Asinoff

Richard Asinoff is an editor of the Washington-based *Environmental Action* magazine. In the following viewpoint, Mr. Asinoff uses the Union Carbide gas leak in Bhopal, India, as an example to generalize about the role of corporations in the environment. He asserts that thousands of Americans lose their lives each year because of corporate irresponsibility. Government must enforce regulations and make corporations pay for industrial accidents, he believes, in order to improve the environment.

As you read, consider the following questions:

1. What is the author's answer to the question, "Could Bhopal happen here?"
2. What right does the author say everyone should be guaranteed?
3. Compare Mr. Asinoff's attitude toward corporations in this viewpoint with Milton and Rose Friedman's attitude in the next viewpoint. How do they differ? Which, do you believe, is more accurate?

Richard Asinoff, "India Accident Raises Question of Corporate Responsibility," *In These Times*, December 19, 1984/January 8, 1985. Reprinted with permission.

What do potato farmers in Long Island, citrus growers in Florida and California and the residents of Bhopal, India, have in common? They are all victims of Union Carbide's production of Temik, a pesticide that the U.S. Environmental Protection Agency once described as "the most acutely toxic chemical ever registered."

Temik's active ingredient is aldicarb, a potent chemical nerve poison 10 to 15 times more toxic than cyanide. When exposed to large amounts of Temik, a person is likely to experience dizziness, nausea, convulsions and eventual death.

"When Union Carbide first introduced Temik to Long Island potato farmers in 1975," wrote Janet Marinelli in the May 1983 issue of *Environmental Action*, "the company assured regulators that this new insecticide would not only wipe out the black-and-yellow-striped Colorado potato beetle and its maggot-like companions, but would biodegrade and never reach the water table. For the next five years, Temik was planted in granular form along with potatoes throughout Long Island's East End farms. After widespread contamination of the groundwater became known in 1979, Temik was voluntarily removed from the market by Union Carbide and is now banned on the island."

The use of Temik has now been banned by counties in New York and California and, most recently, by the state of Rhode Island, following continued incidents of groundwater contamination and ill-health effects. Temik has been found to have contaminated groundwater in Wisconsin, Maryland, Virginia, Maine, Massachusetts, Washington and Florida. And yet, despite the continuing controversy over its use and the unanswered questions about its long-term health impact, Union Carbide is remarketing the pesticide in the U.S. with a new label warning of its dangers in certain applications.

Governments Protect Corporations

In Bhopal it was an intermediate chemical, methyl isocyanate, used in manufacturing Temik and Sevin, that leaked from an underground storage tank and caused what's being called the worst industrial accident—more than 2,500 dead and tens of thousands blinded and disabled. But more than an industrial accident, Bhopal is a testament to how governments are more willing to protect the right of multinational corporations to produce a profit than to protect their people from toxic contamination.

As the death toll mounted in Bhopal and horrific images appeared on television news reports of crying babies, blinded by the gas and pointing to their throats that were burning, I kept thinking back to a comment that Jesse Jackson had made right before he announced his decision to run for president. "Suppose the Russians were doing to us what we are now allowing corporations to do to us," Jackson said. "We would rise up and declare war. Suppose the Russians had poisoned our earth and contaminated our water. We would call that chemical warfare. We would make speeches and mobilize our army saying that Russia had no right to pollute our air and contaminate our water and poison our vegetation. In fact, nobody has that right."

Pressing Questions

In the aftermath everyone is asking the same questions: "Could it happen here?" "What can we do to protect ourselves?" "What should be the corporate liability?" But other important questions need to be answered: "Why were the pesticides Temik and Sevin being produced in India in the first place?" "What kinds of agricultural applications were they being used for?" "Were there alternative pest control methods that could have been applied?" "Where else does Union Carbide operate pesticide factories in the Third World?"

Reprinted by permission of United Feature Syndicate, Inc.

It's been 20 years since Rachel Carson published her exposé of DDT, *Silent Spring*, and yet DDT, banned in the U.S., is still used extensively around the world, particularly in Latin and South America, only to be brought back home here in imported food like bananas and coffee. This "circle of poison" has been well-documented, almost as well as the sordid tale of how multinational corporations seek out "pollution havens" in developing and Third World countries and ravage these countries' natural resources while poisoning their people. As Bob Wyrick, in his 1981 series for *Newsday*, "Hazards for Export," reports:

- Pesticide poisoning has reached epidemic proportions in developing countries—an estimated 22,000 people die each year, according to the Oxford Committee on Famine Relief.
- In India, workers at an asbestos-cement plant that was designed by the Manville Corporation were exposed daily to hazardous asbestos material protected by only the most rudimentary safeguards. Outside the factory, children played in discarded piles of asbestos.
- In Indonesia, at a Union Carbide battery plant outside Jakarta, health and safety provisions at the plant were reportedly so poor that at one point more than half the workforce of 750 were diagnosed as having kidney diseases linked to mercury exposure.
- In Brazil, the factory town of Vila Parisi has become known as "the valley of death," where residents' life expectancy is only 30 years, half the national average, because of the smothering air pollution.

In the past, developing countries welcomed multinational companies and their factories. Pollution was seen as a small price to pay for posterity, and criticism of development efforts was often viewed as a kind of imperialism. As Adeildo Martins de Lucena, editor of *Correio du Sul,* a newspaper in the Amazonian town of Vilhena, Brazil, told a reporter: "We have the same right to destroy our wilderness as the Americans had in the Far West." The Amazon, he declared, "is not the lungs of humanity."

But now, faced with visible scars of resource depletion and feeling the scourge of poorly managed development, Third World countries are beginning to perceive environmental degradation and grinding poverty as two sides of the same coin.

Confronting the Perils

The answer to the oft-heard question "Could it happen here?" is that it is already happening, but most people remain unaware of the extent of it. Last year alone there were more than 14,000 explosions, spills and accidental releases involving toxic chemicals. But unlike the tragedy in India and the Mexico City natural gas explosion before it, people rarely see the immediate effects of toxics that are poisoning the environment—toxics such as the estimated four billion gallons of heavy metals, pesticides, solvents and other hazardous chemicals that companies dumped into U.S. water and air during 1981.

Thousands of Americans Dying

It may take five, 10 or more years before people become ill after drinking water, breathing air or eating food contaminated with toxic chemicals, but the result is no less tragic. Talk to the families of the estimated 100,000 Americans who will die this year from work-related diseases, many of them chemically related. Talk to the residents of Woburn, Mass., where a cluster of child leukemia deaths has been tied to chemical toxic contamination of drinking water. Talk to the residents of Williamstown, Vt., where toxic chemicals trichloroethylene, benzene and napthalene from an industrial dry-cleaning facility contaminated a local elementary school. And talk to the residents of Riverside, Calif., where contaminants from the Stringfellow waste dump threaten to contaminate drinking water for 500,000 people in Southern California.

Society Cannot Permit Murder

The real question is who, and by what authority, can have the power to determine how many illnesses and deaths are acceptable? If someone conspired to kill another, then that person would be legally culpable. . . . But corporations involved in the manufacture and use of poison on the general populace can do this under the umbrella of regulation. The fact that the names of the victims are not known makes it legal but I don't think there's a distinction. Those deaths are statistically certain and morally there is no difference. Society cannot permit random, premeditated murder. It cannot delegate the moral and ethical power to decide life and death in the name of private profit.

Lorna Salzman, quoted in *The Poison Conspiracy*, 1983.

Just as the nuclear accident at Three Mile Island rudely awakened people to the dangers of nuclear power, perhaps, too, the tragic Bhopal accident will force Americans to confront the peril of hazardous waste and toxic chemicals—and take action to protect themselves.

"Every community and every workplace," says toxics specialist Ken Silver at the Waste and Toxic Substances Project of the Environmental Action Foundation, "needs to be guaranteed the 'right to know.' They need to know what kinds of dangerous chemicals are being manufactured at factories in their town, what kinds of toxic chemicals are being stored on site, what kinds of wastes are going up the smokestack and being flushed into the water."

The Right To Know

Workers, Silvers continues, also must have the right to know both the short-term and long-term health hazards from working with toxic chemicals. And residents—not just local health and law enforcement officials—must have the right to know what they should do in case of an accident, and the right to inspect factories to make sure that the community's health and safety is not being threatened.

The Bhopal disaster is a shocking example of why the community's right to know must be respected. While workers at the

Union Carbide plant, according to newspaper reports, had been told what to do if there were a gas leak—check wind direction by looking at the windsocks above the plant, and run the other way—no one told the residents of the shanty-town next to the factory what to do. Nor were there any windsocks in the community.

Citizens in 19 states and more than 40 communities have already enacted laws and ordinances for the "right to know" about toxic chemicals. At their best these right-to-know laws require companies to:

- label containers in the workplace with their chemical identities;
- educate and train employees to recognize and prevent hazards;
- make that same information available to local citizens.

Needed Legislation Ignored

After four years of opposition from the Reagan administration, the Resource Conservation and Recovery Act (RCRA), the law regulating the production and disposal of hazardous waste "from cradle to grave," was finally authorized—with stringent provisions covering underground storage tanks like the one that malfunctioned in Bhopal. Still languishing in Congress, though, are bills renewing Superfund, the Clean Water Act, the Clean Air Act, the Safe Drinking Water Act, and the Toxic Substances Control Act, as well as the Federal Insecticide, Fungicide and Rodenticide Act (FIFRA) that regulates pesticides. . . .

Enforcing Laws

It's not just a matter of enacting new laws but also of making sure that the existing laws are enforced. According to the public watchdog group, Environmental Safety, only 70 of the roughly 40,000 pesticides in the marketplace have been reviewed by the Environmental Protection Agency (EPA), as required by Congress. Many of these products were approved long before there were adequate testing procedures or health and safety standards. Now the agency is supposed to be determining if any of these products may pose a risk to public safety. Clearly, the potential looms for another EDB (ethylene dibromide).

As reports from India indicated that the chair of Union Carbide had been arrested (then later released) for criminal negligence, the strong words of Ira Reiner, the former Los Angeles City Attorney who headed a special task force to crack down on illegal toxic dumping, came to mind: "All that is needed is the will to enforce the law," he said. "Corporate executives [responsible for illegal dumping] need to hear the slam of the jail door behind them."

"The people responsible for pollution are consumers, not producers."

Consumers Must Pay for a Cleaner Environment

Milton and Rose D. Friedman

Milton Friedman, Nobel laureate economist, former *Newsweek* columnist, and presidential adviser, is the author of a number of books including *Capitalism and Freedom,* written with his wife Rose. In the following viewpoint, the Friedmans assert that it is consumers, not corporations, who must bear the brunt of a cleaner environment by a willingness to pay more for goods. They argue that corporations are encouraged by consumers to produce as cheaply as possible. Thus, if consumers showed a willingness to pay more for environmental improvements, they would be made.

As you read, consider the following questions:

1. Why do the authors argue that a world without pollution is not desirable?
2. What, according to the authors, is the right amount of pollution?
3. Why are corporate regulations ineffective, according to the Friedmans?

The environmental movement is responsible for one of the most rapidly growing areas of federal intervention. The Environmental Protection Agency, established in 1970 "to protect and enhance the physical environment," has been granted increasing power and authority. Its budget has multiplied sevenfold from 1970 to 1978 and is now more than half a billion dollars. It has a staff of about 7,000. It has imposed costs on industry and local and state governments to meet its standards that total in the tens of billions of dollars a year. Something between a tenth and a quarter of total net investment in new capital equipment by business now goes for antipollution purposes. And this does not count the costs of requirements imposed by other agencies, such as those designed to control emissions of motor vehicles, or the costs of land-use planning or wilderness preservation or a host of other federal, state, and local government activities undertaken in the name of protecting the environment.

The preservation of the environment and the avoidance of undue pollution are real problems and they are problems concerning which the government has an important role to play. When all the costs and benefits of any action, and the people hurt or benefited, are readily identifiable, the market provides an excellent means for assuring that only those actions are undertaken for which the benefits exceed the costs for all participants. But when the costs and benefits or the people affected cannot be identified, there is a market failure, . . . arising from "third-party" or neighborhood effects.

To take a simple example, if someone upstream contaminates a river, he is, in effect, exchanging bad water for good water with people downstream. There may well be terms on which the people downstream would be willing to make the exchange. The problem is that it isn't feasible to make that transaction the subject of a voluntary exchange, to identify just who got the bad water that a particular person upstream was responsible for, and to require that his permission be obtained.

Government Cannot Determine Fault

Government is one means through which we can try to compensate for "market failure," try to use our resources more effectively to produce the amount of clean air, water, and land that we are willing to pay for. Unfortunately, the very factors that produce the market failure also make it difficult for government to achieve a satisfactory solution. Generally, it is no easier for government to identify the specific persons who are hurt and benefited than for market participants, no easier for government to assess the amount of harm or benefit to each. Attempts to use government to correct market failure have often simply substituted government failure for market failure.

Public discussion of the environment issue is frequently characterized more by emotion than reason. Much of it proceeds as if the issue is pollution versus no pollution, as if it were desirable and possible to have a world without pollution. That is clearly nonsense. No one who contemplates the problem seriously will regard zero pollution as either a desirable or a possible state of affairs. We could have zero pollution from automobiles, for example, by simply abolishing all automobiles. That would also make the kind of agricultural and industrial productivity we now enjoy impossible, and so condemn most of us to a drastically lower standard of living, perhaps many even to death. One source of atmospheric pollution is the carbon dioxide that we all exhale. We could stop that very simply. But the cost would clearly exceed the gain.

Weighing Costs and Gains

It costs something to have clean air, just as it costs something to have other good things we want. Our resources are limited and we must weigh the gains from reducing pollution against the costs. Moreover, "pollution" is not an objective phenomenon. One person's pollution may be another's pleasure. To some of us rock music is noise pollution; to others of us it is pleasure.

The Market and the Consumer

The bottom line is that come what may, we the people shall pay for the energy we consume. And we shall pay far less in total, and have far more energy, if we pay directly and are left free to choose for ourselves how to use energy than if we pay indirectly through taxes and inflation and are told by government bureaucrats how to use energy.

Perfection is not of this world. There will always be shoddy products, quacks, con artists. But on the whole, market competition, when it is permitted to work, protects the consumer better than do the alternative government mechanisms that have been increasingly superimposed on the market.

Milton and Rose Friedman, *Free To Choose,* 1980.

The real problem is not "eliminating pollution," but trying to establish arrangements that will yield the "right" amount of pollution: an amount such that the gain from reducing pollution a bit more just balances the sacrifice of the other good things— houses, shoes, coats, and so on—that would have to be given up in order to reduce the pollution. If we go farther than that, we sacrifice more than we gain.

Another obstacle to rational analysis of the environment issue is the tendency to pose it in terms of good or evil—to proceed as if bad, malicious people are pouring pollutants into the atmosphere out of the blackness of their hearts, that the problem is one of motives, that if only those of us who are noble would rise in our wrath to subdue the evil men, all would be well. It is always much easier to call other people names than to engage in hard intellectual analysis.

Consumer Responsibility

In the case of pollution, the devil blamed is typically "business," the enterprises that produce goods and services. In fact, the people responsible for pollution are consumers, not producers. They create, as it were, a demand for pollution. People who use electricity are responsible for the smoke that comes out of the stacks of the generating plants. If we want to have the electricity with less pollution, we shall have to pay, directly or indirectly, a high enough price for the electricity to cover the extra costs. Ultimately, the cost of getting cleaner air, water, and all the rest must be borne by the consumer. There is no one else to pay for it. Business is only an intermediary, a way of coordinating the activities of people as consumers and producers.

The problem of controlling pollution and protecting the environment is greatly complicated by the tendency for the gains and losses derived from doing so to fall on different people. The people, for example, who gain from the greater availability of wilderness areas, or from the improvement of the recreational quality of lakes or rivers, or from the cleaner air in the cities, are generally not the same people as those who would lose from the resulting higher costs of food or steel or chemicals. Typically, we suspect, the people who would benefit most from the reduction of pollution are better off, financially and educationally, than the people who would benefit most from the lower cost of things that would result from permitting more pollution. The latter might prefer cheaper electricity to cleaner air. . . .

The same approach has generally been adopted in the attempt to control pollution as in regulating railroads and trucks, controlling food and drugs, and promoting the safety of products. Establish a government regulatory agency that has discretionary power to issue rules and orders specifying actions that private enterprises or individuals or states and local communities must take. Seek to enforce these regulations by sanctions imposed by the agency or by courts.

This system provides no effective mechanism to assure the balancing of costs and benefits. By putting the whole issue in terms of enforceable orders, it creates a situation suggestive of crime and punishment, not of buying and selling; of right and wrong, not of more or less. Moreover, it has the same defects as this kind of regulation in other areas. The persons or agencies regulated have a strong interest in spending resources, not to achieve the desired objectives, but to get favorable rulings, to influence the bureaucrats. And the self-interest of the regulators in its turn bears only the most distant relation to the basic objective. As always in the bureaucratic process, diffused and widely spread interests get short shrift: the concentrated interests take over. In the past these have generally been the business enterprises, and particularly the large and important ones. More recently they have been joined by the self-styled, highly organized "public interest" groups that profess to speak for a constituency that may be utterly unaware of their existence. . . .

Consumers, Not Government Should Decide

When products enter the marketplace in the usual course of events, there is an opportunity for experiment, for trial and error. No doubt, shoddy products are produced, mistakes are made, unsuspected defects turn up. . . . Consumers can experiment for themselves, decide what features they like and what features they do not like.

When the government steps in, . . . the situation is different. Many decisions must be made before the product has been subjected to extensive trial and error in actual use. . . . Consumers will inevitably be denied the opportunity to experiment with a range of alternatives. Mistakes will still be made, and when they are, they are almost sure to be major.

Milton and Rose Friedman, *Free To Choose*, 1980.

This is a very brief treatment of an extremely important and far-reaching problem. But perhaps it is sufficient to suggest that the difficulties that have plagued government regulation in areas where government has no place whatsoever—as in fixing prices and allocating routes in trucking, rail travel, and air travel—also arise in areas where government has a role to play.

Perhaps also it may lead to a second look at the performance of market mechanisms in areas where they admittedly operate imperfectly. The imperfect market may, after all, do as well or better than the imperfect government. In pollution, such a look would bring many surprises.

If we look not at rhetoric but at reality, the air is in general far cleaner and the water safer today than one hundred years ago. The air is cleaner and the water safer in the advanced countries of the world today than in the backward countries. Industrialization has raised new problems, but it has also provided the means to solve prior problems. The development of the automobile did add to one form of pollution—but it largely ended a far less attractive form.

"Unlike hurricanes, these [chemical] disasters are preventable."

Environmental Disasters Demand Preventive Action

Jay Barry

Jay Barry, an activist on issues of occupational safety and health, writes frequently for the *Daily World* and other liberal periodicals. In the following viewpoint he compares natural disasters to man-made disasters and lays responsibility for the increase in environmental disasters on multinational corporations. He asserts that corporate executives and regulatory agencies are not doing all they can to reduce risks to the public.

As you read, consider the following questions:

1. How does Mr. Barry compare natural disasters to man-made disasters?
2. Who does he blame for the man-made disasters?
3. According to Mr. Barry, why do chemical corporations do so little to prevent environmental disasters?

Jay Barry, "Preventing Chemical Disasters," *Daily World,* March 13, 1986.

Natural disasters such as the [1985] earthquake in Mexico and Hurricane Gloria [in 1985] remind us that, even in the age of space exploration and genetic engineering, there are natural disasters we have not yet learned to tame. In some cases the best we can do is to warn people of the impending storm, and find ways to evacuate or batten down the hatches.

While hurricanes and earthquakes have always been with us, man-made disasters have mushroomed: . . . explosions at oil refineries, fires at nuclear facilities, and massive chemical leaks. As these chemical disasters multiply, corporate executives and heads of regulatory agencies have begun speaking of them in the same terms as natural disasters.

They argue that the best we can do is to inform ourselves about the hazards, and make emergency evacuation plans.

But unlike hurricanes, these disasters are preventable—although the ounce of prevention may interfere with corporate profits.

The Example of Bhopal

The worst chemical disaster took place in Bhopal, India, [in 1984] . . . when a runaway reaction produced a major leak of deadly methyl isocyanate (MIC) and cyanide gas. Several thousand Bhopal residents were killed, and tens of thousands were left with permanent injuries.

No incident on the scale of Bhopal has occurred yet in the U.S., but a rash of smaller incidents has claimed many lives, exposed local residents to high levels of deadly chemicals, and kept many people in a permanent state of fear.

At Union Carbide's plant in Institute, West Virginia—a close replica of its Bhopal plant—there have been 190 leaks of highly toxic substances such as phosgene gas and MIC in the last five years. Cancer rates in the surrounding Kanawha Valley are double those in clean areas.

In the last five years, at least 135 have died, 1,500 have suffered injuries, and 200,000 people have been evacuated from their homes because of such chemical catastrophes. . . .

A Rash of Disasters

[In a period of only a few months] we have seen: a leak at Kerr-McGee nuclear facility in Oklahoma that killed one worker and injured 32; major leaks at a BASF chemical facility in Louisiana described by Rep. John Conyers' office as "a Bhopal waiting to happen"; explosions at two petrochemical facilities that killed half a dozen workers; and a major leak at an Atlantic-Richfield chemical plant in West Chester, Pennsylvania, that prompted the mayor to declare a state of emergency.

A common response from corporations, the press, and U.S. regulatory agencies has been to claim that chemical corporations had well-maintained plants and did everything reasonable to prevent accidents and that towns and cities should develop evacuation plans for when the next leak or disaster strikes. According to them, the blame for these accidents lies with workers who were careless or on drugs.

The EPA [Environmental Protection Agency] strategy in such matters has been described as: publish lists of dangerous substances and tell everyone to head for the hills.

The Real Fault

An examination of these incidents shows that the real fault lies with corporations that cut corners, fail to perform necessary maintenance, junk safety systems, speed up work and use untrained workers—all in a mad dash for greater profits. . . .

Feiffer by Jules Feiffer. Copyright 1986 Jules Feiffer. Reprinted with permission of Universal Press Syndicate. All rights reserved.

For example, the International Confederation of Chemical Workers found that four separate safety systems—any one of which could have prevented the Bhopal tragedy—had either been shut off deliberately or neglected.

• A refrigeration unit which could have prevented the reaction leading to the MIC production and leak was shut off.

• The cooling element, the freon gas used in refrigerators, had been removed and placed in another part of the plant.

• Chemical scrubbers and flare towers, both of which could have prevented the leak, had been shut down.

• Chemical storage tanks holding MIC were habitually filled above recommended levels.

The Chemical Workers Federation concluded that Union Carbide could have prevented the disaster by allotting funds to make any of these safety systems operable.

A Deadly Pattern

A similar pattern emerged at an explosion at a Union Oil refinery near Chicago. . . . A fire broke out in one part of the plant, and when worker firefighters went in to stem the blaze, they were killed in a secondary explosion. All told, 17 workers died. The same explosion blew a 15-ton smokestack half a mile; it landed on the front porch of a house.

Union Oil officials and the local Occupational Safety and Health Administration (OSHA) office insisted that nothing could have prevented the explosion.

But the fire marshall found that it was caused by gas leaking through a cracked tower, producing an explosive mixture when it met another gas. The fire marshall said the crack was easily visible to the naked eye, and Union Oil could have easily prevented the explosion by patching it.

Preventing the Threat

These chemical disasters are not caused by the movement of vast sheets of rock deep under the earth's crust. They are part and parcel of . . . the crisis of capitalism. They result from heightened competition among chemical and oil giants, their tendency to milk their plants and run them into the ground, the gutting of regulatory agencies, and efforts to destroy trade unions. . . .

Science has not yet developed the means to prevent hurricanes—but preventing chemical leaks, explosions, and fires is well within our ability.

"Disasters . . . just aren't important sources of risk."

The Risk of Environmental Disaster Is Exaggerated

Lester Lave

Lester Lave is James Higgins Professor of Economics at the Graduate School of Industrial Administration at Carnegie Mellon University in Pittsburgh, Pennsylvania. According to the statistics Mr. Lave cites in the following viewpoint, more Americans die from automobile accidents than from environmental disasters. Mr. Lave uses these statistics to reinforce his argument that environmental disasters pose low, not high, risks to the average person. He cautions against restricting the makers and transporters of dangerous chemicals merely to appease a frightened public.

As you read, consider the following questions:

1. According to the author, what percentage of accidental deaths are the result of environmental disasters?
2. What kinds of accidents does he consider a greater risk?
3. Mr. Lave cautions against precisely the type of regulatory measures that Jay Barry advocates in the previous viewpoint. Which attitude toward environmental risks seems more plausible? Why?

Lester Lave, "Disasters: Catching the Mice While Elephants Roam," *Los Angeles Times,* August 20, 1985. Reprinted with the author's permission.

Disaster has filled the headlines: . . . 135 injured by chemical leak in West Virginia, 133 killed in Texas air crash, 520 killed in Japan air crash.

Before dispatching federal inspectors to scrutinize every chemical plant or grounding all aircraft, we need to assess the level of danger posed by such disasters.

About 150,000 Americans are killed each year in accidents. Although these represent only about 8% of all deaths, accidents are the principal killers of children and young adults. Roughly one-third of accidental deaths are highway-related. Less than 1% of accidental deaths are the result of disasters, including commercial air crashes and mishaps at industrial facilities.

A Small Threat

Disasters in general and chemical-plant mishaps in particular just aren't important sources of risk. An Institute, W. Va., parent should be concerned that his children buckle their safety belts in the car and ride their bicycles safely; the Union Carbide plant poses a much smaller threat to them.

Certainly the Union Carbide accident should be investigated, particularly in light of a similar accident at a company plant in Bhopal, India, that killed 2,000. Without . . . judging the results of the inquiry, I am suspicious about the competence of the plant management and executives of Union Carbide; other major chemical companies have much better records.

Airline safety in the United States is exemplary, averaging only 100 deaths each year. Indeed, air travel has become the safest travel mode per passenger mile, about 100 times safer than traveling by car. The Dallas crash was an unfortunate event proving that all human activity is risky. While it must be investigated to see whether similar mishaps can be prevented, the greater danger lies in eroding the convenience of air travel because of an overreaction to such accidents. Is one fewer air crash each decade worth frequent delays due to operating restrictions during storms?

Every year tens of thousands of people are evacuated, several hundred are injured and 30 to 40 people die in accidents involving the transporting of hazardous materials. But rather than focus on tank cars loaded with chlorine, benzene, propane and phosgene—which was used to kill people in World War I—131 state and local governments have banned the transporting of radioactive materials in their jurisdictions. No one has ever been killed because of the radioactivity of substances spilled in an accident; in fact, there has been no major case of exposure.

Contrast the risks of highway accidents with those posed by industrial facilities; compare the transporting of chlorine with the risks of carrying radioactive materials. Society is preoccupied with mice while the elephants go unnoticed.

By following New York, Texas and 13 other states in requiring that safety belts in cars be used, [other states] would do much more to reduce fatalities than by increasing safeguards at all chemical plants. To be sure, when a situation such as Union Carbide's Institute leak occurs, government ought to react swiftly. But a new law mandating more frequent inspection of all chemical plants would be costly and obtrusive, and would tend to divert attention from more important problems. Rather, the bad companies need to be identified and given special attention, as occurs in coal mines, where an inspector is placed on the site full time for a period following a serious accident.

Exaggerated Fear

The public's fear of toxic chemicals is grossly exaggerated but nevertheless it is very real. . . . This fear can be translated into laws and regulations so punitive and so excessively expensive that they would make our operations prohibitive, make new products difficult to develop and commercialize, and make our industry noncompetitive in the international trade arena.

Edwin Holmer, quoted in *The Nation*, April 27, 1985.

My sympathies go out to the victims of these disasters, but their pain should not catapult us into needless change. Risk management requires facts, analysis and a systematic approach. Risks must be viewed as an unfortunate necessity of life. The goal is reducing injuries and deaths to the extent possible, within acceptable budgets and with due attention to the benefits of activities such as flying and having modern chemical products.

Unnecessary Action

To date, the United States has rushed from mishap to mishap, demanding immediate action on the peril most recently in the headlines. As a result, an already safe air-transport system is subjected to more public scrutiny while highway accidents and dangers connected with the transporting of hazardous chemicals are largely ignored.

We live in a world that is permeated by risks. Managing them is far more complicated than condemning the company or the individuals responsible for the next news-making disaster.

"*Union Carbide's posture in the aftermath
of Bhopal has been one of arrogance
and bullying.*"

Union Carbide Responded Inappropriately to the Bhopal Disaster

The Revolutionary Worker

On December 2, 1984, a Union Carbide chemical plant in Bhopal,
India, exploded, spewing poisonous fumes into the air. Death
estimates ranged from 2,000 to 20,000. The media immediately
labeled the accident the worst environmental disaster in history.
Reports of the aftermath brought the debate over liability in such
disasters to the forefront of public discussion. In the following
viewpoint, *The Revolutionary Worker,* the weekly newspaper of the
Revolutionary Communist Party USA, argues that Union Carbide
is solely responsible for the Indian deaths and that, moreover, its
actions following the disaster were grossly irresponsible.

As you read, consider the following questions:

1. What elements of Union Carbide's response to the Bhopal
   tragedy does the author condemn?
2. According to the author, what argument is Union Carbide
   offering in its defense? What does the author think of this
   argument?

Excerpted from "Bhopal One Year Later," by *The Revolutionary Worker,* the weekly
newspaper of the Revolutionary Communist Party, U.S.A., January 6, 1986. Reprinted
with permission.

On the night of December 2-3, [1984], what has been widely acknowledged as the worst industrial disaster in history occurred in Bhopal, India. A cloud of killer gases, now known to have included hydrogen cyanide, escaped from the Union Carbide Pesticide plant and enveloped the city. Between 200,000 to 300,000 people were exposed to the gases. To this day no one knows precisely how many died. The official death toll, at last count, stands at 1,754. Most people in Bhopal feel that at least twice that many perished, with some estimates going as high as ten thousand.

The full magnitude of this chemical massacre is becoming ever more apparent with the passage of time. People continue to die from the after-effects of the gassing—between five hundred and a thousand over [1985]. . . . An estimated sixty thousand people in Bhopal were severely debilitated by the toxic cloud; most of them are still unable to work or engage in normal activities. Many are crippled for life. Three thousand are still treated in Bhopal each day for gas-related afflictions. And the long-term effects of the disaster can still only be guessed.

The battle to establish the cause of and responsibility for the Bhopal disaster, and compensate its victims, is continuing. On the [first] anniversary of the gas leak, over four thousand people, including many of the worst-affected slum-dwellers, marched through Bhopal denouncing "killer Carbide," burning Carbide Chairman Ron Anderson in effigy, and demanding more medical care, adequate compensation and relief, and Union Carbide's expulsion from India.

Arrogance and Bullying

In the face of widespread outrage and horrendous suffering in India, and worldwide revulsion over its Bhopal massacre, Union Carbide's posture in the aftermath of Bhopal has been one of arrogance and bullying—a statement of U.S. imperialism's necessity and determination to continue to operate in brutal fashion in the oppressed nations and to assert its global prerogatives. For example, . . . as the toll in suffering and deaths has become ever more apparent, Carbide's help on the medical front has been next to nothing, and it continues to deny the involvement of cyanide in the disaster.

Carbide's "explanation" of its massacre has been similarly contemptuous. According to Larry Everest—author of . . . *Behind the Poison Cloud: Union Carbide's Bhopal Massacre*—it is now acknowledged that the disaster began when water entered MIC (Methyl Isocyanate) storage tank No. 610 and triggered a runaway chemical chain reaction. This chain reaction generated a tremendous buildup of heat and pressure inside the tank, which quickly ruptured a safety disk, spewing over 50,000 pounds of deadly toxins into the atmosphere over Bhopal. It is widely felt that the source of this water was a worker washing down a pipeline leading into tank 610. That such a flow of water could lead to such a disaster was the result of a confluence of a number of factors: among them were that the plant's design was unsafe, in particular large amounts of deadly chemicals were stored, and the plant's safety systems weren't designed to cope with anything other than minor releases of gases. Also, normal maintenance, training, staffing and company safety procedures were ignored under the pressure of crisis-induced cost cutting. For example, many of the plant's safety systems were totally shut off on the night of the disaster. (It has . . . been confirmed that Carbide had been trying to sell off the plant.) And Union Carbide's Bhopal factory didn't even have the same level of safety equipment as the company's also-dangerous pesticide plant in Institute, West Virginia.

Moir, reprinted with permission from Cartoonists & Writers Syndicate.

While being forced to acknowledge some particular safety failures, Carbide has ignored the mountain of evidence of its own culpability and refused to accept any responsibility for the massacre. Instead it has claimed that the disaster resulted from sabotage—the deliberate introduction of water into tank 610. This amounts to a paper-thin effort to take advantage of . . . hysteria over "terrorism" in the U.S. to not only evade any responsibility for the slaughter in Bhopal, but to contribute to that hysteria as well.

Carbide's thesis rests on two thin reeds. One, a newspaper story in *The Danbury News Times* citing an AP report that one poster was seen in Punjab signed by the "Black June" group claiming responsibility for the disaster. However, no one seems to have the poster now, and more importantly this group was previously unknown in India, and the charge is widely discounted there.

The second part of Carbide's argument rests on its own chemical analysis of the disaster. Carbide admits it has no direct proof of sabotage, and its March 20, 1985 report on the disaster admits that water could have entered tank 610 as a result of the washing of a pipeline. Yet it argues that the introduction of water must have been deliberate and not the result of water washing because between one thousand and two thousand pounds of water (120-240 gallons) were necessary to account for the ensuing reaction, and that that quantity of water could never have traveled through the closed valves between the site of the water washing and tank 610.

Flawed Argument

It has been understood since March 1985 that Carbide's argument concerning the route of water ingress was flawed because it ignored the shoddy quality of the plant's valves, and that a jumper line connected two major pipelines and provided a route of entry from the site of the water washing into tank 610. . . . [More] information from India further undercuts Carbide's sabotage charge. Indian scientists studying the corporation's report and its technical manuals have determined that roughly half the amount of water postulated by Carbide—in other words, between 750 and 1100 pounds—has been sufficient to account for the residue in tank 610. This strengthens the contention that the washing of a pipeline was the source of the water that initiated the runaway reaction because in general the less amount of water, the more likely it could have traveled through a series of pipelines and leaky valves into the tank. In fact Indian scientists . . . claim that this amount of water could have traveled from the site of the water washing into tank 610.

Further, the speed of the reaction indicates that it was mainly the result of contaminants, carried by the water from the plant's corroded pipelines, not simply water by itself (further indicting the quality of the construction and maintenance at the plant). This undercuts the sabotage hypothesis because Carbide has speculated that the saboteur attached a water hose to lines leading into tank 610 at a nearby work station, a route that meant that water did not pass through an extensive length of the corroded pipelines. It would also mean that any saboteur would had to have extensive knowledge of the contaminants in the tank and the pipelines leading to it, not to mention an extremely sophisticated understanding of chemistry.

Carbide has attacked the water-washing thesis because the pipelines, through which water supposedly leaked, were found to be dry. Yet Indian scientists point out that the heat and vacuum created by the gases, which escaped by the same route that the water entered, would have sucked the pipelines dry. Also, journalist Ivan Fera states in a September [1985] issue of *The Illustrated Weekly of India:* "There are no valves or vents or bleeders on either the PVH or the RVH (the two main pipelines) leading directly into the tank, to which a water hose could be applied. Even if there were, a saboteur opening a valve would first be overwhelmed by the gas." . . .

Ripe for Disaster

The . . . Indian government report on the disaster . . . also discounts the sabotage hypothesis and argues instead that design failures, cost-cutting, and mismanagement created conditions that "were ripe" for disaster.

Bhopal Was Murder

Bhopal was murder, if not genocide. To mumble "Sorry" and offer cash is an intolerable response in light of the organized effort that profited from the conditions that produced the disaster. To accept the proposition that people of less technologically advanced regions, abroad and at home, are unfortunate but necessary industrial fodder so that the rest of us may progress to unlimited splendor is unconscionable. It suggests how much we have yet to learn about our common humanity, how genuine freedom may have to be shared before it can be thoroughly lived and enjoyed.

Robert Engler, *The Nation,* April 27, 1985.

The imperiousness of Union Carbide's posture is equally glaring concerning compensating the victims of its massacre. Since the disaster this $10 billion corporation has managed to cough up a total of $3 million in interim relief and services. (The Indian government has so far spent $40 million on relief.) As Carbide lawyer Bud Holman explained to the *American Lawyer* magazine, "One interim payment can lead to another. See how it works? Do you have children? If you have children, you see it's better to give $1 and see what they do with it before you give more." Carbide employees contributed another $150,000, which amounts to less than $2 per employee.

Carbide has offered to settle out of court for $240 million spread over thirty years, which comes to about $100 million today—half its current liability coverage. Its offer—reportedly a sliding scale ranging from $12,000 per death to $45 for non-serious injuries—is based on its calculation of the value of Indian life. Holman declared: "According to the Indian government the average income in Bhopal is $127 a year. The people who were hit were squatters in a slum who are intermittently employed, and many weren't employed. Many of them were children and women. You can't take the squatters you saw on Chhola road (one of the main roads near the Union Carbide plant in Bhopal) and compensate them as if they lived in New York or California or West Virginia." This is a raw example of imperialism's reduction of all human life to cash calculations, and raw hypocrisy as well. Union Carbide located in India in part to take advantage of the abysmal living conditions and low wages of the Indian masses. Now those same abysmal conditions are mustered as an excuse to get off cheaply from the company's criminal neglect of safety in Bhopal.

"We've had a good reputation for health, safety, and the environment."

Union Carbide Responded Appropriately to the Bhopal Disaster

Warren M. Anderson

Warren M. Anderson is the chairman of Union Carbide Corporation, based in Danbury, Connecticut. After the Union Carbide India Limited plant in Bhopal, India exploded, killing thousands of people, Mr. Anderson flew to the city to oversee the corporation's response to the accident. The following viewpoint is excerpted from an interview with the chairman conducted by William J. Storck and David Webber of *Chemical & Engineering News* magazine. Here Mr. Anderson describes the company's response to the disaster and what has happened in the chemical industry as a result of Union Carbide's example.

As you read, consider the following questions:

1. How does Mr. Anderson describe his company's response to the Bhopal tragedy?
2. According to Mr. Anderson, what has happened in the chemical industry as a result of the disaster?
3. Mr. Anderson says it may be fortunate that this kind of incident happened to Union Carbide. Why does he say that?

Warren M. Anderson, "Carbide's Anderson Explains Post-Bhopal Strategy." Reprinted with permission from *Chemical and Engineering News*, January 21, 1985. Copyright 1985 American Chemical Society.

It seems what Carbide is trying to do in dealing with Bhopal is strike a balance between compassion and practicality. What would you like to see happen?

I would like to see all the proper people who represent the survivors, the relatives of the deceased, the city of Bhopal, the state of Madhya Pradesh, the government of India, Union Carbide India Ltd., and Union Carbide Corp. sit down and come up with an answer. The key is to find a way of recompensing—it's hard to say money is going to solve things, but it's the only real means we have—that would be compassionate and reasonable. I would hope that this could be done in a relatively short period of time, because the longer one waits, the more complicated life becomes.

Have you begun some kind of negotiation with the Indians?

Oh yes—right from the word go. From the time I arrived in India . . . Carbide has been saying to a whole host of people that the way to sort this out is to sit down and talk about it. Now the issue has been, how do we get all those people represented in a negotiation rather than in a confrontation. That's what we've been working on. . . .

Find Out How To Help

What did you hope to accomplish on your trip to Bhopal?

We were misunderstood in some ways on this whole issue. There was an article that said the only reason I went over was the litigation issue. That isn't true. As for the litigation issue—nobody was even thinking about litigation. Everybody was in a state of shock. The reason for going was to find out how to help the people who have been hurt. How to cope with this kind of an incident, a kind that I've never been involved in before. The reason for going was also to be supportive of Union Carbide India, to worry about the security of that plant so that nothing else would go wrong, and then to worry about what to do with the MIC [methyl isocyanate] left in the tanks. How could we get it out of the way safely? Then, what in fact did happen there? How do we get our hands on what was the cause?

What progress has Carbide made in its investigation of what happened at the plant?

Trying to replicate or determine exactly what went wrong in a situation such as this is not easy. It's as if an airplane crashes and you put all the pieces in the hangar and then say, "Now I wonder what happened." It takes time.

But we need an answer as soon as we can get it for a variety of reasons. It's incumbent on the company to disclose to the world what happened, because there are other people who make and use MIC. When we voluntarily shut down our MIC unit at Institute, we said that we would not start it up again until we know what happened at Bhopal and until we and the proper authorities are convinced that it's safe. We need to know, government agencies need to know, customers need to know, other producers need to know. . . .

What obstacles do you face in your investigation?

We have not been able to interview our personnel at the plant [because they are under arrest]. We haven't been able to take samples other than from the tank itself.

Industry's Reappraisal

Why was there so much MIC in the tank? Was it necessary?

The question of how much is right is an issue that is dependent on production schedules, demand for product, etc. Product manufacture is a seasonal kind of thing, because application of pesticides is seasonal. The question of adequacy of inventory is complicated by all these issues.

We are reappraising how to work with hazardous materials, not just in India, but all over the world. What procedures should one use? Should one convert it all [to a less hazardous product] immediately? But we're not alone here. There's going to be a reappraisal not only by the chemical industry but by a lot of industries of how they operate in this kind of environment with this kind of product.

In light of this reappraisal, have you sent teams out to check your plants?

Oh yes, we've done as everyone else has done. We've set up a whole new reappraisal structure that's organized and laid on top of the normal line responsibilities for safety, environment, and health. . . .

A Company with Compassion

We have been known as a company that has compassion, that's concerned about our employees and the community as well. I said at that moment in time [right after the accident] that I didn't worry about legal liability. . . . Let's have a way of solving the compensation issue. Let's not get into the legal niceties, because when you go down that road, then you have years and years and years of interminable litigation.

Warren M. Anderson, quoted in *The American Lawyer,* November 1985.

What changes do you foresee coming out of industry's reappraisal of its practices and the public's reappraisal of industry?

First you have the legislative side. This gets involved in transportation of hazardous materials. There is the issue of "right-to-know" laws, the issue of toxic substances. Then there is a whole set of management issues: How to organize, and what new thoughts should be introduced in investment overseas. What kind

81

of controls to exert. How to negotiate and work with overseas countries on issues like siting a plant. On issues [such as locating] a plant out in the country, whose responsibility it is to keep people away from the plants. I can't remember ever going by an industrial location in India that didn't have people living right there. But it's not just India. So I think there are issues about what we do within our plant, and issues about what happens outside our plant.

India is not the only country that requires local control, local construction, local staffing, and so forth. Will you back away from a location with those requirements now?

It may well be that local content requirements—I understand and appreciate why developing countries want them—may be mitigated in areas where there are hazards, because some lessons have been learned. Not by India alone. The world has learned some lessons. So it's not only the industry that's reappraising. It's the countries that are taking a look now and saying they understand they won't have as much currency help [if a company doesn't manufacture here], but on the other hand maybe it's worth that not to go through that hazardous step that they don't really want.

Corporate Obligations

It seems that would be a problem, ideologically, for a lot of developing countries that have been trying to gain the benefits of western technology without becoming shackled to U.S. industry.

I think what is going to happen is an appraisal by the multinationals of Japan, Europe, and the U.S., saying that there has been a new issue introduced here. It's sort of ironic. On one side, you see the problem of Bhopal, and on the other you see people starving in Africa. What's happened in India over the past few years has provided a self-sufficiency in food. A country can't get there unless it has pesticides, herbicides, fertilizers, and so on. So a country has to somehow reach an accommodation of having available to it the technology that permits indigenous production of some of these materials. Otherwise, it has the terrible alternative of starving people.

And yet, we do have a new issue here as to how far to go in bringing high technology into developing countries. It's not just Union Carbide and the chemical industry. It's a whole bunch of other industries too that are sort of sitting back now, saying, "Hey, wait a minute." People have made judgments that [bringing this technology in] was good or bad. I think maybe those same people now might not come out with the same judgments.

I think it has to be good for the world to think through this whole sequence of where to put the material, what kind of control to have, what are the obligations of the governments of developing countries, and what are corporations' obligations? It's not bad to sit and think these things through. It's unfortunate that this has to come about because a lot of people died. . . .

What changes do you foresee in terms of safety practices?

If you had tried [before Bhopal] . . . to get a bunch of different people involved in evacuation plans around a chemical plant, you might have been hard pressed to get everybody's attention. You must get doctors, hospitals, TV stations, radio stations, police, state troopers, the governor's office. Now you can get their attention. Can we come up with plans so that in a location like a Kanawha Valley (W. Va.) or Seadrift, Tex., or Texas City we have the capability of doing even a better job than we've already tried to do? I think that, given the help of the Chemical Manufacturers Association and of the local communities, who now have a much heightened interest in this kind of thing, we're going to be better off. . . .

No Responsibility

There is no need or reason for Union Carbide to agree to an inflated settlement. The corporation did nothing that either caused or contributed to the [Bhopal] accident, and if it comes to litigation, we will vigorously defend that position.

Warren M. Anderson, quoted in *Chemical & Engineering News*, April 29, 1985.

What will be the ultimate consequences of the Bhopal disaster?

You know, I said this before—and I don't even know if people believe me—but maybe it's fortunate that this kind of incident happened to Union Carbide. I say this because we've had a good reputation for health, safety, and the environment; we're a company that has resources; and we can cope with an issue like this one. Maybe out of this will come a whole new approach to this issue of health, safety, and environment. Not only in developing countries, but in the U.S. as well. If it had happened to a company that didn't have Carbide's capabilities, maybe not as much would have been learned. So we have a commitment and an obligation to lead the way if we can. The world's going to be a better place. It's a hard way to learn a lesson, but if you went through a disaster like this and didn't learn anything, that would be the worst.

The Ability To Empathize

This chapter consists of viewpoints dealing with the effects large corporations have on people and the environment, and the corporations' responsibility for these effects. The viewpoints discuss some of the problems that arise when the question of corporate responsibility occurs. This exercise is designed to improve your problem-solving skills through empathizing: the ability to understand situations from another's point of view.

In this activity you will be required to imagine you and your group are involved in the building of a nuclear power plant. Each member in the group will take the part of one of the key figures in the decision-making process. You are not allowed the option of not building the power plant.

After reading the viewpoints in this chapter, the class should break into groups of five people. Each student will take the role of a person who is involved in the confrontation over the power plant and must argue that person's point of view with the other students in the small group. First list the varying concerns each of the characters might have and then discuss different solutions based on the concerns you have listed.

The situation: The nuclear power plant is to be built near a residential area and directly next to a pond containing an endangered species of algae-eating snails that will be destroyed when waste from the plant is dumped into the pond. There is also danger of an accident during the building of the power plant as well as after it is in operation. There are many government safety regulations that must be adhered to in order to allow the plant to begin operation, especially those dealing with the nuclear reactor. Environmental activists are angry about the possible extinction of the snails, the possibility of a nuclear accident, and possible damage to the environment. Company officials are trying to meet deadlines set by the parent company and are running into all kinds of obstacles. The citizens of the nearby town are up in arms over the nearness of the power plant to their town. The residents of the town also suffer from problems with their present energy supply, often going without power because of mechanical breakdowns in their present supply. As you discuss all of the problems of this situation in your respective roles, attempt to reach a compromise that will satisfy all those involved.

The roles:

Chairperson of the board of the corporation responsible for building the power plant: The chair of the board is in charge of making sure that the plant gets built in the least amount of time, with the least effort, at the smallest cost to the parent company.,

Plant manager: responsible for overseeing the construction of the plant so that all the governmental conditions are met.

A parent living near the proposed site: concerned about safety standards, what kinds of accidents could happen at the power plant, what kind of information the company would provide, and what responsibility it would take in the event of an accident.

An environmental activist: believes that the plant would contribute to the destruction of the atmosphere through radiation leaks and the waste from the nuclear power plant would poison the water in the area.

Government agent: responsible for providing power for a certain area of the country, and making sure governmental guidelines are followed.

Periodical Bibliography

The following list of periodical articles deals with the subject matter of this chapter.

Dennis Bernstein and Connie Blitt
"Lethal Dose," *The Progressive,* March 1986.

Richard E. Cheney
"Crisis Communication," *USA Today,* May 1986.

Robert Engler
"Technology Out of Control," *The Nation,* April 27, 1985.

Denise Giardina
"Almost Heaven? Don't You Believe It," *The Washington Post National Weekly Edition,* September 9, 1985.

Steve Lerner and Mary Ellin Barrett
"What You Haven't Heard About Bhopal," *Ms.,* December 1985.

Thomas J. Lueck
"Carbide Says Inquiry Showed Errors But Is Incomplete," *The New York Times,* January 28, 1985.

Ian I. Mitroff and Paul Shrivastava
"Corporate Disasters: Coping with Product Tampering, Sabotage, and Other Catastrophes," *USA Today,* May 1986.

Tom Morganthau with Daniel Pedersen
"Kerr-McGee's Deadly Cloud," *Newsweek,* January 20, 1986.

Meera Nanda
"Secrecy Was Bhopal's Disaster," *Science for the People,* November/December 1985.

The New York Times
"Company's Statement: The Major Points," January 28, 1985.

James H. Senger
"The Aftermath," *Chemical and Engineering News,* March 25, 1985.

Deborah A. Sheiman and David D. Doniger
"To Avoid a Bhopal in the U.S.," *The New York Times,* December 11, 1985.

Union Carbide
"Bhopal Methyl Isocyanate Incident: Investigation Team Report," March 1985. Available from Union Carbide Corporation, 39 Old Ridgebury Road, Danbury, CT 06817-0001.

A. Vaidyanathan
"Accountability Is Bad for Business: Multinationals, Indian Industrialists and Government Balance Their Books," *Science for the People,* November/December 1985.

Have Pollution Regulations Improved the Environment?

THE ENVIRONMENTAL CRISIS

"Federal regulation [is] the most underrated form of preventive medicine in America today."

Environmental Regulations Are Necessary

David Bollier and Joan Claybrook

The federal government has been regulating health, safety, and environmental standards for many years. In the following viewpoint, David Bollier and Joan Claybrook lament the lack of gratitude for these regulations and outline how regulatory agencies protect the public from harm. David Bollier, a political journalist based in New Haven, Connecticut, has written extensively about consumer issues. Joan Claybrook, former administrator of the National Highway Traffic Safety Administration, is the president of Public Citizen, a national consumer organization based in Washington, DC. They co-authored *Freedom from Harm: The Civilizing Influence of Health, Safety and Environmental Regulation,* from which this viewpoint is taken.

As you read, consider the following questions:

1. Who do the authors blame for lack of public appreciation for regulations?
2. What, according to the authors, is the purpose of the regulatory agencies? Do they believe the agencies have accomplished this purpose?
3. According to the authors, why is it dangerous to forget what life was like before health and environmental regulations were enforced?

David Bollier and Joan Claybrook, *Freedom from Harm: The Civilizing Influence of Health, Safety and Environmental Regulation.* Washington, DC: Public Citizen and Democracy Project, 1986. Reprinted with permission.

When Dr. Jonas E. Salk discovered a serum that could prevent the crippling symptoms of poliomyelitis, the vaccine was enthusiatically welcomed by *The New York Times* as "one of the greatest triumphs in the history of medicine." Its widespread use in the mid-1950s lowered the incidence of polio from a peak of 21,269 cases in 1952 to less than 900 in 1962. Dr. Salk was rewarded for his discovery with a cover article in the March 29, 1954, *Time* magazine. A caption beneath a likeness of the doctor described his achievement: "Polio Fighter Salk: Generations will grow up free." Dr. Salk was lionized by his medical peers and the public, and immortalized for his new preventive remedy for polio—the "Salk vaccine."

When the Environmental Protection Agency (EPA) proposed a new rule in 1984 to reduce the amount of lead in regular gasoline—a measure that would save an estimated 50,000 children from the brain-damaging effects of airborne lead—no brass bands or public adulation followed. The story registered a quick blip on the evening news and provoked bitter denunciations from many gasoline refiners. The EPA scientists and regulators responsible for this important advance in the nation's health remain anonymous to the public, and the future beneficiaries will probably never know how a few courageous civil servants fought to enhance the quality of their lives and health.

Complex Science and Reluctant Corporations

So goes another episode in the annals of federal regulation, the most underrated form of preventive medicine in America today. In the 20th century, the bacterial killers of the past have been largely vanquished through basic sanitary reforms, new vaccines and immunizations. What now looms as a far more serious threat to the public health are unprecedented new harms stemming from the proliferation of technologies: unsafe automobiles (and roadways), dangerous consumer products, unsafe drugs, medical devices and cosmetics, contaminated foods, residue-laden meat and poultry, polluted air and water, toxic chemicals, and hazards in the workplace. These "technological epidemics" of the 1980s are at least as debilitating to the public well-being as earlier bacterial scourges.

Yet the crusade to eliminate these documented harms, which are largely preventable in nature, is criticized by prominent political and corporate leaders and beset by countless legal, scientific, political, budgetary and other obstacles. Even measures that will certifiably help innocent young children, such as the leaded gasoline rule, encounter entrenched opposition. It almost goes without saying that actual success in abating harms through regulation receive little public notice or acclaim. Why?

Solutions to the technology-based epidemics of our industrial society remain elusive for two primary reasons: the complexity of the science and technology which generate the hazards, and the intransigence of the corporate dominated economy that sustains them. The dangers of airborne lead, for example, are not only scientifically complex to investigate and confirm. Remedies are expensive to conceive and develop, and the solutions are politically difficult to implement as well. Scientific knowledge and feasible solutions are not enough. A *political transformation* must be effected to alter the institutional practices of industry which give rise to the hazard.

© Alexander-Lawrence/Rothco

So, for example, gasoline refiners must adopt new, more costly ways to boost the octane of gasoline instead of using lead that ends up in children's bloodstreams; auto companies must design cars that are crashworthy, not only flashy; drug companies must undertake more rigorous premarket testing of prospective medicines; industrial polluters must install new control technologies to curb their emissions; food processors must forgo certain unsafe additives; slaughterhouse operators must observe sanitary practices in preparing meat; and so on. Literally thousands of nodes in our economy are affected by the requirements of federal health, safety and environmental regulation. And in thousands of ways, the public well-being is enhanced as a result. . . .

90

Americans benefit from the research, analyses, rulemaking and enforcement decisions and advocacy of the federal regulatory agencies. . . . The six most significant health and safety agencies charged with abating non-catastrophic hazards . . . include the:

- Food and Drug Administration (FDA);
- U.S. Department of Agriculture's Food Safety and Inspection Service (USDA);
- National Highway Traffic Safety Administration (NHTSA);
- Environmental Protection Agency (EPA);
- Occupational Safety and Health Administration (OSHA); and the
- Consumer Product Safety Commission (CPSC).

Agencies' Mandate

These agencies are instructed by Congress to protect the public based on their scientific findings and the best provisional evidence that can be acquired at that time. As William Drayton, a former assistant administrator of the EPA, explained, "Regulators, especially those responsible for protecting human health and safety, are charged by our society to act before all the evidence is in, before every issue is nailed down and ten articles have been published in the rigorous academic literature. Prevention, the key goal of the agencies, is undermined if uncertainty becomes an unwarranted excuse for delay. Delay not only prolongs the hazard, it makes its eventual control more difficult and costly. Once a new technology exists—an automotive feature, pesticide, drug production equipment—it becomes politically explosive and costly to turn that technology off, or to modify it. Investments have been made and expectations set. But allowing that integration into commerce to become even more complete, while the hazard persists, flirts with a Faustian bargain: dependency on a deadly or injurious technology.

It is the rapid acceleration of scientific discoveries and their application in the marketplace that fuels the steady diffusion of new technological hazards. Few of these harms would be investigated let alone controlled if the federal government did not focus its scientific searchlight on them. And without the "public sector" knowledge generated by agency investigation, few preventive strategies would emerge.

Congress realized that ingenuity alone cannot conquer technological hazards that have political and economic origins. Powerful business enterprises "benefit" by not addressing the dangers they create, leaving hapless consumers, workers and taxpayers to pay for the damages they suffer with their dollars and health. To help correct this injustice, the federal health and safety agencies attempt to prevent and control the antisocial behavior of private business decisions and preserve the quality of life.

This is an inherently controversial role because it involves a basic struggle over private property, human values and the exercise of power. Without a government presence industry regulates our lives in accordance with its private, chiefly economic, priorities. It does so by controlling capital investment, scientific research, technological development, product design, economic efficiency in the workplace, the price and availability of products, and the flow of information in the marketplace.

When government "intervention" in the marketplace assists these priorities, American business usually welcomes the help. Indeed, most government activity is oriented to serve business needs in one fashion or another. This assistance can range from direct research and operational and marketing subsidies to indirect assistance in "maintaining order" in the marketplace. The economic regulatory agencies serve this latter function and, in many instances, restrict competition that could unsettle existing business arrangements. Business usually favors this sort of federal regulation. As Republican Senator Paul Laxalt once remarked, "If tomorrow it was announced that all government intervention in business were ended, there would be coronaries in every boardroom."

Regulation Is Needed

Public Opinion magazine found that only 9 percent of the public wants worker-safety regulations reduced, 32 percent wants them as they are, and 59 percent wants them strengthened.

Whatever its periodic errors or excesses, federal environmental and consumer regulation has worked, and the regulation is needed. Product safety standards on cribs and bottle caps have cut infant deaths from crib strangulation and ingestion of poisons or pills by 50 percent. The Clean Air Act has created 200,000 jobs and has provided $21.4 billion worth of economic and health benefits annually. Federal auto and traffic regulations have prevented approximately 100,000 deaths from automobile accidents.

Mark Green, *The New Republic,* March 21, 1983.

Not so for the health, safety and environmental agencies. Their regulation is designed to protect the public health, not promote private wealth. These agencies are authorized to suspend the short-term priorities of the market, upon which most American businesses base their actions, in order to protect long-term needs of the public well-being. Thus, they interfere with "business as usual" by requiring new investments, research, technologies and production procedures.

Power for Americans

The result is to empower the American people in a way that few other federal programs do. Consumers gain new freedoms from harm through regulatory standards. They learn how to make more informed decisions in the marketplace through technical data that the government develops and popularizes. Workers gain new rights to ensure their well-being at work through manufacturing process changes required to meet Occupational Safety and Health Administration standards. Communities acquire new legal tools and funds to protect their air, water and soil. And diffuse constituencies with little political clout gain new levels of protection. Babies unwittingly benefit from quality control rules preventing production of unsafe infant formula (which can be nutritionally deficient) and unsafe crib designs (which have led to strangulations). Artists and woodworkers can use benzene-free paint solvents and varnish-removers (benzene is a carcinogen). The sick and disabled can trust their drugs and medical devices to be reasonably safe and reliable. Asthmatics can enjoy some measure of relief from polluted air.

Regulation is an imperfect but necessary attempt to democratize corporate-owned science and technology. It injects public concerns into otherwise "private" decisions and investments. It helps the public understand and interpret technological information that otherwise is jealously guarded by the corporate scientific elite. Few consumers can make sophisticated scientific judgments about, say, the toxicity of household solvents or the crash strength of automobiles. And even if some highly knowledgeable or wealthy consumer could make such judgments, the principle of *caveat emptor,* ("let the buyer beware"), is truly a primitive basis for conducting commerce in an era of sophisticated technology and mass markets serving millions of consumers. A contamination mishap in a single mushroom canning factory in Pennsylvania can jeopardize the health of millions of people in dozens of states—as it did in 1981. By deciding not to recall a tire which it knew was dangerously defective, a tire manufacturer can endanger the lives of millions of motorists—as Firestone did in 1976. Sulfur oxides released into the air by power plants in the Midwest are causing acid precipitation that is killing fish, wildlife, lakes and vegetation in New England. . . .

Regulation and the Anatomy of Amnesia

It is both ironic and disturbing that the benefits of regulation are not easily recognized or applauded. Why? In part, because new technological hazards are constantly making new claims for government attention even as "old" problems are being addressed. Rarely is there a sense of eradicating a hazard once and for all. Also, since most regulatory victories involve political negotiation and compromise, the outcomes are nearly always qualified and incomplete victories.

Public ignorance of regulatory achievements can also be explained by the very nature of regulatory success: the accomplishments—tragedy averted—are rarely seen or appreciated by the beneficiaries. When harm is *prevented,* the evidence of the payoff from more stringent health and safety protections is highly technical and not readily apparent to the lay person. Few Americans appreciate the fact that federal regulation has eliminated carcinogens from sleepwear, paint solvents, certain drugs and food products, and root beer. Few Americans realize that laminated car windshield designs mandated by federal regulation prevent glass from shattering in a crash and disfiguring and injuring occupants. The tens of thousands of Americans who are alive only because of federal auto and highway safety standards do not know to write a thank-you note to Washington, D.C. . . .

Regulators' Burden

There is a fundamental difference in the choices faced by academic scientists and regulators. Academic scientists can afford to wait for more data before concluding that a chemical does or does not cause a particular effect, and they would be judged careless or remiss if they did not wait. For regulators, waiting is functionally the same as deciding not to regulate. And when human health is at stake and prevention is possible, waiting for more data can cause great harm if a chemical does in fact turn out to pose a risk. Thus, in some cases regulators may have a moral obligation to act even if the available evidence does not meet the criteria of academic science.

J. Clarence Davies, *Issues in Science and Technology,* Winter 1985.

Successful regulation may also go unnoticed because it defies easy measurement. There are, of course, many incremental improvements that can be measured in air quality, crashworthiness in cars, product-related deaths and injuries, and so forth. However, numerical assessments do not measure the many intangible ripple effects that occur simply because a federal agency is paying attention to a hazard. As Professor Lee Preston, Director of the Center for Business and Public Policy at the University of Maryland, states:

The most critical activity [of regulatory agencies] may be the *articulation* of social concerns, rather than the development and implementation of specific means for their achievement. The fact that questions have been raised, issues looked into, and awareness stimulated may amount to satisfactory goal attainment in itself.

Simply "paying attention" is often *not* enough to control a hazard; actual regulation and enforcement is frequently necessary. However, most economically oriented observers of regulation fail to acknowledge the fact that when a regulatory agency looks into technology-based problems or proposes regulations, it sparks a wide variety of salutary if unquantifiable results: for example, new research by university scientists; a more vigilant surveillance of hazards by companies; more press coverage and thus more public awareness of a hazard; new consumer behavior in avoiding/selecting certain products and in asserting consumer rights; and a greater number of product liability lawsuits to obtain relief through individual means. One auto industry was exhilarated by the regulatory challenges of the late 1970s. Robert Alexander of Ford Motor Company commented in 1978 " . . . the lion's share of the burden of meeting these stringent standards and mandates will fall on the shoulders of the engineers. In fact, I like to call this the 'age of the engineer'—and I, for one, couldn't be happier." This sort of reaction is overlooked in orthodox evaluations of regulations.

Emphasis on Economics

Also because the economics profession has come to dominate evaluations of health and safety regulation, economic categories of thought predominate in the scholarly literature and political debate about regulation. It is therefore not surprising that *benefits* receive short shrift. After all, how is it possible to really "measure" the value of having milk pasteurized? The value of stronger doors in cars to protect occupants in side-impact crashes? The value of government inspections to reduce harmful nitrosamines in bacon and contaminants in meat? The value of a smog-free Grand Canyon? Economists habituated to number-crunching feel secure with the measurable, and indifferent to the unmeasurable, though immense, benefits of avoided injuries and death.

The ascendancy of the economic paradigm in assessing federal regulation tends to obliterate the memory of why regulation was needed in the first place. Cost-benefit analysis exemplifies this tendency. It is not just that strict numerical cost-benefit analyses run contrary to most of the statutes governing public health, regulatory programs; or that they neutralize and obscure issues of fairness; or that they are time-consuming, costly, often arbitrary and highly imperfect. Worse, cost-benefit analyses seek to substitute a specious economic test for a distinctly moral, social criterion for regulating—to prevent human and environmental harm that is ethically distasteful and violates societal standards of decency. . . .

Strong Public Support

Regulators carrying out the laws demonstrate . . . that regulation ultimately is an ethical judgement based on the best provisional evidence, not an economic decision based on elusive numbers. While conservative critics of regulation might view this

95

notion of regulation as quaint and uninformed, it is the underlying reason why public support for specific regulatory programs remains so strong. In a major survey of consumer attitudes conducted by Louis Harris in 1982, it was found that:

> Anti-regulation opinion outnumbers opinion favoring more regulation by a ratio of two to one. However, this indicator of opinion at a general or abstract level does not translate into public disfavor with all concrete forms of regulation. Quite the contrary, consumers strongly support many specific types of regulation. . . .
>
> Instances of protective innovation by the government typically receive public endorsement averaging about 80 percent. Instances of economic intervention by the government receive endorsement averaging about 40 percent. Virtually no support is found for rolling back or dismantling consumer protection regulation.

Other surveys of public opinion have come to similar conclusions that the public strongly supports health, safety and environmental regulation. . . .

The Long, Hard Struggle

It took years for the evidence of filthy slaughterhouses to come to the attention of the American people and galvanize a sluggish Congress; for the inadequacies of drug regulation to become tragically apparent; for the design defects of the Chevrolet Corvair to become known publicly and spark creation of an auto safety agency; for feeble environmental statutes to be replaced with technology-forcing laws containing more stringent enforcement provisions; for the accretion of consumer product injuries to inspire creation of the Consumer Product Safety Commission; for death and injury on the job to become a national scandal resulting in the establishment of the Occupational Safety and Health Administration. But once these changes occurred, the need for them seemed so obvious in retrospect. But of course, the many regulatory benefits came only after years of long hard political struggle.

So it will also take years for our society to recognize the many benefits that an earlier generation bestowed on us through regulation.

"Pollution regulation is not only inefficient, it also stifles innovation."

Environmental Regulations Are Unnecessary

Richard L. Stroup and John A. Baden

Richard L. Stroup is professor of agricultural economics and co-director of the Center for Political Economy and Natural Resources at Montana State University. He has served as director of the Office of Policy Analysis in the US Department of the Interior. John A. Baden is Director of the Center for Political Economy and Natural Resources at Montana State University. In the following viewpoint, taken from *Natural Resources: Bureaucratic Myths and Environmental Management,* Doctors Stroup and Baden argue that federal pollution regulation is ineffective and unnecessary. They believe taxing producers of hazardous wastes for the amount of waste they generate would be a much better way to clean up the environment.

As you read, consider the following questions:

1. Why do the authors believe that capitalism and technology have been unfairly blamed for pollution problems? What do they blame for excessive pollution?
2. The authors list two methods for controlling pollution. What are they? Do they favor one over the other?
3. The authors claim that some environmental groups now favor taxing hazardous wastes rather than regulating them. Would such a system be more effective? Why or why not?

Permission granted by the publisher to reprint material from *Natural Resources: Bureaucratic Myths and Environmental Management,* by Richard L. Stroup and John A. Baden, published in 1983 by Ballinger Publishing Company.

For many individuals, all other natural resource problems pale when compared with a continued pollution of our environment. Despoliation of air and water is compelling evidence to some that, in the relentless pursuit of material wealth and well-being, our environment has been intentionally and maliciously mistreated. It is still difficult, for example, to erase the mental image of the Cuyahoga River in Ohio—so polluted by industrial waste that it caught fire.

Many people believe that pollution problems are a natural result of our capitalist system, with its emphasis on profits instead of people, and of our pursuit of higher technology. Even though it is convenient to blame capitalism and the pursuit of sophisticated technology for pollution and diseased wildlife, neither of these so-called culprits can be held truly responsible. Pollution problems also exist in countries with planned (that is, nonmarket) economies. Even more to the point, technology is neutral and will respond to whatever signals (economic incentives) are given in the economy. If natural resources are being overexploited, it is because improper signals are directing users away from conservation.

Incentives To Do Good

In an economy with well-defined and transferable property rights, individuals and firms have every incentive to use resources as efficiently as possible. Furthermore, they will take into account the opportunity costs of their actions; that is, the highest valued alternative use of a human, technological, or environmental resource.

For example, if the owner of a factory also owns an adjacent stream that is good for fishing, he can charge fisherman for access to that stream. If the factory dumps pollutants into the stream, reducing the value of fishing, revenues from the fishermen will decrease. Therefore, the owner will rationally consider reducing the amount of pollutants his factory emits into the stream. The socially efficient solution would be to reduce pollution until the marginal cost of pollution control equals the marginal revenue from selling fishing permits. Under such an arrangement, the owner would benefit from the additional revenue and fishermen would benefit by having a pleasant place to practice their sport.

Alternatively, what if another individual has clear, easily defended rights to the stream? Just as factory owners cannot dump garbage on someone else's car, they could not dump waste in someone else's water. They must respect the rights of others or risk being taken to court.

No Profit, No Preservation

But what if no one owns the adjacent stream? Suppose the stream is considered common property. Under these conditions, factory owners can no longer receive revenue from the sale of fishing rights. Nor would they fear prosecution in court. For factory owners, then, the opportunity cost of the stream is essentially zero, and they have no incentive to reduce pollution of the stream. As a result, everyone bears the cost.

This helps explain why pollution can be a problem in a market-oriented economy. The lack of property rights in certain resources can result in economic agents ignoring the true opportunity costs of their actions. It follows directly that air and common water resources will be overpolluted. It also follows that nonmarket-oriented economies, with even fewer direct incentives, will have pollution problems as well.

New Game in Town

Federal regulation is not the only game in town—perhaps not even the most important one. Even the most efficient regulations cannot eliminate all health, safety, and environmental hazards. Therefore, we must rely more heavily on private alternatives even while regulators are taking their ball and going home.

J. Raymond Miyares, *Technology Review,* July 1983.

Pollution is the residual or byproduct of a production process—the smoke from a factory, the sewage from a chemical company, or the exhaust from an automobile. When air and water are common pool resources, it is easy to ignore the social costs of pollution. When calculating the cost of owning an automobile, for example, we usually consider gas, oil, depreciation, insurance, and the like. But an automobile's exhaust emissions contain noxious substances that pollute the air, and, in an area like Los Angeles, driving contributes to often toxic air conditions. Smog can cause respiratory problems and burning eyes and can eventually kill some forms of plant life. In the Lake Arrowhead area, for example, just sixty miles east of Los Angeles, pine trees are dying from the city's smog. We can conclude, then, that spewing poison into the air we breathe represents one cost of driving. The major cause of this health hazard is not the unfeeling, unthinking automobile owner, but the common property aspects attached to the air itself. No one owns the air and, therefore, everyone is at liberty to misuse it without bearing any personal cost.

Society would be better off if all individuals were made responsible for the damages they inflict on the environment. But how can this best be accomplished? A socially efficient solution demands that pollution emissions for any activity be reduced until the marginal damage (measured in dollars) from one additional unit of pollutant equals the marginal cost of reducing pollution by one unit. If the law required that pollution be at a level where marginal pollution control costs exceed marginal damages, then society would lose because a more desired activity is being restricted too much. For instance, if eliminating one unit of pollution reduces pollution damages by ten dollars but the cost of controlling that unit is fifteen dollars, then pollution has been reduced too much.

Taxes or Regulation?

Aside from extending property rights to air and water resources, two methods can be used to control pollution: (1) Price it by imposing a tax based on the amount of pollution emitted, or (2) require a fixed reduction in the amount of pollution produced. For both efficiency and equity reasons, most economists favor the tax method, more commonly known as effluent fees. Nevertheless, most pollution control legislation calls for a uniform reduction in pollution emissions. Yet direct pollution regulation is not only inefficient, it also stifles innovation by requiring specific pollution control devices or techniques and by implicitly encouraging firms to ignore the regulations by providing insufficient monitoring and enforcement.

Consider two plants in the same area that emit the same amount of SO_2 (sulfur dioxide), causing damages estimated at ten dollars per unit of pollutant. Legislation is enacted that requires a 50 percent reduction in pollution emission for each plant. The marginal cost of reducing pollution for the first plant is six dollars and fourteen for the second plant. The difference in pollution control costs may be due to the kinds of products produced, the quantity produced, or the production techniques used in each plant.

Does legislation lead to an efficient resolution of the problem? Clearly not. For the first plant, the reduction in pollution damages exceeds marginal control costs (ten dollars is greater than six dollars), and the reverse is true for the second plant. If, instead, an effluent fee equal to pollution damages is charged, different results would ensue. . . .

Regulation Not Equitable

The case is often made that direct regulation is more equitable than effluent fees because an equiproportionate reduction in pollution is required for all firms. But unless all firms are identical, there will be a disparity in pollution control costs. With effluent fees, on the other hand, all polluters pay the same for the use of the resource—that is, the air or water. Because of this, many economists contend that effluent fees are the most equitable method for controlling pollution. . . .

Given that a system of effluent fees is the most efficient way to handle damage caused by pollution, it may seem odd that some businesses favor direct controls. For insights into this seeming inconsistency and for other responses to approaches in pollution control, we turn to an examination of federal legislation.

Pollution Control Legislation

Until the mid-1950s, responsibility for pollution control lay primarily with state and local governments. As the nation became more concerned with environmental matters, however, federal involvement in pollution control was inevitable. Decentralized control, for obvious reasons, gave states little incentive to abate pollution that crossed their boundaries. Prior to 1970, federal programs were administered by a number of agencies, primarily the Department of the Interior and the Department of Health, Education, and Welfare. Then in 1970, the Environmental Protection Agency (EPA) was created to administer all important federal environmental programs.

The first comprehensive legislative act concerning water pollution was the federal Water Pollution Control Act of 1956. The act made federal grants available to local governments for constructing sewage treatment plants. In addition, the federal government was given the authority to study water quality in interstate water bodies. If it was found that pollution was hazardous to human health, a federal-state conference could be convened. Although the authority has rarely been exercised, the act also permits the federal government to file suit in federal court to force dischargers to take required actions.

Not Even a Pencil

I think in today's [regulatory] environment you couldn't invent the pencil. It has a very sharp point. You can stick it in your eye or your ear. Yet children use it.

I doubt that you could get the pencil introduced into the market today.

Warren M. Anderson, quoted in *The Spotlight*, November 4, 1985.

The Water Pollution Control Act was amended in 1965 to establish ambient quality standards on interstate waterways. These standards were established in an attempt to ease the circumstances under which the courts could be used to force polluters to take action. It was reasoned that water quality falling below the standards was prima facie evidence that the dischargers were violating the law. Enforcement remained elusive, however, because the government had to prove that violation of a standard was caused by a particular discharger.

The act was amended in 1972 over President Nixon's veto. Under the Water Pollution Act Amendments, the EPA was charged with establishing a permit system for pollution discharge. After all permits have been issued, it will be illegal to discharge wastes from a point source without a permit. . . . Congress set a goal of eliminating *all* discharges by 1985.

Burdensome Task

The EPA's task is a burdensome one. By 1976, nearly sixty-three thousand industrial and municipal dischargers had been identified. To determine "economically achievable" abatement technology, the EPA must be aware of available production and waste treatment technologies for *each* discharger. In addition, their progress has been impeded by their involvement in many lengthy court challenges of the proposed standards.

Edwin S. Mills has nicely summarized the evolution and current state of federal water pollution control:

> National policy in this area has been characterized by increasing boldness and stridency, if not wisdom, since 1956. . . . In principle, almost nothing an industrial firm does is outside the purview of EPA. Its activities are limited mainly by the budget Congress provides. Major industrial decisions were formerly made on the basis of competitive and profitability considerations; they are now made jointly with government lawyers and technicians.

The passage of air pollution legislation and management has followed a similar path. The Clean Air Act of 1963 gave the federal government its first enforcement powers in the abatement of air pollution. Similar to the Water Pollution Control Act of 1956, the Clean Air Act authorized the study of areas where health problems are potentially caused by air pollution. The regulatory power of the act applied only to stationary sources. The Motor Vehicle Air Pollution Act of 1965, however, authorized the first auto emission standards, beginning with 1968 models. Modest reduction levels in carbon monoxide (CO) and hydrocarbon (HC) discharges were set. For 1970 models, the standards were much stricter, as emissions of CO and HC were cut to one-half the preregulatory levels.

The Air Quality Act of 1967 designated a set of air quality regions and asked the appropriate states to establish ambient air quality standards for these regions. If these standards were deemed unsatisfactory, the federal government could then establish its own standards.

Setting EPA Standards

The major piece of air pollution legislation, the 1970 Clean Air Amendments, gave the EPA the responsibility for setting air quality standards. The EPA set the primary standards, below which human health was threatened, and gave the states only a short time to implement them. For stationary sources, the EPA undertook the same detailed approach as it did for water pollution. It also required reductions of pollution emissions from new cars, beginning in 1975, that were 5 percent of pre-1967 emission levels for CO and HC. In addition, the EPA established standards for nitrogen oxides (NO_x). The 1970 act is unique in that it stated what the ambient standards were, rather than establishing guidelines for the EPA to use in setting its own standards.

Pollution can be seen in two very different ways. When viewed as an abnormal occurrence, regulation takes an all-or-nothing attitude toward pollution control. If a firm exceeds the established pollution limits, it is subject to criminal sanctions and the police powers of the state. On the other hand, pollution can be seen as a normal consequence of activities whose costs are incorrectly reflected in market prices. In this view, the problem can be alleviated by establishing corrective prices, or effluent fees. By and large, government has adopted the first position. . . .

Encouraging Stagnation

The current regulatory environment actually encourages stagnation in pollution control. An industry that develops a new technique for reducing harmful discharges may be unwilling to use it because it may lead to a tightening of emission standards for the entire industry. For example, the EPA discovered that cement plants were capable of filtering out significant levels of harmful particulate emissions. As a result, the agency imposed emission levels for cement plants that were more stringent than emission levels for electric power plants. In other words, electric power plants were allowed to pollute more. Angered by the supposed inequities sanctioned by the EPA, a Portland cement plant challenged the agency's rate structure in court. In denying the challenge, the court argued that if an industry can more effectively control emission, is should be required to do so. Because of such cases, many critics accuse the EPA of penalizing innovation, leading to continued rather than reduced pollution levels.

The same perverse incentive applies to firms within an industry. If a firm has many plants and develops a new pollution control technology for one of them, it may become the standard that must be met as the "best available technology" for all of the firm's plants. Under the present institutional structure, the costs of doing research and development on pollution control devices are often prohibitive. Regulatory agencies depend on negative reinforcement to effect industry compliance to pollution standards, but such perverse incentives lead to discontent and stagnation. . . .

The costs of complying with direct pollution control are very high. It is estimated that required pollution control expenditures will reach nearly one-half trillion dollars for the 1980s. Yet, business tends to favor direct control. Why? There are three possible reasons. First, effluent fees, once enacted, are not easily avoided. Second, under direct controls, firms can attempt to avoid compliance by negotiating with regulators or by charging inequities in the courts. Many corporations have successfully delayed complying with pollution control standards for up to ten years by challenging the regulations in court. Third, direct control could limit the entry of new firms into polluting industries, thereby increasing the profits of existing firms.

Political Motivations

We must not ignore the political motivations involved in the pollution control process. Congressional legislation creates agencies that hold sweeping power, providing concrete evidence that "action" is being taken against pollution. Compare the political palatability of direct control with effluent fees that, after all, are merely licenses to pollute. Yet, even potential special interest supporters of the EPA believe that direct control is not the best way to proceed. In fact, effluent charges are now favored by the National Audubon Society, the Sierra Club, and other environmental organizations.

"The presence of an enormous governmental effort was—and is still—called for."

The Federal Government Should Manage the Environment

John E. Schwarz

For the past several decades, environmental groups have depended on Washington to write into law the environmental protections they lack the power to enforce themselves. These environmentalists believe government management of natural resources is imperative. In the following viewpoint, John E. Schwarz begins with a description of the environment at its most polluted, and shows how federal management repaired the damage. He concludes that government involvement is still the best way to protect the environment. An associate professor of political science at the University of Arizona in Tucson, Mr. Schwarz has written widely on the politics of both the United States and Europe.

As you read, consider the following questions:

1. According to the author, what was the federal government's first and unsuccessful attempt to deal with increasing pollution? Why did this tactic fail?
2. To what does the author attribute the nation's effective clean-up of pollution in the '60s and '70s?

Excerpted from *America's Hidden Success, A Reassessment of Twenty Years of Public Policy*, by John E. Schwarz, by permission of the author and the publishers, W.W. Norton & Co. Inc. Copyright © 1983 by John E. Schwarz.

I was there in 1961, just after finishing college, walking along the edge of Lake Erie. The memory remains vivid. Beach after beach was polluted. Signs were posted in the shallow water warning against swimming. Sledge and oil slime appeared to the naked eye, perhaps the result of passing ships. I walked farther. Garbage spewed into the lake from the great hulk of a manufacturing plant that I passed. Off in the distance, I could see dozens of other industrial plants lining the shore. Everywhere around me, it seemed, the walleye pike of this famous lake floated atop the water. The signs were unmistakable: The lake was dying. I did not stop to consider whether the process was reversible. To me, at that time, the death of our lakes was simply the inevitable price of industrialization.

Now, twenty years later, it seems of little surprise that in the affluent and prosperous post-Eisenhower years a public outcry would follow the degradation of our environment, and that following the outcry the federal government would intervene. This stands as the second major undertaking of the nation's government during the post-Eisenhower years. When Rachel Carson's *Silent Spring* was published in 1962, it ignited the environmental movement. Between 1963 and 1980, Congress adopted legislation intended to bring air and water pollution under control, foster coastal zone and other land-use planning, control strip mining, protect Alaskan lands, and regulate toxic wastes.

Government Intervention Still Necessary

As in the case of the poverty programs, the environmental programs have come under heavy fire. Repeatedly, attempts are made to reduce their funding and to confine their power. Like the poverty programs, too, the environment programs enacted by the government have brought about substantial progress in some areas and at the least have prevented great backsliding in others. Still a third characteristic shared by the environmental and poverty programs is that success could not have been achieved without massive governmental intervention. The presence of an enormous governmental effort was—and is still—called for.

By the late 1950s and the early 1960s, environmental pollution had become an expensive problem in the United States. In a whole string of urban areas across the nation, more than one-third of the year was marked by hazardous or unhealthful air pollution. Estimates for 1968 indicated that without environmental controls air pollution in the nation would have cost more than $16 billion in damage. About $5 billion of that cost would stem from air-pollution damage to residential and commercial property, requiring large expenditures for resurfacing and rebuilding. But the cost to the nation in the deterioration of buildings and housing was only one element. Substantial costs would also arise from the harmful effects of air pollution on health. Reflected in such items as increased medical bills and days lost at work, these costs would have amounted to more than $6 billion in 1968.

Failure at the State Level

Throughout the late 1950s and the 1960s the federal government had prodded state governments and private industry to deal with the growing problems of pollution voluntarily. The Water Pollution Control Act of 1956 and the Clean Air Act of 1963 called upon the states and other interested parties to convene conferences to study the increased incidences of pollution and to develop standards and plans by which to control pollution. The Clean Air Act of 1963 enabled the federal government to provide financial grants to states and localities. Following the act, spending to combat air pollution increased by more than 50 percent in the first two years and sixfold by the end of the decade. By 1965-66, 58 percent of the urban public was served by local air-pollution-control programs. The spending in these localities for the programs had reached about 40 percent of what was considered adequate for effective action.

A Better Environment

As a nation, we have made significant strides in many environmental areas where laws and institutions have been explicitly devised to address specific problems. Most of the conventional air pollutants no longer pose a health threat to nearby communities. The majority of our rivers are suitable for fishing and swimming. For some specific toxic substances—lead, PCB's, and pesticides such as DDT—exposure has declined, representing a clear success story for past regulatory efforts. The populations of many wildlife species are increasing. Progress on these and other problems should be a source of significant encouragement.

William K. Reilly, *USA Today,* September 1985.

But far less action had taken place at the state and the regional levels and even in some urban localities. Indeed, by 1970, no state had yet fully implemented an air-quality plan. Moreover, the standards to control water pollution were inadequate in almost every state, a result of the fear that stronger measures would discourage new industry. As a consequence, the standards set in states with the worst water quality became the *norm* for states across the nation.

Stronger Federal Measures Needed

The period 1956-70 demonstrated that while some progress could be achieved through voluntary action and federal grants, stronger federal measures were needed to move the states as well as the more resistant urban areas into action. Thus, the Congress amended the Clean Air Act in 1970 and the Water Pollution Control Act in 1972. Even many leading conservative economists had come to agree that firm governmental action was needed, although they disagreed with the particular form that such action was to take.

Considering the policy of the past, the actions that the Congress took involved radical policy changes. The 1970 amendments to the Clean Air Act gave a national agent, the Environmental Protection Agency, the authority to set national air-quality performance standards. Should states not draw up plans within a reasonable period to meet the standards, the amendments gave the EPA the power to do so. The Water Pollution Control Act amendments of 1972 likewise established goals for water quality that were to be met nationwide. Private businesses and industry were directed to adopt the "best practicable" technology for waste treatment by 1977 and the "best available" technology by 1983. A nationwide discharge-permit system was authorized, and the EPA was given the power to administer and enforce the system. A discharge permit specified the amount of pollutant that could be emitted from each installation. Finally, to help state and local governments meet sewage disposal needs, federal funding would contribute three-quarters of the financing for constructing local waste treatment plants, with a projected cost of $6 billion annually. . . .

Pollution Reversal

The nation . . . experienced an absolute reversal in air pollution trends during the 1960s and 1970s; it also avoided further deterioration of its waters, the area in which governmental regulation was most confined. As with progress against poverty, these accomplishments are well worth attention, though certainly they remain some distance from perfection.

"The best hope for the long run conservation of . . . the environment rests with privatization."

The Private Sector Should Manage the Environment

E. Barry Asmus and Donald B. Billings

A growing trend in US politics has been to turn over federally-operated programs or property to private ownership. This process, known as privatization, has had an effect on environmental discussions. In the following viewpoint, Doctors Barry Asmus and Donald Billings advocate the increasingly popular position that the private sector of the economy could more efficiently manage natural resources than does the federal government. E. Barry Asmus is an economist and national speaker living in Phoenix, Arizona. Donald B. Billings is professor of economics at Boise State University in Idaho.

As you read, consider the following questions:

1. What differences do the authors describe between the private sector and the federal government? Which do they think is the most effective?
2. Why, according to the authors, do the government's good intentions produce poor results?
3. John E. Schwarz, the author of the previous viewpoint, believes the federal government can best manage the environment. Doctors Asmus and Billings believe private owners can do better. Which viewpoint is more convincing? Why?

E. Barry Asmus and Donald B. Billings, *Crossroads: The Great American Experience.* Lanham, MD: University Press of America, 1984. Reprinted with the authors' permission.

Self-interest aside, the environmental movement has appropriately focused our attention on environmental degradation and the importance of our natural surroundings in general. The issue, however, is not whether conservation and pollution are important. The crucial problem is how to develop institutional arrangements to protect our planet's physical and social habitability in the most efficient and equitable way. In that discussion, environmentalists, with very few exceptions, have *assumed* government to be the necessary custodian of the natural environment, since capitalism, in the name of profits, will exploit the minerals, forests, wildlife, and other natural values to the detriment of the environment. The idea that self-interest and the market economy are at fault has been shown to be in error by the biologist Garrett Hardin in his classic description of the environmentally destructive implications of the commons. (See "The Tragedy of The Commons," *Science,* December, 1968.) The promise that government will manage the natural environment in the "public interest" remains to be challenged.

Advantages of Private Management

In contrast to the private sector of the economy, where the quality of managerial decisions is brought to light by the signals of profit and loss, managers in the public sector are seldom totally accountable for their decisions. When resources are not held privately, and therefore are not transferable to others by those in control, the public bureaucrat is rarely held accountable for any wasteful and exploitive use. Efficient resource allocation in the government sector requires informed voters and legislators. Unfortunately, existing political institutions guarantee neither. Good intentions and good people are not enough. The problem is not one of bad people running the Bureau of Land Management, the U.S. Forest Service, or the National Parks Department. Natural resource economists Richard Stroup and John Baden have identified the fundamental dilemma: "Even with good intentions and expertise, public servants are likely to generate environmental problems because they lack the feedback and reality checks inherent in the price system and markets." (See *Natural Resources: Bureaucratic Myths and Environmental Management,* Pacific Institute, 1983.)

Political Struggle Inevitable

Government stewardship of natural resources guarantees bitter conflict over the use of the "public domain." As the mountain valley, lake, river, forest, or desert becomes popular due to rising incomes and growing population, a political struggle is the inevitable consequence of public ownership. Irresolvable conflict among competing users leaves the government bureaucrat in the middle of the argument. Hearings are held, special interests lobby their legislators, but almost inevitably good intentions produce poor results. One group lobbies to save the wild horses in the American West; consequently the horses multiply in great numbers and consume the forage which supports other wildlife species dear to the hearts of other special interest groups.

Bureau of Land Management grazing policies, determined in the political arena by special interests, destroy the land. Federal irrigation projects subsidize farmers at the expense of free flowing rivers. "Multiple use" policies guarantee political confrontation over access to "public lands" and necessarily produce inefficient results. Quality in the management of natural resources, whether in the public or private domain, is largely determined by the structure of the property rights in force. When resources are treated as common property, the tendency of fast depletion and environmental destruction is assured. However, when resources are exclusively under the control of a private owner who has an absolute right to the capital value of the assets, the owner will have a direct interest in conserving and protecting those values. In addition, the profit motive assures that the resources will be moved to their highest valued use.

Inevitable Conflict

Part of the inefficiency of environmental programs is due to the amount of conflict they engender. Siting hazardous waste facilities or even cleaning up existing hazardous waste dumps, for example, is an inefficient process because every step is fraught with argument and conflict.

William K. Reilly, *USA Today,* September 1985.

Stroup and Baden in *Natural Resources* persuasively argue that an efficient management of natural resources involves three interrelated issues. First, the authority to control resources must be coupled with the personal responsibility for actions taken. Decision makers must have a personal stake in the consequences of their decisions. The public sector inevitably breaks this link and therefore inhibits accountability. Second, it must be recognized that we live in an imperfect world, and while the market system is not ideal, it does not follow that government solutions are preferable. The competitive market process, even when not operating perfectly, has otherwise unobtainable beneficial effects. Finally, it must be recognized that individuals respond to the incentives they face. Unfortunately, institutions in the past have encouraged wasteful exploitation of publicly owned property. For

111

emotional and philosophical reasons the assignment and enforcement of private property rights have been falsely condemned as a surrender to "big business" and the profit motive.

The fact of the matter is that individuals conserve, husband, save, protect, and expand their stocks of valuable resources if they have exclusive claims on the proceeds resulting from their sale. Black Angus cattle on private ranches thrive, while the wolf nears extinction. Lion populations in private game reserves flourish, while their numbers are threatened in the wild. Hawk populations on public lands dwindle, but domesticated chickens, turkeys, and geese are harvested in great numbers in the private sector. The private forests in the southeastern United States are much more productive than the public forests in the Pacific Northwest. The contrast has been starkly stated by Stroup and Baden: "Private ownership allows the owner to capture the full capital value of his resource, and thus economic incentive directs him to maintain its long-term capital value. . . . In contrast when a resource is owned by everyone, the only way in which individuals can capture its economic value is to exploit the resource before someone else does."

The Example of Rainey

A profound illustration is provided by the National Audubon Society's management of its privately owned Rainey Wildlife Sanctuary in Louisiana where environmental values of preservation and wildlife protection exist in harmonious partnership with gas wells and grazing cattle. Nevertheless, in stark contrast to their practice at Rainey, the Audubon Society continues to advocate public ownership of federal lands to prevent mineral exploitation and development. At Rainey, "reality checks" that produce management decisions in which opportunity costs must be squarely faced are available to the Society. In the political arena, bureaucratic managers produce outcomes which are pleasing to no one because they are faced with ill-defined multiple use mandates and have no personal stake in decisions.

The environmental movement's preference for government ownership of natural resources has the potential of producing results opposite of what they desire for yet another reason. Government can both give and take away. The reliance on government for environmental protection is a double-edged sword which can just as easily swing in the direction of environmental destruction. The election of President Reagan in 1980 and his appointment of James Watt as Secretary of the Interior should remind us of how rapidly political circumstances can change and how the reins of government power can be shifted to those who would oppose our favorite interest. Given the speed and degree by which governments can change their mind, depending on which individuals occupy power, the ultimate security for places of beauty rests with secure and enforceable *private* property rights.

Government Sacrifice of the Environment

There are many examples of how the environment can be sacrificed on short notice because of emergencies declared by government. For example, the oil embargo by the OPEC countries in November 1973 quickly produced a suspension of the National Environmental Protection Act by a Congressional vote so that the Alaskan Pipeline might be built. The Wilderness Society's court action was quickly circumvented. And this was the same government which held energy prices *down* during the 1970s and thereby stimulated energy use in the U.S. While spending billions to encourage energy conservation with their right hand, government simultaneously "encouraged" consumption, through price controls, with their left hand.

Jon McIntosh, reprinted with permission.

In the summer of 1979, largely as a result of the government created "energy crisis," President Carter and important members of both parties in Congress advocated a new Federal Energy Mobilization Board which would have had broad powers to override all existing environmental legislation. A little emergency here, another there, and the political atmosphere shifts to a stance which argues that the environment must be sacrificed to the latest *political* difficulty.

The Private Property Alternative

The essence of politics is compromise, which hardly assures confidence that environmental concerns will have priority. The government limits the liability of private power companies from nuclear accidents under the Price-Anderson Act, and thereby contributes to the proliferation of nuclear power stations like the Diablo operation on the coast of California. This is the very same government that most environmentalists wish to assign the responsibility of conserving, preserving, and protecting our physical environment. To a degree, fortunately, the environmental movement is coming to recognize the risks associated with government's stewardship of the land and wildlife. Audubon's experience with the Rainey Wildlife Sanctuary is difficult to ignore. Nature Conservancy and Ducks Unlimited have demonstrated their recognition of the importance of private ownership and, therefore, control of valuable wilderness and other environmental treasures.

Capitalism and the profit-motivated capitalist are not fundamentally to blame for the various classes of environmental decay witnessed on spaceship earth. Indeed, private ownership for profit generates an incredibly powerful incentive to conserve and cultivate resources in order to increase their value to other users. It is our conviction that the best hope for the long run conservation of natural resources and the environment rests with privatization and the enforcement of private property rights in a free-market setting.

114

"We need laws on toxic substances that take advantage of the chemical industry's desire to lower costs . . . and avoid risks."

Better Federal Regulations Should Clean Up the Environment

Carl Pope

Carl Pope is the political director of the Sierra Club, one of the most prominent environmental groups in the nation. He is co-author of *Hazardous Waste in America,* an exposé of the harmful toxic waste disposal procedures used by American companies. In the following viewpoint, he gives an example of effective federal environmental regulation and laments industries' penchant for violating such regulations. He advocates that regulations and federal legislation be improved to ensure public safety from hazardous products.

As you read, consider the following questions:

1. What does the author find commendable in the Environmental Protection Agency's ban on certain wood preservatives?
2. Why does he feel this regulation falls short of the goal to change the chemical industry's behavior?

Carl Pope, "An Immodest Proposal." Reprinted with permission from *Sierra,* the magazine of the Sierra Club, Vol. 70, No. 5.

[In] July [1985], *The Wall Street Journal* reported that the Environmental Protection Agency, "capping six years of internal deliberation and industry efforts to block strict controls," was banning the use of wood preservatives containing creosote, pentachlorophenol, and inorganic arsenic-based compounds. The EPA made its decision based on the Federal Insecticide, Fungicide and Rodenticide Act, one of nine major statutes designed to protect the public from exposure to toxic chemicals.

At first glance, the wood-preservative decision represented exactly the kind of responsible oversight that the EPA is supposed to provide. The agency carefully reviewed voluminous documents on the risks of wood preservatives, balanced these risks against the benefits, and tailored a set of rules that would best serve the interests of society. . . .

The EPA's action affected 97 percent of the wood preservatives and more than a third of all pesticides used in the United States. So while the regulations had been slow in emerging, they dealt moderately but comprehensively with a large part of the total pesticide problem. Critics might feel that the regulations were too weak, but at least the public would, in some measure, be protected.

So goes the theory of toxics regulation. But industry proceeds on its own course.

Side-Stepping the EPA

One month later and 3,000 miles away, some 500 sawmill employees in Korbel, Calif., voted to strike if Simpson Timber Company went ahead with its plan to treat redwood timber with tetrachlorophenol, a close relative of pentachlorophenol, but one never studied or regulated by the EPA.

Simpson defended its decision to spray with "tetra," promising to follow the EPA worker-safety standards applied to "penta" even though it was not legally required to do so. Reichold Chemicals, the manufacturer of tetra, argued that these precautions would provide workers with adequate protection. The EPA was less certain. "We don't have the test data to support tetrachlorophenol's use," said the agency's Henry Jacoby. "We don't know what the long-term worker or public health risks really are." . . .

The public, however, seeks a higher standard of safety. People want chemical products that will not cause injury when used as directed. They do not want to be told a decade after a product is marketed that is can cause birth defects and that pregnant women should not be exposed to it.

People want a margin of safety to ensure that they are being protected. The task of toxics laws and regulations is to provide the public with this "margin of error," a measure of protection against an industry with a very different, very limited concept of responsibility toward public health and the environment.

The chemical industry does not accept the legitimacy of the public's desire for safer chemicals and larger margins of error. It particularly does not accept the right of government regulators to interfere with how the industry makes internal decisions. It resists what it sees as the public's "chemophobia" and the government's bureaucratic red tape. Each new effort by the government to deal with a particular facet of the toxics problem is met with resistance from the industry. Administrative appeals, political pressure, and lawsuits slow down the regulatory process, and the government's energy and resources are exhausted long before the problem can begin to be solved. Across the board, whatever their approach, America's major laws for controlling toxic materials are not working. . . .

"Where there's smoke, there's money."

Drawing by Joe Mirachi; © 1985 The New Yorker Magazine, Inc.

Suppose a company is faced with the choice of using a very toxic chemical or one that is less hazardous. If the more toxic substance is cheaper to develop and produce, or more easily protected by a patent, the company can pursue its development with little fear of regulatory restriction. The present system leaves a company little incentive to proceed with the safer formulation instead.

We need laws on toxic substances that take advantage of the

chemical industry's desire to lower costs, increase markets, raise prices, and avoid risks. We need a climate in which the industry will consider the degree of possible toxicity *before* it spends millions of dollars to develop and market a product.

Alternatives Are Possible

Alternatives to conventional, American-style regulation are possible and may be more effective. We could do worse in the hazardous waste area than to borrow heavily from what has been done in other countries. Can we devise approaches to deal with different facets of the toxics problem? Can we create a climate in which industry voluntarily chooses to shift its emphasis from toxic chemicals to safer ones?

We can—if we shed our ideological blinders and act comprehensively. We must design an approach that will affect each of the major factors industry considers in the decision to produce and market a particular chemical: production cost, market price, volume of sales, and overall risk.

There are two key ways that we can make toxic chemicals more costly to produce than safe ones. First, workers have the right to know the hazards of the materials they are exposed to. Providing workers with full information on the chemical composition, testing data, and other health-related findings regarding workplace chemicals would have a major impact on the cost of producing toxic chemicals. When manufacturers are forced scrupulously to inform their work force about dangerous chemicals, the costs of production will rise. In contrast, when these costs are passed on to workers in the form of illness and death, the production costs of toxic chemicals appear artificially low to corporate decision-makers.

Simpson Lumber Company, for example, paid a high price for using tetrachlorophenol: a disrupted plant. If the Simpson workers had not known they were being exposed to a hazardous chemical, they would not have threatened to strike. Many workers do not have the organizing focus provided by a union, but clear identification of chemicals and their hazards would be a major step forward.

Hazard Fees

A second mechanism for increasing the cost of producing potentially hazardous chemicals is the imposition of "hazard fees." Clearly, the production and use of unsafe chemicals is going to cost society massive sums for medical care and environmental restoration. Hazardous waste alone may cost from $40 billion to $100 billion to clean up. To the extent that these costs can be recovered by levying fees on unsafe chemicals, the repair process can be turned into a preventative program to encourage the use of less risky substitutes. Although it does not distinguish between hazardous and relatively safe chemical production, the tax levied on chemical-industry feedstocks to finance the Superfund is a crude example of such an approach.

Right-to-know laws are also the key strategy for reducing the market price of hazardous chemicals. In order to decide whether they are willing to run the risks of being exposed to certain chemicals, workers and consumers must know the identity of those chemicals. But industry jealously guards the chemical composition of its products under the legal doctrine of trade secrets.

The industry has good reason to fear that competitors will use information reported to government agencies to their economic advantage. Corporations have been the major users of provisions of the Freedom of Information act that apply to product data supplied to federal agencies. It is probably safe to assume that these corporations are not seeking environmental enlightenment.

A Right To Know

The vast majority of dangerous exposure to hazardous chemicals is through long-term routine or regular releases, not the dramatic Bhopal-type incident that killed more than 2,000 people [in 1984]. The effect of exposure to these chemicals is not discernible overnight. The corpses are not in Indian streets, but are waiting in American hospitals and hospices. They come from American playgrounds, blue-collar neighborhoods and nursing homes. . . .

Americans have a right to know where the strange odors in their neighborhoods are coming from. They have a right to know what toxic substances are mixed in the soil on which their children play. And they have a right to know what poisonous chemicals are contaminating their drinking water.

Gerry Sikorski, *St. Paul Pioneer Press and Dispatch,* December 30, 1985.

The chemical industry uses this fact as an argument against right-to-know laws. However, if right-to-know requirements are applied more stringently against chemicals that are toxic than against those that are safe, a manufacturer will discover that it can protect its product from competition far more easily if it uses safe chemicals. Properly designed right-to-know requirements will threaten the most toxic chemicals with competition, and consequently demand a lower market price—a powerful incentive to develop safer products.

Product Labeling

Above all, chemical companies want to know that their products will find buyers, and they concentrate on products they believe can attract and hold firm markets. The key to reducing the market potential of products containing toxic chemicals is consumer information—specifically, labeling.

Labeling requirements for all products that can expose consumers to toxic chemicals will give manufacturers a strong reason to come up with products that do not contain toxics. . . . A comprehensive labeling rule would dramatically restructure the marketplace.

For example, some shampoos contain captan, a chemical shown to cause cancer in lab tests. If these shampoos were required to carry a prominent label that read, "This product contains captan, which is suspected of causing cancer and has failed to pass safety tests," consumers would know what they were buying. More important, right next to these shampoos would be others, also heavily advertised and slickly packaged, without any warnings. It's easy to guess which type of shampoo most consumers would choose.

Thus, comprehensive labeling requirements on toxic ingredients would enlist the chemical industry's potent marketing and sales divisions in the battle to encourage development of safer products.

Inadequate Tort Law

Risk, or the desire to avoid it, is the final incentive for the chemical industry. Theoretically, if a chemical goes wrong, the manufacturer can be sued for damages. But tort law, which governs such damages, works poorly when it comes to toxics.

If a defectively designed skyscraper collapses, tort law works. It's fairly easy to find out why the building fell, prove that it should not have fallen, and identify the architect, builder, and contractor. It's also easy for those injured to know that the building caused their broken bones.

But health problems caused by chemicals, such as birth defects, learning disorders, pulmonary disease, and cancer, are harder to handle. It's difficult to show that a particular chemical caused a given cancer, and even if the chemical is identified, there may be many manufacturers—whose vinyl chloride was it? Finally, companies may plead that the chemical was not defective by the standards of the day. This "state-of-the-art" defense says, "We did what everyone else did, and the product was safe as far as we knew." Thus the collective historical irresponsibility of the chemical industry becomes a legal defense for the individual irresponsibility of a particular corporation.

However, more and more "toxic torts" are being brought to trial. While some of these lawsuits do provide compensation to victims of the more spectacular chemical incidents—asbestos, Agent Orange, Love Canal—they leave most victims in limbo. Legal changes are needed. None will be perfect, and none will result in exactly the right compensation to each individual, but we can improve a victim's chances of recovering losses. More important, we can make the risks of marketing toxic chemicals a major factor in industry decisions.

First, we should outlaw state-of-the-art as a defense. Chemical manufacturers should be held strictly liable for the damages their products cause. This doctrine already applies to such "dangerous instruments" as dynamite; applying it to toxic chemicals would give the industry a major incentive to make certain their products are properly tested and used.

Second, once a chemical has been shown to cause a particular health problem, manufacturers should be required to show that they are *not* responsible when an individual using it suffers injury. Shifting the burden of proof to industry would also be a strong argument to a chief executive to move his company away from marketing hazardous products.

Increasing the ability of victims to recover damages for chemical injury will also recruit a powerful new ally to the cause of safer chemicals. Insurance companies are already beginning to refuse the chemical industry "environmental hazard" insurance because of the unpredictable nature of losses. An explicit legal separation between liability for manufacturing safe and unsafe chemicals would put immediate pressure on companies to start producing safe products.

Within Our Reach

It will not be easy to pass laws to change the incentives that currently encourage the proliferation of teratogens, carcinogens, mutagens, and nerve poisons in the marketplace. Large chemical companies are massive, ponderous bureaucracies. They deny the legitimacy of the public's desire for less risky products. They resent the intrusion of government and outside institutions on their operations. A shift from chlorinated hydrocarbons, heavy metals, and other types of toxic chemicals may well mean greater profits in the long run, but it will introduce a short-term period of massive change. Some companies will prove more nimble—or more lucky—than others. They will gain. Their clumsy, technically less deft, or unlucky competitors may lose. Few industry executives will want to bet their companies on their ability to adapt to the new climate. They will resist such a change fiercely, tenaciously, sometimes irrationally.

Public fervor on this issue is now running high. More than a decade has been wasted trying to regulate toxics with laws that do not go to the source of the problem. But safe chemicals and a responsible chemical industry *are* within our reach—if we give them sufficient priority.

"If corporations were accountable . . . there would be no need for most of our regulatory agencies."

Corporations Should Clean Up the Environment

Barbara M. Heller

Barbara M. Heller served as Deputy Undersecretary of the Department of the Interior for three years. Prior to her work at the Department, she was a co-founder, board member, and director of oil, gas, and energy programs of the Environmental Policy Center, a nonprofit organization in Washington, DC. In the following viewpoint, Ms. Heller acknowledges that government has some role in regulating protection for the environment. She believes, however, that it is ultimately the responsibility of corporations, not government, to clean up the environment.

As you read, consider the following questions:

1. How does Barbara Heller characterize the three sectors involved in environmental protection?
2. According to Ms. Heller, why don't corporations take a more active role in protecting the environment?
3. What does the author want corporate executives to do before they make decisions affecting the environment?

These are times of controversy and even turbulence in the realm of environmental policy, when sagebrush-rebellion advocates use bulldozers to defy federal rulings, . . . when National Park rangers in Alaska literally fear for their physical safety, and when federal regulations are every politician's favorite target. And the controversies will not diminish; . . . they will intensify. We cannot know what the results of all of these controversies will be in the long run; but I think we can, and indeed must, speculate about the future. To make any predictions, however, we must have a base from which to work.

The Players

Let us look first at the roles of the different sectors with which we are particularly concerned today—private enterprise, "public interest," and government—and then let us examine some of the historical reasons for current policies and regulations. Traditionally private enterprise has had one primary goal: the financial health and stability of the company. Without that as its first concern, a company obviously cannot compete or survive.

Public-interest groups (and I do not imply that the other sectors are non- or anti-public interest) are generally organized around more abstract commitments than private enterprise. That is important to remember. For the most part they have no individual economic stake in the programs or policies they support or oppose. Their staffs are generally poorly paid compared to the rest of society, and their budgets are miniscule compared to those of the corporate world. Call them do-gooders if you like, but their commitment is not to be sneered at—nor is their broad public support.

No one views government through rose-colored glasses. In fact it seems to be seen mostly through bifocals. Take the Department of the Interior, for example. Environmentalists, seeing it through one half of the glasses, see rapacious exploiters, always on the side of industry, leasing too much too fast, whether we are speaking of offshore oil acreage or grazing lands. Through the other half of the glasses, industries see the Department of the Interior as a computerized "Bigfoot," an enormous environmental bureaucracy whose only commitment is to step all over them and put them out of business.

We hear a lot about the problems with government but very little about what government ought to be doing. The role of government, as I see it, is to protect people, their rights and their property, for this and future generations: to protect individual liberty and to promote the common good.

Private Development

Most environmental problems and occupational safety and health problems are caused by private-sector development.

Granted these developments are often in response to consumer demand. We would have far fewer air-quality problems if people did not buy automobiles or if they did not want electricity from power plants. But we do have these demands, and the development, and they do pollute the air. By now we are all familiar with the impacts of air pollution: respiratory illness, agricultural damage, and financial losses to businesses in large population centers. Who pays for this pollution? The elderly emphysema victim pays in medical costs, the farmer pays in crop damage, the homeowner pays, the small businessperson pays.

Abiding by the Law

After all, the corporation is a creature of law. Laws established its right to exist in the first place, and laws—made by the people in a democratic society—allow it to continue to exist. Among those laws, created by that society, are the environmental regulations. . . .

So the issue, quite properly, is not avoiding environmental regulations, but adapting to them. Ultimately the fact that one corporation is more successful than another will depend on which one understands the origin of changes mandated by the society at large, and successfully adapts to those changes.

William D. Ruckelshaus, *Corporations and the Environment: How Should Decisions Be Made?* 1981.

Whose job then is it to protect these people from damage to their property and their health? Is that now what government's role ought to be? There are areas in which it may not be in the financial interest of industry to act. These are areas where expenditures do not contribute to a company's profit, but rather to the profit of society as a whole. These areas include some aspects of environmental protection and occupational safety and health. In fact these areas were neglected by industry for many years, in some instances because the impacts were unknown. As a result serious problems, sometimes disasters, occurred: black-lung disease in coal miners, the Santa Barbara oil spill, Love Canal. These events and others like them drew enormous public attention and often outrage, as a result of which Congress acted and required control and regulation.

We knew for years that underground coal miners were dying from black-lung disease. Despite devastating costs in terms of health and even life for thousands of miners and their families, an act of Congress was required to set standards for permissible amounts of dust in mines, and even to require that miners be tested for the disease. It was cheaper for companies to hire new miners than to take care of the ones they already employed. In an area as poor as Appalachia, where unemployment was high and people were begging for work, people could not afford to complain.

Corporate Irresponsibility

Delaying environmental or worker protection usually costs far more than preventing it. . . . If Hooker Chemical had spent the time and money to prevent problems, it would not be spending $15 million to clean up contaminated groundwater in Montague, Michigan. If the Life Science Products Company had spent $250,000 in 1975 to clean up the source of kepone in the James River, instead of delaying, it could have avoided $13 million in damage suits, and the taxpayer would not have to foot the bill, estimated at nearly $2 billion, to purify the river. In virtually every instance more is spent to correct a problem than would have been spent to prevent it.

Yet companies continue to say that government acts irresponsibly. The bureaucracy, they say, has not carefully evaluated either the hazards associated with these chemicals or the costs associated with various regulations. All of which raises a crucial question: who should bear the burden of proof that something is harmful? Should private industry be responsible for the safety of its products and workplaces? Should government be responsible for the safety of privately produced products? If your answer to the last question is yes, then let's hear no complaints about government spending or bureaucratic regulations. I would prefer that government not need to be responsible for the safety of privately produced products or for environmental protection. Whether or not government should be responsible, in fact it is. Government is responsible because public concern has compelled Congress to pass laws requiring it to be. It is responsible because people believe that private corporations have abdicated their responsibilities. . . .

If corporations were accountable for the safety of their workers and their consumers, for the consequences of their own corporate actions, there would be no need for most of our regulatory agencies or for their regulations. Although many do, most corporations do not feel that responsibility. If business spent less time and money trying to defeat laws and regulations and more campaigning among its own for a higher level of self-regulation, the impetus and the need for much of what industry considers burdensome would disappear. Profitable private enterprise and environmental protection are not mutually exclusive.

Too Many Regulations

It is true that government has often overreacted in the regulatory sphere. There have been too many regulations, and many of them have been too complicated. . . . However, simply eliminating regulations in a way that leaves people unprotected in their jobs and their homes would result only in discord. It would not result in fewer expenditures but more—more money to clean up problems and more to litigate.

I hope we are moving toward a vision of the future where the government's role, regulatory and legal, will be increasingly unnecessary. It would, however, be foolish and ill-advised to assume that environmental policies and programs are temporary. Environmental consciousness runs very deep in this nation. It will not disappear. The extent and the type of the government's role in the future depends in large part on how seriously the private sector views its responsibilities toward the rest of society. . . .

Make Corporations Pay

It's time to:

Send executives to jail for knowingly poisoning our water and making our children sick, not slap them on the wrist with token fines.

Make utility executives and investors pay the multi-billion dollar cost overruns on the dozens of nuclear "white elephants" now entering service, instead of *rewarding* their mismanagement by sticking the excess costs on ratepayers.

Eliminate tax subsidies for nuclear and coal power plant construction, timber overproduction, groundwater depletion and other harmful activities.

As long as we allow corporations to be insulated from the true costs of their practices (or worse, bribe them with tax breaks to do exactly the wrong thing), we shouldn't be surprised when our laws fail.

Alden Meyer, *Environmental Action Visions*, 1985.

If cooperative changes are in sight, they will come from new corporate accountability. Our government mechanisms are inordinately slow, and they do not materialize out of thin air. They are reactions to problems. The appropriate question is how to minimize the problems.

Distinguishing Between Fact and Opinion

This activity is designed to help develop the basic reading and thinking skill of distinguishing between fact and opinion. Consider the following statement as an example: "Despite Governmental regulations, the number of pollution disasters has risen by almost 150 percent in the last ten years." This statement is a fact with which few people who have looked at the research could disagree. But consider another statement about pollution regulations: "Governmental regulations have caused the number of chemical disasters to increase drastically by interfering with companies that had good safety records before the regulations took effect." The connection between governmental regulations and chemical disasters is arguable and this statement includes nothing to factually connect the two.

When investigating controversial issues it is important that one be able to distinguish between statements of fact and statements of opinion. It is also important to recognize that not all statements of fact are true. They may appear to be true, but some are based on inaccurate or false information. For this activity, however, we are concerned with understanding the difference between those statements which appear to be factual and those which appear to be based primarily on opinion.

Most of the following statements are taken from the viewpoints in this chapter. Consider each statement carefully. *Mark O for any statement you believe is an opinion or interpretation of facts. Mark F for any statement you believe is a fact.*

If you are doing this activity as a member of a class or group, compare your answers with those of other class or group members. Be able to defend your answers. You may discover that others will come to different conclusions than you. Listening to the reasons others present for their answers may give you valuable insights in distinguishing between fact and opinion.

If you are reading this book alone, ask others if they agree with your answers. You too will find this interaction valuable.

O = *opinion*
F = *fact*

127

1. The EPA says that reducing the amount of lead in regular gasoline would save an estimated 50,000 children from the brain-damaging effects of airborne lead.

2. Health, safety, and environmental agencies are designed to protect public health.

3. Sulfur oxides released into the air from power plants cause acid precipitation that kills fish, wildlife, lakes, and vegetation.

4. In 1961, according to an eyewitness, Lake Erie was too polluted to swim in. The visible sledge, oil slime, and dead fish all indicate this.

5. Pollution is the result of both natural and man-made processes.

6. New legislation requires a 50 percent reduction in pollution emissions in every plant.

7. Some pollutants, now regulated, have potential health risks that current regulations do not account for.

8. Congress passes legislation to protect the air, land, and water.

9. The current approach to pollution control should be changed from treatment to prevention.

10. When corporations treat natural resources as common property, the natural resources are depleted and environmental destruction occurs.

11. "Big Business" cares only about profit and nothing about the environment.

12. Louisiana's Rainey Wildlife Sanctuary contains not only wildlife, but also cattle and gas wells.

13. Congress suspended the National Environmental Protection Act to build the Alaskan Pipeline.

14. In July 1985, *The Wall Street Journal* reported that the EPA had banned wood preservatives.

15. The laws in the US for controlling toxic wastes, which are designed to protect consumers, do not work.

16. Workers have the right to know the hazards of the chemicals with which they work.

17. An act of Congress regulated amounts of dust in coal mines and required black-lung disease tests for miners.

Periodical Bibliography

The following list of periodical articles deals with the subject matter of this chapter.

Doug Bandow — "Environmental Protection the Private Way," *The New American*, November 11, 1985.

J. Clarence Davies — "Coping with Toxic Substances," *Issues in Science and Technology*, Winter 1985.

David D. Doniger and Deborah A. Sheiman — "Toxic Safety: No Room on the Bottom Line," *Los Angeles Times*, February 21, 1986.

Mark Green — "The Gang That Can't Deregulate," *The New Republic*, March 21, 1983.

Kitry Krause — "Toxic Chemicals and 18-Wheelers: The Dangers of Deregulation," *The Washington Monthly*, November 1985.

R. Shep Melnick — "Deadlines, Common Sense, and Cynicism," *The Brookings Review*, Fall 1983.

J. Raymond Miyares — "Controlling Health Hazards Without Uncle Sam," *Technology Review*, July 1983.

Lawrie Mott — "Regulation Breaks Down, but Pesticides Linger On," *Los Angeles Times*, August 12, 1985.

Peter Osterlund — "Can Government Improve Safety of Chemical Plants?" *The Christian Science Monitor*, January 28, 1986.

Peter Osterlund — "Is US Chemical Industry Safe?" *The Christian Science Monitor*, January 27, 1986.

William K. Reilly — "The State of the Environment," *USA Today*, September 1985.

David J. Sarokin and Warren R. Muir — "Too Little Toxic-Waste Data," *The New York Times*, October 7, 1985.

Philip Shabecoff — "Pesticides Finally Top the Problem List at EPA," *The New York Times*, March 6, 1986.

Jim Sibbison — "The Agency of Illusion," *Sierra Club Bulletin*, May/June 1985.

Fred Smith and Eric Shaeffer — "The Flawed Logic of Superfund," *Cato Policy Report*, November/December 1985.

Is Nuclear Power an Acceptable Risk?

**THE
ENVIRONMENTAL
CRISIS**

"Nuclear power is going to be an essential generating source for American electricity . . . and we must be ready to provide it."

America Needs More Nuclear Power Plants

John S. Herrington

John S. Herrington is the United States Secretary of Energy. The following viewpoint is excerpted from a speech he delivered to the Commonwealth Club in San Francisco, California. In it, Mr. Herrington argues that nuclear power is safe, efficient, and essential and can be provided in a way that complements, rather than compromises, the environment. He contends that nuclear and coal resources combined with technological advances will provide a limitless supply of energy for the future.

As you read, consider the following questions:

1. In the opinion of the author, what are the lessons that Americans should have learned about energy since the Arab oil embargo?
2. Mr. Herrington states that America has fallen behind in the use of its nuclear technology. What does he feel America's nuclear role in the world should be?
3. What arguments does the author give to support his belief that nuclear energy is safe?

John S. Herrington in a speech before the Commonwealth Club in San Francisco on September 13, 1986.

A few years ago, you couldn't open a newspaper without reading that America was losing its technological edge—or that the spirit of American innovation was fast following the route of the dinosaur toward extinction.

Well, those reports were wrong. The revival of the American spirit in the last few years is due in large part to a renewed sense that America is still the most fertile breeding ground for new ideas and new technologies. . . .

Foundation of the Environment

Threading every American's environment like a spider's web is energy. It doesn't matter where one turns in our country or in our economy, energy will always be there, touching the foundation of every issue, and the core of our society.

We are now well into our second decade since the Arab oil embargo brought oil, and the American hunger for energy, into the world spotlight. During that time, we've seen energy ride a roller coaster of public sentiment . . . from complacency to crisis and now, perhaps, back to complacency again.

We've seen surges of energy exploration and development, followed by market corrections that have struck deeply into every corner of the energy industry—and into each of your homes.

We've seen long lines at gasoline stations turn into an oil surplus. We've seen both price hikes and price downturns. It has been an extraordinary decade . . . a decade in which energy touched the very fabric of our social consciousness. It should have left an indelible impression. We have learned lessons in the 1970s that we must never forget.

We should have learned for example that energy security doesn't emanate from Washington, D.C., but from places like the Mobile Bay, the Santa Maria Basin, Kansas, Colorado, Louisiana, and Texas. We should have learned that energy conservation isn't something that can be regulated into existence, but instead, must be instilled through economics and competitive innovation.

Most Important Lesson

But perhaps most importantly, we should have learned that government policy doesn't have to be one of allocating shortages and misery, but instead, it can be one of optimism and progress . . . one that returns the business of energy to the collective wisdom of our nation's consumers.

Think back for a moment . . . to where we were a decade ago, 10 years ago, we faced a future we felt we couldn't control . . . energy prices had just quadrupled, sending economic shockwaves around the globe. Experts were predicting that oil was on its way to $100 a barrel, interest rates would never see the lower side of 20 percent, and double digit inflation was here to stay.

We pulled ourselves out of the turbulent '70s by rebuilding confidence in our abilities. We achieved major successes in returning the business of energy to the expertise of the private sector and taking it out of the hands of regulators.

We have made great strides in diversifying our energy resources, moving toward those that are most abundant and away from those in least supply. . . .

World's Energy Appetite

Americans cannot be blind to events taking place outside our borders particularly in the area of energy consumption. America's future will be shaped largely by the strength and vitality of its energy producers. . . .

Let me turn to nuclear power—the misunderstood story that affects our energy future. Two years after Shippingport, our first nuclear reactor, the French took Westinghouse technology and built the first nuclear reactor in France. Since that time, pursuing an aggressive program, the French have come to the point where 65 percent of the electricity generated in their country is by nuclear power.

Nuclear Is a Benign Fuel

Too bad. The world's greatest technological nation still heats the boilers of its steam-generating plants the way early man warmed his cave in the Ice Age—by burning carbonaceous fuels such as wood, coal, and oil. . . . Burning oil for heat makes as much sense as burning your furniture. It works, but it isn't very bright.

Uranium, on the other hand, has no redeeming qualities except that it produces about 100 million times as much heat energy per atom as the combustion of carbon, without the worrisome by-products of combustion. . . . According to Herbert Inhaber in *Science* magazine, nuclear is among the most benign of fuel sources. Failure to use it costs the environment dearly.

Although once the leading nation, we are now in 13th place in percentage of electricity generated by the atom. . . . Those who foster the delays that make us—the inventors—the "slowest" in building nuclear power plants, should realize that the increased cost of electricity and the health costs that have resulted make us all poor.

Charles Osterberg, *The Washington Times*, October 8, 1985.

During this same period of time the United States has managed to reach only 15 percent nuclear power generation in its electricity mix. France engages in advanced breeder technology but our Clinch River breeder reactor project is dead. France lines up in a row four to six nuclear generating plants of 900 to 1300 megawatts each using standardized plans and we labor over each individual plant. France builds a plant in seven years and we take 12 to 14. By 1995 France will have 73 percent of its electricity supplied by nuclear power.

The rest of the world has followed suit. Fifteen years ago the Japanese looked around the world and asked themselves who is doing the best job with nuclear power? The answer was France. Since that time, using the French model, the Japanese have engaged in an ambitious construction program developing standardized nuclear plants at central locations under a modified and simple licensing process.

The People's Republic of China will build 12 reactors in the next few years using imported technology. So the story goes for Korea, Taiwan, Germany, Finland, and others.

America Is Behind

America has fallen behind in the utilization of this valuable technology for the 21st century. The Shoreham Nuclear Power Plant in Long Island, New York has taken 17 years to build and it is still not operating—the cost is five billion dollars. It is indisputable that the Shoreham Nuclear Power Plant replaces 100 percent of imported oil—nine million barrels a year. Shoreham is in an area where the New York State Regulatory Agency predicts brownouts and blackouts.

There are similar stories across our land. There are no new domestic orders for nuclear power plants. Our industry must rely totally on the foreign market where competition from France and Germany is fierce. We have carefully constructed 96 nuclear power plants in this country—each one different—each one unique. Since Three Mile Island, we have regulated ourselves with a clumsy licensing procedure, duplication, and a process which inhibits the effective and economic construction of safe nuclear facilities in this country.

The Department of Energy has submitted this year a nuclear licensing reform bill simplifying the process to bring it in conformance with the rest of the world. The rest of the world grants a permit for a nuclear plant at a certain site and it is also the operating permit.

We have a nuclear waste act and we have a nuclear waste plan. The federal government will be ready in 1998 to accept the first shipments of high-level waste for deep geologic storage using vitrification and the latest technology. We are developing the most extensive and the most technologically advanced uranium enrichment process in the world today putting us back at the forefront of competition for the world market.

America taught the world how to harness the atom. We simply cannot allow the rest of the world to walk away from us as leaders in this technology.

Nuclear power is safe, efficient and necessary for our nation's future energy security. In the course of 800 reactor years, not a single member of the public has been injured or killed and for more than 2900 reactor years, American naval personnel have lived and worked alongside nuclear reactors traveling 60 million miles without a nuclear accident. No other technology can make similar claims, yet the critics of nuclear energy persist in calling it unsafe. By any reasonable calculation nuclear power is going to be an essential generating source for American electricity in the next 30 years and we must be ready to provide it. . . .

Given the right market signals, the right mix of federal cooperation, and the right regulatory climate, American industry has the competitive instincts and the indigenous strengths to take new technologies off the drawing boards and put them into commercial practice. I believe we have an almost limitless supply of energy if we can only learn to manage the future properly.

"The construction of new nuclear power plants will be unnecessary for the foreseeable future."

America Does Not Need More Nuclear Power Plants

James J. MacKenzie

James J. MacKenzie, Ph.D., is senior staff scientist for the Union of Concerned Scientists in Washington, DC. In the following viewpoint, Mr. MacKenzie argues that nuclear power is not safe or economical and doubts that the nuclear industry can meet all the conditions necessary to make it an acceptable source of energy. He believes that the United States does not need to build any new nuclear power plants and cites deteriorating public confidence and energy conservation as reasons.

As you read, consider the following questions:

1. What are the reasons that the author gives to support his belief that energy use is not linked to economic growth?
2. According to the author, why wouldn't nuclear power contribute to the reduction of oil imports?
3. Mr. MacKenzie doubts the safety of the nuclear energy industry. What are some of the problems he cites?

James J. MacKenzie, "The Decline of Nuclear Power," *engage/social action,* April 1986. Reprinted with permission.

As of January 1, 1986, there were 98 nuclear power plants licensed for operation in the United States; these units accounted for about 14 percent of US electricity production. Another 30 plants have construction permits and some of these will be completed over the next few years.

Despite the sizeable contribution it makes to domestic energy supply, nuclear power in the United States is in serious trouble, a fact acknowledged by even its most ardent supporters. No new nuclear plants have been ordered since 1978 and more than 110 have been canceled since 1972.

The decline of nuclear power cannot be attributed to any single factor. Rather, it is the result of numerous problems that promoters of nuclear power have failed to address adequately over the years:

- Unnecessarily high limits for the routine release of radioactivity.
- Untested vital safety systems.
- The Three Mile Island (TMI) accident.
- Huge cost overruns and breakdowns in quality control during construction.
- Most recently, a poorly-managed but quickly-moving federal program to dispose of radioactive wastes.

All of these have taken their toll to the point that there is little support on the part of the public for the construction of new reactors.

Nuclear industry spokespersons have countered this gloomy outlook with a series of claims in support of building more reactors. New nuclear plants are needed, they claim, to support economic growth and reduce our oil imports. Moreover, they also claim, nuclear power is already safe enough, and, if federal regulation were reduced, it would once again become the energy source of choice for utilities.

More Nuclear Plants Necessary?

Will more nuclear plants be needed to meet domestic needs for electricity and economic growth? This question must be addressed in two parts, the first concerned with the quantity of electricity that will be required and the second with the choice of supply for providing that power. No one seriously disputes that energy is a vital element of economic growth, and that—at least at the point of use—electricity is a clean and convenient energy carrier. For many years analysts have linked growth in energy use with economic growth, as measured by the Gross National Product. The trend over the past decade, however, shows that, whatever the linkage may have been in the past, it is not very tight today. Between 1973 and 1985 the amount of energy required to produce a (constant) dollar of GNP fell 25 percent. . . .

Studies strongly suggest that there are still vast opportunities

137

to use energy more efficiently. In August, 1983 the Congressional Research Service (CRS) published "A Perspective on Electric Utility Capacity Planning." The CRS study reviewed in some detail the future of domestic electricity demand. The study explored the opportunities for "least cost" methods—conservation, load management, solar, cogeneration, and small-power producers such as wind machines and small hydro dams—to reduce electrical capacity requirements by the year 2000. CRS compared the relative costs of meeting US needs through new power plants versus least-cost methods. CRS's bottom line was that no new large central power plants beyond those then under construction need to be built during the rest of this century, provided that the least-cost actions outlined in the report were actually implemented.

Public Opposes New Nuclear Plants

Polls consistently have shown that while the public does not favor the immediate shutdown of operating plants, they would prefer that no new nuclear plants ever be built. Until the nuclear industry solves the basic problems of waste disposal, safety, decommissioning, and high priced energy that have plagued it since its inception, it is unlikely the public will change its mind on this point. Overcoming public opposition to nuclear power will be far more difficult for the industry than changing the regulatory climate.

Michael Mariotte, *Multinational Monitor,* May 1986.

Other studies by the Union of Concerned Scientists, the Energy Conservation Coalition, and the Mellon Institute's Energy Productivity Center have reached parallel conclusions. Taken together, these reports provide compelling evidence that cost-justified efficiency improvements (such as more efficient lights, appliances, and electric motors) supplemented with the increasing use of renewable resources, could essentially hold electricity demand constant for at least two decades, even in the face of healthy economic growth. In these circumstances, neither new coal nor new nuclear plants would be needed.

Necessary To Reduce Oil Imports?

Is nuclear power needed to further reduce US oil imports? Oil consumption can be cut by any of several courses of action, including efficiency improvements and the substitution of other energy sources. Over the past few years both of these approaches have been successful in this country.

US oil consumption has been declining since 1978 when it reached an all-time high of 18.8 million barrels per day. Since 1978 demand has fallen to about 15.7 million barrels per day in 1985.

138

Most of this reduction has resulted from improved efficiency. Thus, oil use in buildings declined by 40 percent between 1978 and 1984. Since the same period saw only a modest increase in electricity use in buildings, most of the reduction must be attributed to conservation.

Industrial oil use declined by 19 percent over the same period, with no significant increase in any other energy source; again, this demonstrates the effects of conservation. Petroleum use in transportation—virtually the only energy source for this sector—declined by 3.6 percent, reflecting contained efficiency improvements in both air and ground vehicles.

Increased Energy Efficiency

Electric utilities burn oil in peaking, intermediate-load, and base-load plants. Only about 5 percent of all electricity is generated in oil-fired units. The total amount now burned is rather modest, about 560,000 barrels per day—a two-thirds reduction from 1978. This reduction has most likely resulted from the substitution of coal-fired and nuclear plants for intermediate and base-load oil fired units.

Thus, the bulk of the reduction in US oil use over the past six years—and the corresponding reduction in imports, about 3.3 million barrels per day—has been the result of increased energy efficiency, with only a modest contribution from direct electrical substitution.

Transportation (16 percent) and industry (26 percent) currently account for the lion's share of oil consumption. Unless electric vehicles are widely introduced, there is little prospect that nuclear power will displace oil in the transportation sector.

The potential to displace oil in industry is much greater. In many industrial applications, electricity could economically substitute for the direct use of oil and natural gas. However, industrial purchases of electricity could still decline because of continued efficiency improvements and the use of cogeneration technology. In residential and commercial buildings, oil is used primarily for space heating; it would generally be very costly to replace central heating systems with electric space conditioning. Hence, the prospects for significantly reducing oil use in existing buildings are not great.

To summarize, electricity—and therefore nuclear power—offers some potential for further reducing US oil imports by substituting for direct fuel use in industrial processes. However, offsetting trends in improved industrial efficiency could readily nullify or reverse the increase in electricity use resulting from these substitutions. On the other hand, there appears to be only a very limited potential for electricity to displace oil in other sectors of the economy.

139

Is nuclear power a safe, reliable, and economic means of generating electricity? Like many simple questions, this one has no simple answer. Nuclear reactors are beset with persistent safety problems that threaten the industry's future in several ways. Another serious accident would likely lead to the complete loss of public confidence in the technology. Economic burdens, arising from a seemingly unending list of safety retrofits, reduce capacity factors and place large economic drains on utilities.

Conservation Works in America

Atomic power plants seem very much on the decline. The reasons are partly financial, partly political. With soaring construction costs and a stabilizing level of energy demand, atomic power is simply no longer a reasonable investment—if it ever was. Since energy costs have skyrocketed in the wake of the 1973 Arab oil embargo, the American public has found it can conserve large quantities of energy and still survive quite nicely. Utilities that were essentially coerced into going nuclear at the outset now find that conservation can ultimately increase profits and cause fewer headaches than the wonders of atomic fission.

Harvey Wasserman and Norman Solomon, *Killing Our Own*, 1982.

The principal unresolved reactor safety problems stem from steam generator degradation at pressurized water reactors (PWRs), the embrittlement of pressure vessels in older PWRs, the cracking of large diameter recirculation pipes in boiling water reactors (BWRs), and the potential inability of electrical safety systems to function under the conditions of high pressure, steam, and radiation expected during a serious accident. In principle, these problems appear to be solvable. But progress has been exceedingly slow.

Deteriorating Public Confidence

In addition to reactor safety, the challenge of long-term disposal of radioactive wastes remains unmet 45 years into the nuclear era. The Atomic Energy Commission and its successor, the Department of Energy (DOE), consistently underestimated the technical difficulties of storing wastes as well as the public's concern about the issue. Tanks holding high-level wastes have leaked unnoticed, as have dumps where low-level wastes were buried. Unfortunately, DOE appears to have learned little from these incidents and is pressing for quick site selection for a permanent high-level repository. Reflecting the concerns of local citizens, a number of potential host states have sued DOE. The end result will almost certainly be a continued deterioration in public confidence that the government can competently deal with the problem.

Nuclear reactors are not only faced with many unresolved safety problems, they are also increasingly uneconomic compared with coal-fired plants. Why have nuclear costs risen so dramatically? According to a study on nuclear costs completed by Cambridge Energy Research Associates, the principal reason for increases has been poor management. An audit of the canceled Zimmer, Ohio project concluded that the utility's lack of experience and unwillingness to spend enough for staff with expertise were major factors in the plant's troubles. Utilities with good management and prior nuclear experience have a much better chance of building plants on time and on budget. Unfortunately, many American utilities are building their first units. This is a major difference between the United States and other countries such as France, Great Britain, Japan, and West Germany with one or, at most, a few utilities that use relatively standardized plant designs. . . .

No New Plants Are Needed

To sum up, we conclude that, if a range of economically attractive conservation measures are taken, the construction of new nuclear power plants will be unnecessary for the foreseeable future. No new electric power plants of any kind, beyond those now under construction, would be needed to meet economic growth; indeed, an emphasis on efficiency improvements would represent the cheapest path to meet the future electric demands. Nor can nuclear plants contribute in any major way for the foreseeable future toward reducing our oil imports.

Nuclear power plants are beset by serious technical problems that pose continued safety and economic risks for their owners. These problems, along with the inherent complexity of the plants, has led to their high construction costs and poor reliability.

It has become conventional wisdom that, if nuclear power is ever to make a comeback late in this century, several conditions will have to be met. First, the industry will have to develop a few standardized plant designs that are relatively simple, reliable and as free of generic safety defects as possible. Second, the quality of management in plant construction and operation will have to greatly increase; no more TMIs can be allowed. If these conditions can be met, nuclear power may once again become an acceptable domestic energy source. In our view, though, the prospects of this happening are not bright.

"More than 30 years after the first nuclear reactor started producing electricity, a viable decommissioning strategy has yet to be formulated."

A Strategy for Dismantling Nuclear Power Plants Is Needed

Cynthia Pollock

Cynthia Pollock is a researcher with the Worldwatch Institute. She is a graduate of the University of Wisconsin-Madison where she studied economics, environmental studies, and international relations. She is the author of *Decommissioning: Nuclear Power's Missing Link.* In the following viewpoint, Ms. Pollock argues that the development of decontamination and dismantling techniques have been neglected by atomic energy authorities, and there exists a need for a viable plan for the disposal of retired nuclear plants.

As you read, consider the following questions:

1. What does the author mean by the term "back end" of the nuclear fuel cycle?
2. According to the author, why is waste disposal site selection a major obstacle to the full dismantling of a reactor?
3. Why does the author believe it is important to begin funding for decommissioning while a plant is still operating?

Cynthia Pollock, "Decommissioning Nuclear Power Plants," in *State of the World 1986,* published in 1986 by the Worldwatch Institute/W.W. Norton. Reprinted with permission.

Nearly four decades and 350 power plants into the nuclear age, the question of how to safely and economically dispose of nuclear reactors and their waste is still largely unanswered. Unlike other electric generating technologies, nuclear plants cannot simply be abandoned at the end of their operating lives or demolished with a wrecking ball. Radioactivity builds up each year the plant operates, and all the contaminated parts and equipment must be securely isolated from people and the environment. Some radioactive elements decay quickly, but others remain hazardous for millennia.

No one knows how much it will cost to decommission the hundreds of units in service or under construction around the world. Estimates range from $150 million to $3 billion per plant. . . .

Expense of Decommissioning

At the turn of the century, when growth in the demand for power is likely to be slow, nuclear decommissioning could be the largest expense facing the utility industry, outstripping plant construction. Given current policies, most of this bill will be paid by a generation that did not take part in the decision to build the first round of nuclear power plants—and that did not use much of the power generated.

Although nuclear power supplied 13 percent of the world's electricity in 1984, not a single large commercial unit has ever been dismantled. Nuclear engineers have been attracted to the exciting challenge of developing and improving a new technology, not in figuring out how to manage its rubbish. But as a growing number of plants approach retirement age, the problem of dealing with reactors that are no longer usable will demand attention. Not one of the countries currently relying on nuclear power is adequately prepared for this challenge.

The oldest commercial nuclear reactors are already nearing the end of their useful lives, and some plants have closed prematurely because of accidents or faulty designs. In the United States, dozens of tiny research and military reactors are no longer used, four small commercial units are shut down and awaiting decommissioning, and the Nuclear Regulatory Commission estimates that another 67 large commercial units will cease operations before the year 2010. Worldwide, more than 20 power reactors are already shut down, 63 more are likely to retire by the turn of the century, and another 162 between 2000 and 2010. Countries with advanced nuclear programs will soon start to feel the pressure associated with managing the new and broadened "back end" of the nuclear fuel cycle. . . .

Decommissioning is waste management on a new scale, in terms of both complexity and cost. Following plant closure, the company or agency responsible must first decide which of three courses to follow: decontaminate and dismantle the facility immediately after shutdown, put it in "storage" for 50-100 years to undergo radioactive decay prior to dismantlement, or simply erect a "permanent" tomb. Each option involves shutting down the plant, removing the spent fuel from the reactor core, draining all liquids, and flushing the pipes. Elaborate safeguards to protect public and worker health must be provided every step of the way.

Under the immediate dismantlement scenario, irradiated structures would be partially decontaminated, radioactive steel and concrete disassembled using advanced scoring and cutting techniques, and all radioactive debris shipped to a waste burial facility. The site would then theoretically be available for "unrestricted" use.

Plants to be mothballed, on the other hand, would undergo preliminary cleanup but the structure would remain intact and be placed under constant guard to prevent public access. After 50 years in storage, most of the short-lived radioisotopes would have decayed, further safety gains would be negligible, and the facility would be dismantled. Entombment, the third option, would involve covering the reactor with reinforced concrete and erecting barriers to keep out intruders. Although once viewed as the cheap and easy way out, entombment is no longer considered a realistic option because of the longevity of several radioisotopes.

Decommissioning Deserves More Attention

The formidable issue of decommissioning is getting far less attention than it deserves. Utility companies and ratepayers balk at yet another expense associated with using nuclear power. Politicians are reluctant to tackle an issue that will not come to the forefront until after their political careers have ended.

Cynthia Pollock, *Multinational Monitor*, May 1986.

A survey of 30 electric utilities in the United States revealed that 73 percent planned to promptly dismantle and remove their reactors following shutdown. Yet utilities in Canada, France, and West Germany are planning to mothball most of their reactors for several decades prior to dismantlement.

Radiation Contamination

Regardless of the method chosen, decommissioning a large nuclear power plant is a complex engineering task, without precedent. The high levels of radioactivity present at recently closed reactors place numerous constraints on the decommissioning crew. . . .

Many activities are so dangerous that workers cannot perform them directly. Remote-control technologies, often used behind protective barriers, are thus a focus of industry research. . . .

Much of the radioactivity in a retired nuclear plant is bound to the surface of structural components. The type of material and its exterior surface determines the depth of penetration—the range is typically from as little as several millimeters to as much as 15 centimeters for unsealed concrete. . . .

The other source of radiation that confronts decommissioning crews is "activation" products. When nuclear fuel undergoes fission—the splitting of uranium atoms—stray neutrons and other particles escape and enter the surrounding structures. These neutrons bombard the nuclei of many atoms, and the resulting change in composition causes some elements in the steel and concrete that encircle the reactor core to become radioactive. . . .

Limited Dismantling Experience

Following preliminary decontamination, the reactor and surrounding structures must be dismantled into smaller pieces for transportation and burial. . . . Remote operations and the need to keep dust formation to a minimum complicate the dismantlement. . . .

Practical decommissioning experience is limited to very small reactors. The 22-megawatt Elk River plant in Minnesota is the largest that has been fully decontaminated and dismantled. The U.S. Department of Energy (DOE) completed the three-year project in 1974 at a cost of $6.15 million. Underwater plasma arc torches cut apart the reactor, and 2,600 cubic meters of radioactive waste were disposed of at government burial sites. Today's reactors can produce 50 times more power and will have operated for over seven times as long as Elk River. Since radioactivity builds up in proportion to plant size and operating life, a 1,000-megawatt reactor used for 30 years would be considerably more contaminated. . . .

In Europe, dismantlement of several commercial reactors is currently being planned. The first three projects are the 100-megawatt Niederaichbach unit in West Germany, the 33-megawatt Windscale advanced gas reactor in the United Kingdom, and the 45-megawatt French G-2 gas reactor at Marcoule. Although the French and U.K. plants are small, each operated for about 20 years—long enough to become well contaminated. The larger, German reactor was in service for only two years before technical difficulties resulted in its closure. Each unit has a different design, and problems unique to specific technologies are likely to be discovered. . . .

The overriding consideration in selecting a decommissioning schedule and the appropriate decontamination and dismantlement methods must be worker and public safety. Although radioactivity

145

'Quick, Look Over There—See What A Clean, Beautiful Plant We Have'

Engelhardt in the *St. Louis Post-Dispatch*. Reprinted with permission.

declines more than tenfold during the first 50 years after plant closure, thereby reducing worker exposure, the reactor is a potential hazard during the cool-down period. . . .

Waste Disposal Dilemma

Considering the volume of radioactive waste being accumulated around the world, the lack of progress in its management is disturbing. Few nations have commercial disposal facilities for low-level radioactive wastes. And not a single country has developed a permanent repository for the most dangerous, high-level, wastes—spent fuel and the byproducts of fuel reprocessing. Dismantlement and burial of nonoperating and dangerous commercial nuclear facilities will not be possible until there are safe places to put the radioactive remains. . . .

Where to put these disposal sites is a contentious issue of each of the 26 countries that produce nuclear power. The lack of high-level waste repositories is an omission that will limit the decommissioning of commercial facilities until at least the turn of the century. It is impossible to fully dismantle a reactor if there is nowhere to put the spent fuel cooling in utility storage ponds. . . .

Several high-level waste repositories have been proposed and tested over the years, most extensively in the United States, but none has yet proved acceptable for receiving commercial spent fuel. Political opposition may be a more difficult obstacle than finding a geologically appropriate site. Waste disposal is likely to be particularly tough where population densities are high, such as in Japan and many European nations. Some countries—the Netherlands, for example, where there is strong public opposition to domestic waste disposal—are hoping that international sites will become available, perhaps operated by reactor suppliers. Yet the likelihood that any nation would want to accept large volumes of waste not generated internally is small. China has reportedly offered to store West German spent fuel in the Gobi Desert, but discussions are still at an early stage. The Soviet Union is the only country that takes back the high-level wastes generated by the reactors it sells, most of them to Eastern European nations. . . .

Final site selection has already become a political hot potato. Potential host states and environmental groups have filed lawsuits challenging the adequacy of the siting guidelines. According to James Martin, a staff attorney with the Environmental Defense Fund: "First, there are concerns that, in its haste to site a repository, [the Department of Energy] has relied on the pre-NWPA studies of dubious quality and is delaying analysis of waste transportation risks that cannot be deferred. Second, there is evidence that politics are creeping into and tainting the decision-making process. These factors pose grave threats to the integrity and public acceptance of the siting process." . . .

As experience is gained in decommissioning and waste handling, regulations are likely to become more strict. If worker radiation exposure limits are lowered, if residual radioactivity standards are set at levels more stringent than predicted, or if transportation and disposal rules are tightened, costs could rise substantially.

Although hundreds of nuclear power plants have been erected around the world, the cost of decommissioning them is highly uncertain. The bill for all the plants now in service could total several hundred billion dollars. The experience necessary to clarify these cost estimates is sadly lacking and urgently required. In order to be manageable, expenses of this magnitude must be budgeted for; they cannot be allowed to come as a surprise.

The lack of reliable cost estimates makes financial planning for decommissioning extremely difficult. But some mechanism needs to be put in place to assure that there will be enough money available, at the right time, to do the job. When a reactor stops producing power, it also stops earning money for its owner. To ensure that the company can pay for decommissioning, funds need to be set aside during the years that the reactor is operating. . . .

No Viable Strategy

More than 30 years after the first nuclear reactor started producing electricity, a viable decommissioning strategy has yet to be formulated. Even if reactor ordering ground to a halt tomorrow, the international nuclear community will eventually have to dispose of more than 500 plants, including those currently under construction. If it costs $1 billion to decommission each unit, the total bill would amount to a staggering $500 billion. Mountains of radioactive waste will be created, and dozens of waste disposal sites will be required. Aggressive, well-funded research and development programs are needed at both the national and international levels. . . .

Decommissioning planning has lagged far behind reactor development. . . . This blatant neglect of the back end of the nuclear fuel cycle has been replicated by national atomic energy authorities everywhere.

The biggest stumbling block for all nations with nuclear plants is the lack of permanent disposal facilities for radioactive wastes. Although many reactor operators around the world agree that plants should be dismantled as quickly as practicable after shutdown, that option has been foreclosed until at least the turn of the century. No country currently has the capability to permanently dispose of the high-level wastes now stored at a single reactor. Just as today's cities would not be habitable without large fleets of garbage trucks and extensive landfills, the international nuclear industry is not viable without a sound decommissioning strategy.

"The application of the known decommissioning techniques will provide the public with a safely decommissioned [nuclear] plant."

Dismantling Strategies Are Well Established

American Nuclear Society

The American Nuclear Society, founded in 1954, is a not-for-profit scientific and educational society of 13,500 scientists, engineers, and educators from universities, government and private laboratories, and industry. It issues *Public Policy Statements* which are the considered opinions and judgments of the Society in matters related to nuclear science and technology. In the following viewpoint, the Society concludes that the established alternatives for dismantling nuclear facilities are environmentally and technically acceptable.

As you read, consider the following questions:

1. Why does the Society believe that radioactive material can be safely disposed of?
2. What does the Nuclear Regulatory Commission state the primary goal of decommissioning should be, according to the Society?
3. Why does the Society believe that public health and safety have been adequately addressed during the decommissioning process?

American Nuclear Society, "Decommissioning of Nuclear Generating Stations: A Policy Statement of the American Nuclear Society." Copyright 1983 by the American Nuclear Society.

Regulations have been promulgated, and alternatives for decommissioning commercial nuclear electric generating facilities have been identified. Conventional and safe processes and techniques exist and have been demonstrated.

Mechanisms for financing decommissioning through the ratemaking processes are available and are in use in some utilities. The radioactivity in wastes from decommissioning represents only a small fraction of the radioactive wastes generated during operation of the facility. Experience has shown that public health and safety have been adequately addressed during the decommissioning phases of plant life.

The viability of alternatives for decommissioning and site restoration is well established. The option for continued use of the site is becoming more important since sites for new power stations are becoming more limited.

Public Health and Safety

Once a nuclear facility has reached the end of its operational life, it must be placed in a condition such that future risk to public health and safety from the facility remains acceptable. The activities and processes involved in achieving such a condition are generally referred to as the "decommissioning" of the nuclear facility. This is accomplished in accordance with a preapproved plan that ultimately results in termination of the Nuclear Regulatory Commission license to operate a facility or to possess radioactive material (10CFR50, Section 50.82).

The primary source of radioactive materials in all nuclear power plants is the nuclear fuel in the reactor core. When the fuel fissions, it generates heat and radioactive material, including fission products, actinides, and activation products. Fission products and actinides are contained within hermetically sealed fuel rods as long as rod integrity is maintained. Two additional barriers are provided—reactor system piping and containment building—to prevent release of radioactive material to the environment. Thus, most of the radioactivity in a power reactor is contained in the fuel rods and leaves the plant when the fuel is shipped for disposal. The last fuel discharged from the reactor will be shipped away during or following the decommissioning period.

The residual radioactivity in the plant after the fuel is removed is of two types: (a) neutron-induced activation on the surface and in the metal components of the reactor system and (b) low-level surface contamination of metal components by fuel, fission products, and actinides.

Disposal Methods

The basic approach in disposing of neutron-induced radioactive material (the pressure vessel internals, the pressure vessel itself and immediately adjacent piping, and the first few inches of the primary shield) is to cut or break it up into pieces small enough to fit into standard waste shipment packages for shipment to a licensed waste burial site. Its radioactivity would be in the same range as material routinely disposed of today as low-level waste. An alternative is to ship major components in specially fabricated shipping casks for disposal as a unit. Exposure considerations may make this the most practical alternative.

Decommissioned U.S. Reactors

Reactor	Decommissioning Mode Selected	Present Status of License	Location
Saxton	Mothballed	Possession only	Saxton, PA
SEFOR	Mothballed	Byproduct, state	Strickler, AR
WTR	Mothballed	Possession only	Waltz Mill, PA
NASA Plumbrook	Mothballed	Possession only	Sandusky, OH
GE EVESR	Mothballed	Possession only	Alameda Co., CA
B&W	Dismantled	Byproduct, NRC	Lynchburg, VA
Hallam	Entombment	Terminated	Hallam, NE
Piqua	Entombment	Terminated	Piqua, OH
Elk River	Dismantled	Terminated	Elk River, MN
Bonus	Entombment	Terminated	Puerto Rico
VBWR	Mothballed	Possession only	Alameda Co., CA
Fermi 1	Mothballed	Possession only	Monroe Co., MI
CVTR	Mothballed	Byproduct, state	Parr, SC
Peach Bottom 1	Mothballed	Possession only	York Co., PA
Pathfinder	Conversion and mothballing	Byproduct, NRC	Sioux Falls, SD

The well-established methods for removing the radioactive contamination remaining in the system (activated impurities and corrosion products deposited in the steam generators, the piping, or the primary water cleaning system) are chemical cleaning and conventional low-level liquid radioactive waste processing, followed by disposal at a licensed waste burial site. All of these steps can be accomplished safely with currently available technologies.

Several Decommissioned Facilities

Decommissioning of nuclear installations in the United States has resulted in the existence of several decommissioned facilities. These include early experimental and production plants run by the Manhattan Engineer District, Department of Energy (DOE) facilities, university research, industrial and mining facilities, as well as the power, demonstration, and test reactor facilities such as those in the accompanying table.

The plants listed demonstrate successfully the main processes that have been used for decommissioning nuclear reactors in the United States. All of them were small or pioneer units. Each site had special characteristics that dictated the alternative chosen. These operations demonstrated safe and uneventful removal of large components, the subsequent disposition of wastes, and provided a basis for estimating the efforts and costs required in decommissioning strategies. The forthcoming decommissioning of the Shippingport reactor will provide further valuable practical experience.

Regulatory Guidelines Established

The guidelines for terminating the operating licenses for nuclear reactors are presently provided in Regulatory Guide 1.86, which was issued by the Nuclear Regulatory Commission in June 1974. This regulatory guide identifies four alternatives for the retirement of nuclear reactor facilities that are considered acceptable by the regulatory staff. These are as follows:

Mothballing: This is defined as ". . . putting the facility in a state of protective storage. In general, the facility may be left intact except that all fuel assemblies and the radioactive fluids and waste should be removed from the site. Adequate radiation monitoring, environmental surveillance and appropriate security procedures should be established under a possession-only license to ensure that the health and safety of the public are not endangered."

Entombment: This is defined as ". . . sealing all the remaining highly radioactive or contaminated components (e.g., the pressure vessel and reactor internals) within a structure integral with the biological shield after having all fuel assemblies, radioactive fluids and wastes, and certain selected components shipped offsite. The structure should provide integrity over a period of time in which significant quantities . . . of radioactivity remain with the material in the entombment. An appropriate and continuing surveillance program should be established under a possession-only license."

Removal: This is defined as ". . . all fuel assemblies, radioactive fluids and waste, and other materials having activities above accepted unrestricted activity levels . . . should be removed from the site. The facility owner may then have unrestricted use of the site with no requirement for license. If the facility owner so desires, the remainder of the reactor facility may be dismantled and all vestiges removed and disposed of."

Conversion: Renewal of steam generating system is permitted: conversion to a new steam supply system to furnish steam to the existing turbine-generator, with the old steam supply system to be disposed of in accordance with one of the previous three alternatives.

An NRC reevaluation plan was published in March 1978 and revised in December 1978, then supplemented in August 1980, and March 1981. Revision 1, Supplement 2 redefines the decommissioning alternatives as follows:

DECON means to immediately remove all radioactive material to permit unrestricted release of the property.

SAFSTOR means to fix and maintain property so that risk to safety is acceptable for a period of storage followed by decontamination and/or decay to an unrestricted level.

ENTOMB means to encase and maintain property in a strong and structurally long-lived material (e.g., concrete) to assure retention until radioactivity decays to an unrestricted level.

The NRC issued a draft generic environmental impact statement on decommissioning in January 1981 and further is considering rulemaking revisions relative to decommissioning. A draft report discussing some thoughts on decommissioning was issued by the NRC in August 1980. This report states that the primary goal of decommissioning should be DECON. However, since it may not be the most effective because of occupational exposures, SAFSTOR, perhaps followed by ENTOMB to allow decay of the radioactivity to unrestricted levels in about 100 years, should be considered.

The Challenges Will Be Met

You might call it a delayed reaction. Nuclear power, which until recently appeared down for the count in the United States, is coming off the canvas with a flurry of plant openings in the next few years. . . .

Government and industry experts indicate that the travail of the past couple of decades has not been without its rewards. The lessons of Three Mile Island and other less dramatic setbacks have been taken to heart by both industry and regulators. . . .

It is also expected that other challenges—particularly the cost of "decommissioning" worn-out reactors and the safe disposal of spent but still radioactive fuel—will have been met within a decade.

Already the NRC has extended the period for which nuclear licenses are valid by 10 years—from 30 to 40, and researchers say it may be possible to extend the life of reactors even further.

Leon Lindsay, *The Christian Science Monitor*, October 11, 1985.

The American Nuclear Society believes that the decommissioning alternatives are environmentally and technically acceptable. Regulations for decommissioning have been promulgated, and alternative procedures have been described.

ANS further believes that the selection of the alternative is site- and utility-specific and is dependent on plant and site characteristics, financial considerations, and possible future needs for power and land availability.

In short, selection of the appropriate decommissioning method by a thorough cost-benefit analysis and the application of the known decommissioning techniques will provide the public with a safely decommissioned plant and continued safe and economic use of nuclear power in the United States.

"The consequences of [abandoning nuclear power] will be to stifle growth in the countries that need it most."

Nuclear Energy Should Not Be Abandoned

The Economist

The Chernobyl nuclear accident awakened the world to the safety and health hazards involved with nuclear energy according to the authors of the previous viewpoint. But, *The Economist*, a London magazine, asserts that economics rather than technology should be considered before making any decision about the future of nuclear energy. In Part I of the following viewpoint, *The Economist* editors provide three reasons why they believe that the elimination of nuclear energy as a power source is a poor choice. In Part II, they present their view of world energy consumption and explain why they believe renewable energy will not fill the gap if nuclear power is phased out.

As you read, consider the following questions:

1. In the opinion of the authors, why is a non-nuclear answer a poor one?
2. What are the effects that rising energy prices would have on developing countries, according to the authors?
3. What do the authors say are the problems with renewable energy? What do they believe would fill the gap if nuclear power were phased out?

The Economist, "Life Without Nuclear" and "Energy Brief: Power Without Nuclear," May 24, 1986. © 1986 The Economist, reprinted by permission from Special Features.

I

A century from now, Chernobyl will be seen in one of two ways: as the beginning of the end of nuclear energy or as an unfortunate hiccough in its adolescence. The verdict will depend on politics, not technology. Chernobyl has persuaded many people . . . that nuclear power is too dangerous at any price. Few people yet understand the price of doing without it.

Life Without Nuclear Power

That price is not unbearable; few prices are. Mankind is not so dependent on nuclear power that a decision to abandon it would cripple civilisation. A mere 5% of the world's energy and 15% of its electricity (but four times that much in France) come from nuclear reactors. There are plenty of ways in which, given time, even Frenchmen could meet their energy needs from other sources without returning to the dark ages. Oil, natural gas and coal, though finite, are all in temporary surplus and much cheaper—for the moment—than they were in 1980. If energy prices tripled, many other resources, from windmills to sugar cane and tar sands, could profitably fuel the world.

The issue is not technology. With enough time and money, men in white coats can meet most technical challenges. The questions that matter for energy's future are duller: cost, safety and environmental acceptability. A non-nuclear answer is a poor one, for at least three reasons: it would mean dearer energy; more pollution; and slower economic growth.

The Reasons for Going Nuclear

The world had good reasons for going nuclear. Countries wanted to reduce their dependence on dirty, dangerous-to-mine coal, and later their dependence on cartelised oil. They wanted a way of generating electricity that was reliable, smokeless and untouched by OPEC [Organization of Petroleum Exporting Countries]. And they wanted to keep energy prices low. By the year 2000, the OECD [Organization for Economic Cooperation and Development] countries will, on current trends, rely on nuclear power for a quarter of their electricity. Without nuclear power, they will have to use that much more oil, coal or gas. Since few renewable sources could make much of a contribution by then, it is a fair bet that energy prices would have to double—at least—in a non-nuclear world.

Would that matter? Energy and prosperity are twins that march together. Between 1949 and the Yom Kippur war of 1973, every extra dollar of real gross national product increased energy consumption by 30 megajoules. So static did the ratio between growth and energy consumption become during that period that it began to look like an iron law.

It wasn't. After the oil shock of 1973, the twins fell out of step. Although America's real GNP grew by 31% between 1973 and 1984, its consumption of energy dropped by 1%. Conservationists have seized on such statistics to show that—given thrift—prosperity can grow without more energy. They pose a reasonable question: since cheap power from finite fossil fuels will not last, and since economies can grow without a matching growth in energy consumption, why not let the underlying scarcity of oil drive up the price of energy and so encourage both conservation and the development of renewable sources of power?

Tomorrow's Industrial Countries

What they leave out of account is the special position of tomorrow's industrial countries. Conservation is one reason for the falling demand for energy in today's industrial countries, but changes in the structure of their industry are just as important. Each year, more Americans, Japanese and Europeans earn their livings by moving electrons around computer screens or working in salad bars, fewer by wielding blowtorches.

Soviet Economy Will Suffer

The loss of nuclear power to generate electricity, already in great need if any kind of economic growth is to be achieved, will put an added strain on other Soviet energy sources. It has long been a central goal of Soviet policy to remain self-sufficient in energy while increasing hard currency earnings from energy exports. Between now and the year 2000, Moscow hopes to do as much as it can to substitute natural gas, coal and nuclear power for oil, which accounts for more than half of Soviet hard currency exports. Even without the accident, this effort has consistently fallen short of its targets—and it will surely face greater difficulty now. . . .

The Chernobyl accident is likely to slow Soviet economic growth and industrial development for some time to come.

Joseph J. Sisco, *The New York Times*, May 4, 1986.

The poorer countries are still hungry for energy. As a nation industrialises, its demand for energy goes up faster than its growth; only later does the ratio stabilise or fall. It happened in America, where energy use per unit of GNP grew by 15% between 1900 and 1914. It is happening in every developing country now, and will do so even more as peasants find fewer trees to cut down and switch to commercial sources of power. If energy prices are pushed up by today's Chernobyl-shocked rich, they will stunt the future Americas and Japans in their infancy. You do not have to drive a gas-guzzler to want cheap energy.

Still the question remains: why nuclear, since splitting atoms is not the only new way of making electricity? The world's demand could be satisfied by huge new windmills, solar panels or sugar cane. The price, however, would be unaffordable for at least half of mankind: if a developing country installed enough photovoltaic cells to satisfy demand at today's energy prices, it would bankrupt itself in servicing the loans that financed the investment.

To which the champions of alternative energy have a riposte: if as much money had been spent on developing solar or other renewable sources as has been spent on nuclear power, such techniques might now produce energy as cheaply as reactors. They are almost right, but not right enough. There are inherent problems with renewable energy that will always keep the cost high. It needs large areas of land; it is intermittent; and the sun cannot be turned up simply because 50 million people turn on their kettles during the commercial break in "Dallas".

This is not to disparage renewable energy, but to recognise that its limited future is in the next century, not this one. The lessons of Chernobyl may yet be so awful that mankind should abandon nuclear power. But be aware that the consequences of doing so will be to stifle growth in the countries that need it most.

II

Nuclear power is good at producing large quantities of electricity. Barring a big change in the world's pattern of energy consumption, that is the kind of energy that will be most in demand if economic growth is to remain rapid. . . .

Electricity is only part (though a growing part) of the world energy mix. About 35% of the energy which countries consume each year is committed to generating electricity. Nuclear power accounts for only around 5% of total energy use, and, because of the heat lost in power generation, 2-3% of the energy delivered to end users. Some countries, though, are much more dependent on nuclear power: like France with 65% of its energy coming from nuclear reactors. . . .

By the Year 2000

The end-of-century nuclear capacity will probably be barely half what was predicted ten years ago, although double what it is today. If nuclear power were phased out, that would leave a lot of energy, and electricity, to be produced in other ways.

The actual size of that gap will depend partly on energy conservation. If the world can continue to conserve energy at the rate it has done since the first oil crisis in 1973, it will have no trouble in making up any shortfall in nuclear power, at least this century. But can it? Since 1974, the amount of energy used per unit of gross domestic product in the non-communist world has fallen by 13%. . . .

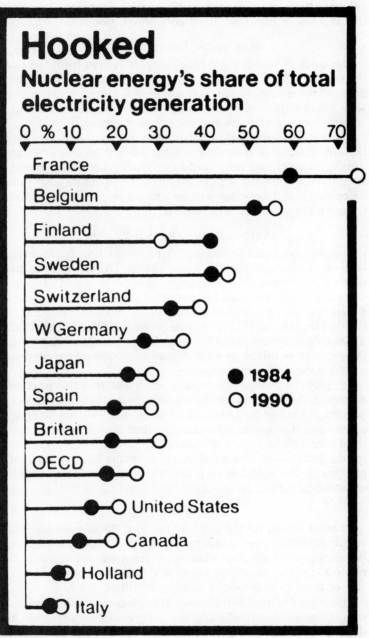

Hooked

Nuclear energy's share of total electricity generation

Source: Nuclear Energy Agency

Developing countries, on the other hand, because they are developing basic energy-intensive industries, increase their energy use at a faster rate than their economies grow. . . .

Renewable Energy Sources

The earth is brimming with energy. It arrives from the sun at the rate of 178 billion megawatts, 20,000 times as much as world demand for energy. Fossil fuels are merely stored supplies of that solar energy, trapped by ancient plants. So why not short-cut the storage process and use the energy as it arrives?

Renewable sources of energy cannot run out, and they do not pollute, blow up or melt down. After the first oil shock, some optimists claimed that they could eventually meet all demand for energy. That optimism is fading. The money spent by governments on research and development into renewable energy has halved from its 1980 peak of $1.2 billion.

Intermittent and Unreliable

The reason is that the renewables have two inherent drawbacks: they are diffuse and they are intermittent. The diffuseness means that a 1,000-megawatt solar farm might occupy about 5,000 acres, compared with less than 150 acres for a similar-capacity nuclear power station. A 1,000-megawatt wind farm would be several times larger still. A wave-power station generating 1,000-megawatts might be 30 miles long. If crops were grown for conversion to oil or gas by digestion, 1,000-megawatts-worth would occupy 200 square miles.

Because renewable energy is intermittent, it is also unreliable. Although the wind often blows strongest when most power is needed, it cannot be relied on to do so, nor—as any Briton will agree—can the sun be relied on to shine. Any renewable supply must therefore be attached to an efficient means of storing energy for the lean times. Energy storage—by using big batteries, or by pumping water uphill or air into underground caverns—is getting more efficient but still wastes at least one-fifth of the energy. . . .

Filling the Gap

So what would fill the gap? By the year 2000, even on conservative estimates of economic growth, OECD countries would be generating 25% of their electricity from nuclear power. Total nuclear capacity would be about 400,000 megawatts. That is the size of the gap that would have to be filled.

These are the least-bad guesses, though they are still rough. The rate of economic growth and the progress of conservation both depend partly on the price of energy—and the price of energy depends on the speed and extent of any nuclear phase-out. But if nuclear power stations were shut overnight, power cuts would be impossible to avoid in several countries and electricity-generating costs would soar. Only oil, gas and coal could fill the gap. Consumption of either oil or coal would have to rise by 10%.

Replacing nuclear power over say 20 years would be less disruptive, but still costly. Some new sources—oil from tar sands and shale, more hydroelectric power, perhaps fuel cells—would fill the gap. But they would not prevent energy prices from rising to at least double their present levels in real terms. Indeed, they would require such a rise, because without it they would make no commercial sense.

"Nuclear energy is super-dangerous and we must face up to this fact."

Nuclear Energy Should Be Abandoned

Russell Peterson and Jeannine Honicker

Russell Peterson is the former governor of Delaware and former president of the National Audubon Society. He served on the Kemeny Commission investigating the Three Mile Island nuclear accident. In Part I of the following viewpoint, Mr. Peterson argues that the Chernobyl nuclear accident should awaken world leadership to the hazards of nuclear energy. He believes that humanity must develop other, renewable forms of energy. Jeannine Honicker, the author of the second viewpoint, is a guest columnist for *USA Today* and has for a long time fought the construction of nuclear power plants. In Part II, Ms. Honicker points out the dangers of nuclear power and calls for a worldwide end to it.

As you read, consider the following questions:

1. What are some of the ways in which nuclear energy threatens world security, according to Mr. Peterson?
2. Why does he believe that renewable forms of energy will adequately fulfill future energy needs?
3. What does Ms. Honicker mean by her statement "Let's save ourselves from ourselves"?

Russell Peterson, "It's Time for Less Perilous Energy Sources," *Los Angeles Times*, May 1, 1986. Reprinted with the author's permission.

Jeannine Honicker, "To Save Ourselves, Stop Nuclear Pollution," *USA Today*, April 30, 1986. Copyright, 1986 USA TODAY. Reprinted with permission.

I

The [Chernobyl] nuclear reactor disaster . . . in the Soviet Union should awaken world leadership to the need to expand research and development on alternate sources of energy.

Government and Industry Mind Set

Over the next few decades the opportunity exists to fulfill our needs through more efficient use of energy and through development of solar and other renewable energy forms. But as research, development and commercial successes of these alternatives continue to mount, most national governments—especially ours—have markedly reduced their support for such ventures while continuing to promote and subsidize nuclear energy.

Leaders in government and industry continue to extol the safety of nuclear energy, a mind set that threatens the world's security.

Not only Chernobyl, but the fiasco at Three Mile Island in 1979 and the recent tragic failure of the space shuttle Challenger should warn us all how fallible we humans are.

Nuclear Is "Super-Dangerous"

Nuclear energy is super-dangerous and we must face up to this fact.

Why else would we spend a billion or more dollars for safety devices for a single reactor? Why else would we install a containment building with 3- to 4-feet thick steel reinforced walls around the reactor? Why do insurance companies refuse to cover the nuclear industry's potential liability? And why did the industry refuse to go ahead with the construction of nuclear plants until the federal government drastically limited the amount of damages that the utilities would have to pay out in the event of an accident? Why, after seven years and the expenditure of hundreds of millions of dollars, is the damaged reactor at Three Mile Island still not cleaned up? Why do the news media and government leaders cry out hour-by-hour about the great hazards of the Chernobyl accident? Is it because nuclear energy is safe?

The Soviet disaster, which may have killed thousands and incapacitated many more, and which will probably make a substantial part of the Ukraine uninhabitable for decades, is just the current debacle. More will certainly follow.

The world now has 361 nuclear power reactors in operation, with another 144 under construction or on order. Many of the older ones are increasingly susceptible to failure. The serious financial problems of the nuclear industry and the waning interest in technical careers in this field bode ill for adequate staffing and management of the reactors in the future.

Forty years into the nuclear era, the world still doesn't have the means to dispose of the highly radioactive waste accumulating at nuclear plants. Each year about one-third of the used fuel loaded with highly dangerous fission products is placed in pools of water outside the protection of the containment buildings, waiting for a decision on what to do with it—or for some accident or terrorist act to spread it around the countryside.

The nuclear industry is now calling for the decommissioning of plants after a 25- to 30-year useful life. It has yet to be determined whether these plants will be mothballed and guarded for decades as off-limits to humanity, or will be chopped up with remote-control devices and shipped to some guarded, off-limits burial ground.

Ask not for whom the reactor tolls; it tolls for thee.

The most serious threat from nuclear energy plants—one far beyond another Chernobyl-type disaster—is their production of plutonium, the ingredient of nuclear bombs. It is now becoming an article of international commerce. Little imagination is required to picture a terrorist with a homemade bomb holed up in a rooming house on Capitol Hill in Washington.

Must Have Alternatives

It appears essential, then, to provide humanity with alternate choices of energy supply.

When a society reduces its waste of energy or develops the means to use energy more efficiently, such as getting more miles per gallon of gasoline, it reduces the need for building more energy-producing plants. With a modest effort over the last decade, the United States saved more energy than is produced by all our nuclear plants today. With an all-out effort, we could save an even greater additional amount by the year 2000.

The potential for renewable forms of energy is large enough to fulfill all of our needs over the long run. As demonstrated by the forest-products industry, the burning of wood under proper controls already rivals the energy production of the nuclear industry. And photovoltaic devices that use sunlight to produce electricity stand out as the great hope for the world's energy future. Clearly a photovoltaic plant would be a much more friendly neighbor than a nuclear plant.

II

The proof is in: Nuclear plants can and do have catastrophic accidents.

But we see only the tip of the iceberg. The total costs are impossible to measure.

The Effects of Radiation

How can the cost of a birth defect caused by the fallout from the Soviet reactor meltdown or the partial meltdown at Three Mile Island, the fire at Brown's Ferry, or the routine emissions at every step of the nuclear fuel cycle be traced to its source?

How can leukemias and other cancers be traced to radioactive particulates ingested years earlier?

At least the Chernobyl disaster may help dispel the old lie that no one has ever died from the operation of a nuclear plant. But the bodies being counted in the Ukraine represent only a small percentage of the total casualties.

Radioactive iodine causes thyroid cancer.

Strontium 90, a bone-seeker, causes leukemia but is not clinically detectable for up to five years.

Some hard-tumor malignancies may not show up for 20 or 30 years after the initial radiation dose.

165

Fallout effects are magnified when particulates reach the ground in the form of rain or snow or sleet, concentrating in plants and animals. Some fish, according to a 1952 Atomic Energy Commission study, concentrate radiation up to 100,000 times. Thus, the food, milk, water chain is the critical pathway to man.

Our own water-treatment systems are not equipped to remove radioactive particulates. Nor can our health departments monitor every bite of food we eat.

Nuclear Energy Is Inherently Unsafe

As the dark stain of Chernobyl covers the shadow of Three Mile Island, nuclear power accidents have moved from the impossible to the unthinkable.

Its message is unmistakably clear: Nuclear power is not inherently safe, as its advocates have long claimed; it is inherently unsafe.

Arthur H. Purcell, *Los Angeles Times,* April 30, 1986.

Unfortunately, some people are more prone to radiation damage than others. Fetuses are at the highest risk. Some genetic damage may not show up for several generations..

Must Have Non-Nuclear Sources

We don't need nuclear pollution. We can and must produce electricity from non-nuclear, renewable sources.

Harness the wind, the sun, the tides. Burn municipal garbage to cool and heat homes and offices; tap methane from existing landfills. Cogenerate electricity from industrial waste steam. Turn wood waste into charcoal, dig for geothermal power, burn alcohol.

Enforce coal mine safety and strip-mining laws. Mine coal safely and burn it cleanly; Australia does. The Tennessee Valley Authority has perfected fluidized-bed combustion for cleaner, more efficient use of coal. The Russians have demonstrated MHD (magneto-hydrodynamics), a clean method for burning coal.

For a fraction of the money dumped into nuclear power, we can tap renewable resources.

Worldwide, let us join hands and shut down the nuclear fuel cycle. Let's save ourselves from ourselves.

a critical thinking skill

Understanding Words in Context

Readers occasionally come across words which they do not recognize. And frequently, because they do not know a word or words, they will not fully understand the passage being read. Obviously, the reader can look up an unfamiliar word in a dictionary. However, by carefully examining the word in the context in which it is used, the word's meaning can often be determined. A careful reader may find clues to the meaning of the word in surrounding words, ideas, and attitudes.

Below are excerpts from the viewpoints in this chapter. In each excerpt, one or two words are printed in italics. Try to determine the meaning of each word by reading the excerpt. Under each excerpt you will find four definitions for the italicized word. Choose the one that is closest to your understanding of the word.

Finally, use a dictionary to see how well you have understood the words in context. It will be helpful to discuss with others the clues which helped you decide on each word's meaning.

1. We've seen energy ride a roller coaster of public sentiment from *COMPLACENCY* to crisis and now, perhaps back to *COMPLACENCY.*

   COMPLACENCY means:

   a) sarcasm
   b) resentment
   c) emergency
   d) a feeling of satisfaction

2. We pulled ourselves out of the *TURBULENT* '70s by rebuilding confidence in our abilities.

   TURBULENT means:

   a) agitated
   b) moderate
   c) uneventful
   d) interesting

3. Studies strongly suggest that there are still *VAST* opportunities to use energy more efficiently.

   VAST means:

   a) enormous
   b) small
   c) profitable
   d) useful

4. Tanks and dumps holding nuclear wastes have leaked. The Department of Energy has learned little from these incidents, and wants to quickly choose a permanent *REPOSITORY.*

REPOSITORY means:

a) cover-up
b) container
c) development
d) point

5. The oldest commercial nuclear reactors are already nearing the end of their useful lives, and some plants have closed *PREMATURELY* because of accidents caused by faulty designs.

PREMATURELY means:

a) instead
b) normally
c) on time
d) unexpectedly early

6. First the reactor and other parts are decontaminated, then they get *DISMANTLED* into smaller pieces so they can be moved and buried.

DISMANTLED means:

a) produced
b) promised
c) separated
d) taken forward

7. These operations show how a nuclear reactor can be removed safely and how to handle the *SUBSEQUENT* disposal of wastes.

SUBSEQUENT means:

a) succeeding
b) prior
c) mistaken
d) useless

8. There are *INHERENT* problems with renewable energy that will always keep the costs high.

INHERENT means:

a) foreign
b) many
c) new
d) innate

9. Because renewable energy is *INTERMITTENT,* it is also unreliable.

INTERMITTENT means:

a) broken up
b) recent
c) regular
d) untested

Periodical Bibliography

The following list of periodical articles deals with the subject matter of this chapter.

George E. Brown Jr.   "We Lust for Energy, But Not for Its Risks," *Los Angeles Times*, May 2, 1986.

Jay M. Critchley   "Three Mile Island Historic Nuclear Park," *Utne Reader*, December 1985/January 1986.

W. Jackson Davis   "Putting the Future at Risk in Oceans of Nuclear Waste," *Los Angeles Times*, June 29, 1986.

Mikhail Gorbachev   "The Chernobyl Accident: Nuclear Energy and Radiation," *Vital Speeches of the Day*, June 15, 1986.

Tom Johnson   "Lessons of Chernobyl," *The New Republic*, July 14/21, 1986.

Amory Lovins   "The Cheap Energy Myth," *Multinational Monitor*, May 1986.

Russ Manning   "The Future of Nuclear Power," *Environment*, May 1985.

L. Manning Muntzing   "There Are Good Reasons To Defend Nuclear Power," *Los Angeles Times*, June 15, 1984.

R. D. Prosser   "Atomic Waste: Solving the Nuclear Waste Issue at Hanford," *Vital Speeches of the Day*, March 1, 1986.

Michael Rogers   "The Nuclear Bargain," *Newsweek*, May 12, 1986.

David J. Rose   "Nuclear Power," *Bulletin of the Atomic Scientists*, August 1985. For responses, see also November 1985 issue.

Joseph Sisco   "The Soviet Economy Will Pay," *The New York Times*, May 4, 1986.

Union of Concerned Scientists   "Chernobyl Is a Warning To Improve Nuclear Safety," *The New York Times*, May 7, 1986.

USA Today   "The Debate: Nuclear Dangers," April 30, 1986.

How Dangerous Are Toxic Wastes?

THE ENVIRONMENTAL CRISIS

"Synthetic chemicals improperly used or disposed of can cause great harm."

The Chemical Industry Is Poisoning America

Ralph Nader, Ronald Brownstein, and John Richard

Ralph Nader, a noted citizens' advocate and author of several books, is the sponsor of the Public Interest Research Group, a consumer advocate organization based in Washington. Ronald Brownstein and John Richard are two of his associates. They co-edited *Who's Poisoning America: Corporate Polluters and Their Victims in the Chemical Age,* from which this viewpoint is taken. They argue, along with many environmentalists, that chemical poisons from toxic wastes are threatening the health of all Americans and that the chemical industry has reneged on its responsibility to protect the public.

As you read, consider the following questions:

1. What are some examples the authors describe of toxic pollution in the environment?
2. What, according to the authors, keeps chemical corporations from adequately protecting the environment?
3. The authors express hope for a cleaner environment. After reading this viewpoint, do you agree that toxic wastes can be reduced?

Chemical waste dumps number in the tens of thousands throughout this country. Additional volumes of waste have been illegally thrown into sewers, ravines and parking lots, or have been abandoned in urban warehouses. Millions of Americans are drinking water contaminated with toxic substances or finding water sources quarantined by health authorities. Residues of chemical pesticides pervade the food supply. Thousands of new chemical compounds are entering the human environment each year, and each year the evidence grows of even greater danger.

This epidemic of chemical violence spilling across the land and waters of America provokes a new patriotism: to stop the poisoning of the country. It invites a new kind of neighborhood unity: to defend the community, the children and those yet unborn. It highlights the severe deficiencies in our laws, in the flow of information and in the response of our public officials. It reflects a destruction of civilized standards by corporate executives. It is victimization without representation and, for the most part, without realization. It is a massive flood of quiet, cumulative, often invisible violence, too charitably called pollution. Although it usually avoids immediate pain it silently generates future devastation.

Worse To Come

But the future is now, and there may be worse to come. The names "Love Canal," "Kepone," "West Valley," "Reserve Mining," "2,4,5-T," "PBB," and "PCB" will be remembered for early tragedies in America's long struggle for self-defense against callous internal chemical warfare. The names of the companies responsible for these toxic spills and toxic dumps are seen on television or in the press. However, almost no one knows the names of the managers behind the company images.

In contrast, the victims know one another's names. Ask the farmers whose land and kin were contaminated with a fire retardant called PBB that was carelessly mixed with feed grain sold in Michigan. How well the families at Love Canal came to know each other as they learned that they themselves were going to have to impose accountability.

If at the outset the liabilities of a technological choice are known to society, faustian bargains are avoidable. Information about the effects of new substances should be made available to the public before the food chain and drinking water are contaminated. People need to know that many industrial materials are not necessary for a prosperous standard of living. Alternatives to these hazardous chemicals have been found—but, as a rule, only after an environmental disaster prompted a reevaluation.

PCB, PBB and Kepone are no longer produced, and most uses of 2,4,5-T are suspended; industry has adapted, agriculture continues. Reserve Mining Company could have disposed of its daily wastes onshore as did its smaller competitors nearby. And Hooker Chemical Company certainly knew how to contain its myriad of chemicals more safely.

Corporate Guilt

The economic burden on society would have been a tiny fraction of the cleanup and compensation costs had the companies introducing these products acted responsibly. The human casualties would have been avoided, along with the profound community and family disruptions. It was not lack of knowledge, but the lack of corporate interest, that resulted in the transformation of the living environment into the lethal sewers of industry. Interest in controlling the damaging aspects of technology is more likely to come from the potential victims and from parents who care for their children than from the corporate perpetrators. . . .

The environmental movement that questioned . . . chemicals began in earnest as part of the reexamination of values engendered by the war in Vietnam and the civil-rights campaign of the early 1960s. Environmentalism offered an alternative to the consumption ethos of the Depression/World War II generation. This alternative was called ecology, after the branch of study that examines the "intricate web of relationships between living organisms and their living and non-living surroundings," as one writer put it. "Ecology" was, at the time, a way of life as much as a science. . . .

An Onslaught of Deadly Chemicals

Nature was caught off guard, utterly unprepared for *this onslaught* of artificial elements. Nowhere in the earth's crust nor in the ocean was there the capability of disassembling these complex new substances strung together by the ingenuity of man. Many of the chemicals, sophisticated hydrocarbons such as DDT, were based on long molecular chains solid enough to withstand degradation by sunlight, dissolution by water, or breakdown by acids, clay minerals, or metal ions. These chemicals, deadly to the human metabolism, found the earth and its waters a congenial way station; and now they remained permanently available to exact a terrible price for human indifference and greed.

Mike Brown, *Laying Waste: The Poisoning of America by Toxic Chemicals,* 1979.

In those heady days of environmental optimism, few had any idea that the worst was yet to come. "We . . . gained success in combatting gross threats to our air and water," said Gus Speth, chairman of the CEQ [Council on Environmental Quality] in 1980, "only to discover whole new phalanxes of subtle menaces, whose danger and obstinacy often vary in inverse proportion to their ability to be quickly and easily understood."

173

The need for so many different laws, offering protection from such a broad range of exposures, illustrated how thoroughly dangerous chemicals had dispersed in the environment. The chemical companies had become a large and powerful industry. Consider:

— In 1979, 32 companies each had annual chemical sales of $1 billion or more. DuPont, the largest chemical company, had sales of $9.7 billion; the Dow, Exxon, Union Carbide and Monsanto companies each had sales of more than $5 billion.

— Sales are increasing. Each of the top 50 chemical producers sold more chemicals in 1979 than in 1978. Each sold more in 1978 than the year before. In 1978, only DuPont had sales greater than $5 billion; in 1979 the other four companies mentioned above each passed that total. Overall chemical production increased after 1968 at an annual rate of 6 percent; by comparison, all manufacturing grew at the rate of only 3 percent.

Sagging Public Image

Though the 1980 recession . . . hurt the industry, the chemical lobby has been a loud and effective voice in Washington and across the country. Its trade group, the Chemical Manufacturers Association (CMA), has undertaken an expensive, highly visible campaign to restore the industry's sagging public image. (The association not long ago raised its dues 85 percent.) In one . . . poll, the chemical industry ranked the lowest among 13 industries in public image. In a June 1980 "confidential" CMA poll, majorities in all but one sample category "felt the industry was . . . 'unconcerned' about the welfare of the average person." "I don't need any polls to tell me that the chemical industry is not held in high esteem," Robert Roland, the head of the CMA, has said. "The public accepts the benefits of chemicals out of hand, but they do not believe the industry is doing enough to manage the risks. We believe we are acting responsibly."

Whether the public even has been given a chance to balance the benefits against the risks of the industry, . . . no doubt can exist that chemicals are ubiquitous. Some 55,000 different chemicals now are in commercial use. "We are living in a time of organic chemicals," notes author Dr. Samuel S. Epstein, "not just familiar ones, but exotic ones which have never previously existed on earth and to which no living thing has previously had to adapt."

This proliferation of chemicals has raised an elemental concern: Is America being poisoned? Questions about the health effects of pollution and chemicals have been raised before. Air pollution combined with atmospheric inversions caused tragedies in several cities, from London, England, to Donora, Pennsylvania, in the late 1940s and early 1950s. In 1958, the Delaney clause (named for

174

New York Congressman James J. Delaney) prohibited the use of food additives proved to cause cancer in "man or animal." Rachel Carson's epic book *Silent Spring* had questioned the use of pesticides in the early 1960s.

© Carol*Simpson/Rothco

In the mid-1970s the questions raised in the forties, fifties and sixties were answered with chemical disasters that crowded each other off the front page. The synthetic chemicals that appeared after World War II in products of all shapes and sizes also were appearing where they never were meant to be, and often with tragic results. One of those places was the Niagara Falls community of Love Canal. Chemical wastes buried there more than 30 years ago reached into the lives of hundreds of middle-class families living in neat rows of homes. Women there have had more miscarriages than normal; an unusual number of children have been born with birth defects; serious illnesses have wracked families. Love Canal is the site of the first federal emergency declared in response to a human-made disaster.

Love Canal has brought home the threats of the new industrial era. That synthetic chemicals improperly used or disposed of can cause great harm no longer is a theoretical proposition. The polluted lakes and streams, the fish kills and eyesores of the fifties and sixties were only the first, most visible manifestations; the real impact of the belching smokestacks and autos is being realized only many years later—in the elevated levels of lead measured in the bloodstreams of young children and in the more frequent occurrence of respiratory diseases. The true cost of dirty rivers is revealed in higher rates of cancer among the people who draw their drinking water from those waterways.

At Love Canal, these delayed effects of the new technology have become piercingly evident. And a few months after the public heard about Love Canal, the Three Mile Island nuclear accident sliced through the rhetoric of the nuclear industry. Invulnerability to accident cannot be designed into a reactor. Nor has any means of handling the long-lived nuclear wastes been found; the Three Mile Island accident followed the failure of the nuclear reprocessing plant in West Valley, New York. Evidence mounted of the menace of pesticides. DDT was removed from the market. Other pesticides, too, have been banned. But their residues remain, in the environment and in our bodies.

Saving Ourselves

Workers have been exposed to toxic chemicals since their production began. Every few years, the increases in the production of chemicals are punctuated by the uncovering of occupational disease epidemics in such towns as Hopewell, Virginia. The stricken locales emerge, then vanish from the public eye, like augurs. But now the danger, no longer confined to the workplace, pervades the country. This increasing threat is reflected in the continued spread of cancer, the only cause of death to rise in the United States since 1900—and a disease with deep environmental roots. . . .

None of [the] . . . tragedies, however, has turned up in the ledgers of the giant corporations producing the chemicals or of the power plants and steel mills and other industries pouring wastes into the air and water. And this . . . is the essence of the environmental dilemma. Environmental and occupational health regulations have been a belated attempt to assess industries for the true social costs of their products. That accounts for those regulations being so fervently resisted; to want a free ride prolonged forever is natural.

But in the wake of Love Canal and Reserve Mining and Kepone and PCBs and all the other disasters of the decade, the extent of this free ride's cost began to emerge. Protecting the environment was no longer a question only of cleaning up rivers unfit for swimming or of protecting farm lands threatened by suburban sprawl, or even of saving waterfowl endangered by oil spills (though all these remained concerns).

It was a question of saving ourselves.

176

"Is the chemical industry poisoning America? No, and it's unqualified nonsense even to suggest that it is."

The Chemical Industry Is Not Poisoning America

William G. Simeral and Robert C. Cowen

Since 1979, when a whole neighborhood was evacuated from Love Canal in New York to escape the poisons of hazardous wastes, the public has feared for its health and safety and has blamed the chemical industry for placing it at risk. But not everyone believes that such fear is necessary. In the following viewpoint, two authorities argue that wastes from chemical companies are no more a threat to public health than are the chemicals in ordinary household products. Part I is written by William G. Simeral, a former president of the Chemical Manufacturers Association (CMA) and executive vice-president of the DuPont Company. Robert C. Cowen, natural science editor of *The Christian Science Monitor*, is the author of Part II.

As you read, consider the following questions:

1. According to Mr. Simeral, whose responsibility is it to mend public misunderstanding of the chemical companies?
2. How does Mr. Cowen feel about excessive fear of chemicals in light of the fact that consumers use so many in their homes?

William G. Simeral, "The Public Is Afraid of Chemicals Says Industry Leader." Reprinted from *The Journalist*, Winter 1984 by permission of the Foundation for American Communications.

Robert C. Cowen, "Beware the Excessive Fear of Toxic Chemicals," *The Christian Science Monitor*, April 16, 1985. Reprinted by permission from *The Christian Science Monitor* © 1985 The Christian Science Publishing Society. All Rights Reserved.

I

To put it bluntly, the public's perception of what we do is fraught with misunderstanding. . . . We have witnessed one sensational media story after another in which our products have been depicted as direct threats to the safety of people and the environment: PCBs, saccharine, fluorocarbons, formaldehyde—the list goes on. The problems of hazardous wastes and abandoned dumps have almost become syndicated features in many newspapers.

There is a tendency to consider the public's negative attitude toward the chemical industry as part of the anti-business sentiment every industry faces in this country. That may explain some of our problems; but it doesn't explain all of them and certainly not the most crucial ones.

Fear of Chemicals

I submit that the fundamental cause of the chemical industry's public perception problem is basic fear of chemicals. I do not use the word fear in a figurative sense, as in worry or concern. I mean genuine phobia and anxiety.

This fear of chemicals is *the* issue facing the chemical industry in its relationship to the government and the public, which means that it is *the* issue facing CMA [Chemical Manufacturers Association]. In a sense, we have a one-item agenda: All the major issues facing us flow from the fear of chemicals, their presumed toxicity, and their potential impact on human health. Unless we can get the issue of chemical toxicity into proper perspective in the public's mind, we will never make genuine progress in the public policy arena, and our industry will never reach its full potential.

Everywhere we turn, the issue of chemical toxicity confronts us. Toxic pollutants are an issue in connection with the Clean Water Act and Clean Air Act. Toxic chemical waste disposal involves both scrutiny of present practices and the cleanup of old dump sites. Compensation for individuals who might be injured by exposure to chemical waste is a growing issue and a potential Pandora's box. And older issues like toxicity of food additives and agrichemicals are still with us. All contribute their share to the public phobia.

The Public's Ignorance

The intensity of public concern over these issues may surprise those of us who have spent our careers in the management field of risk. And the public's ignorance of the constructive work we have done to minimize risks is a constant source of frustration. We have long been aware of the toxicity problems associated with our industry, and we have taken appropriate steps to deal with them. To us toxicity is one of many concerns that we have tackled—with considerable success—over the years.

To the public, however, it is the *only* concern. If you asked the man on the street whether chemical toxins are a bigger problem today than they were in the forties and fifties, he would probably say that they are—contrary to fact and all documentation.

Is the chemical industry poisoning America? No, and it's unqualified nonsense even to suggest that it is. But the American public does not share this belief. The average person does share the common anxiety over chemicals which is grounded in the irresponsible statements of some scientists and politicians and sustained by the mass media.

Chemical-Phobia

For the past decade, Americans have been in the grip of a virulent strain of "chemical-phobia." Most people seem convinced that an array of sinister industrially-produced chemicals has invaded their air, water, homes, and even their muffin mix. The news media regularly carry anxiety-provoking stories about pesticides such as ethylene dibromide (EDB), aldrin, and dieldrin; environmental contaminants like dioxin; industrial chemicals like formaldehyde and PCBs; and alleged chemical nightmares at sites such as Love Canal, Times Beach and the whole state of New Jersey.

Norman E. Borlaug, *Toxic Terror*, 1985.

In the face of this, some in our industry have responded by saying, "So what?" And we might ask ourselves whether it really matters if the public feels this way. I would answer that it probably doesn't hurt anything but our self-esteem if we are merely disliked; people who dislike you tend to avoid you and go their separate ways. But it does matter if people are afraid of you: People who fear you write their congressman; they take part in demonstrations, and they vote against your interests on election day. A false perception of the chemical industry *does* matter, and we owe it to ourselves, as well as to the public's peace of mind, to set about correcting it.

How can we correct this false perception? Let's begin by recognizing that we'll never do it with words alone. Public relations and advertising campaigns have their place, but what the public really wants is concrete action.

What should we do? *To start, we can clean up the dumps.* I know that this is easier said than done. But let's state the issue up front. It doesn't matter whether your company or mine has anything to do with a specific site. We are all being tarred with the same brush. It also doesn't matter whether a given site poses a genuine health hazard; the public perceives the potential for one.

Abandoned dump sites are the single, most obvious symbol of every-thing the public believes to be wrong with the chemical industry. Whatever their impact on the environment, rusted drums are poisoning the climate for the chemical industry in Washington and across the nation. As long as we let the problem persist, we don't stand a chance at winning the confidence of the people. Individual companies must get involved—literally—in the cleanup. Several companies have been studying possible ways to offer our exper-tise to the government—a way to mount a proactive program aimed at speeding up the cleanup of selected Superfund sites.

What the public needs to understand—and what we have to con-tinue to remind ourselves—is that the chemical industry represents the major resource of technical capability that the country has for dealing with this problem.

The bottom line is that doing something about abandoned dump sites doesn't mean talking about the problem; it doesn't mean hold-ing press conferences; it doesn't mean conducting studies. *What it means is rolling up our sleeves, assigning project managers and go-ing to work.*

In Plain English

Concurrent with getting the dump site problem under control, we must address the misconceptions of the public about chemi-cals and the chemical industry.

What the public needs is plain English information pertinent to their basic question: Are chemicals going to hurt me? We are not dealing with a scientific concern so much as we are dealing with a public health concern.

Promoting a better understanding of chemicals and public health is another top priority objective of CMA. We are seeking to in-volve objective scientists with impeccable credentials from out-side the industry whenever possible, and we are making public understanding of the health effects of chemicals part of our on-going communications.

A New Authority Needed

But what we really need is a new way to deal with public health issues involving toxic substances. There are now a number of government agencies involved in various aspects of the problem—environmental or occupational health, for example. Present proce-dures place the health experts in a secondary role at best. Instead, when it is discovered or suspected that a toxic substance may cause a health problem, the health issues should be dealt with first by experts in human health matters. Such people are the only ones qualified to assess risk to human health and to inform the public about the risks. Frequently, conclusions as to health risks which should be based on medical knowledge are reached by officials with no proper qualifications. Such conclusions are much too important to be placed in the hands of untrained laymen. The public deserves to hear from the people who understand all of the ramifications of human health matters.

If we had such an authority today—which the media would call an unimpeachable source—everyone could look to it for basic information, and we could eliminate much of the hysteria, fear and unwarranted action that characterizes the issue of toxic substances today.

II

Excessive fear of toxic chemicals has swept through the news media and into US public thinking since the tragedy at Bhopal, India. That fear needs to be held in check by a realistic appreciation of the public risk, lest overreaction and needlessly punitive regulations stifle an essential basic industry.

How frightening, for example, modern daily living would seem if you overreacted to the warning labels on common household products. Washing the dishes involves chemicals dangerous to eyes and skin. Household ammonia solutions emit a familiar toxic gas. This is to say nothing of what happens when laundry detergents and bleaches enter a septic tank. They give rise to pollutants high on the Environmental Protection Agency's hit list. When you put fuel in a car, there's a warning on the pump against breathing the gasoline vapors.

It's enough to make one seek the sanctuary of a nice, safe chemical plant where monitoring instruments, automatic controls, and trained personnel generally keep health risks to a low minimum—Bhopal notwithstanding.

Drawings by Redinger

Why then, if we live with and safely use so many "dangerous" chemicals, has public fear of the chemical industry reached a pitch where the industry itself fears for its future? It would seem that the familiar copper pot cleaners, toilet bowl disinfectants, or quick-setting glues are not perceived in the same light as the mysterious "chemicals" that circulate through the awesome piping and retorts of the public conception of a chemical plant. The fact that the chemical industry handles hazardous materials with such skill and care that it has the best industrial safety record of any major industry in the US seems overlooked.

The chemical industry is important to the world. It is a powerful economic engine and source of many essential products. In the United States, for example, its $200 billion-a-year activity employs more than a million people and outcompetes other countries in international trade. Were overreaction to public fear to cause Congress or local legislatures to hobble chemical manufacturers with excessive restrictions, the United States would, economically speaking, shoot itself in the foot.

Concerned Leaders

Leaders in the chemical industry have been so concerned that this might happen that, even before Bhopal, chairmen and chief executive officers of major chemical companies such as Dow or Exxon Chemicals have "gone public" with a campaign to ensure plant safety as a way to convince the public that any risk is minimal. They have sent a message to their subordinates and their colleagues that the public concern with safety is also a top-priority concern of their companies. They are no more tolerant of dangerous toxic waste dumps than is Greenpeace or Friends of the Earth.

Some of these senior executives have joined personally with environmentalists in programs to deal with toxic waste sites and other chemically related environmental problems. Members of the Chemical Manufacturers Association have organized a Clean Sites program with environmental groups to bring the expertise of the industry to bear on the problem and to add muscle in lobbying Congress for a more effective Superfund program. And, reversing a long-held position, industry leaders urged Congress last month to enact stricter uniform controls on emissions from chemical plants.

These and other steps being taken may not satisfy the industry's critics or quickly calm public fear. But they are earnest and represent a high-priority effort on the part of many industry experts and executives. The sincerity of these industry leaders is enforced by the realization that they have no choice. They believe that they must work with legislators, environmentalists, and other concerned citizens to ensure that their industry is safe and perceived to be safe.

"A major potential threat to the life and health
of every single American exists in the pervasive
presence of poisonous chemicals in the
environment."

Toxic Wastes Are Causing a Cancer Epidemic

Lewis Regenstein

Lewis Regenstein is vice president of The Fund for Animals, an
influential environmental group. He has written two books on the
environment, *The Politics of Extinction* and *America the Poisoned*.
In the following viewpoint, excerpted from the latter, Mr. Regenstein finds a direct link between the toxic chemicals being poured
into the environment and an increase in the rate of cancer. He
believes that this growing rate of cancer is exploding into an
epidemic.

As you read, consider the following questions:

1. On what does Mr. Regenstein base his conclusion that
   America is facing a cancer epidemic?
2. Mr. Regenstein calls the present rate of cancer "the
   foremost health and environmental crisis of our times." Do
   you agree with him? Why or why not?

With permission from AMERICA THE POISONED, by Lewis Regenstein, copyright ©
1982, Acropolis Books, Washington, DC 20009.

Some of the pesticides . . . are so long-lasting and so pervasive in the environment that virtually the entire human population of the Nation, and indeed the world, carries some body burden of one or several of them.

Library of Congress study accompanying
Surgeon General's report on toxic pollution,
August, 1980

Man-made toxic chemicals are a significant source of death and disease in the U.S. today.

Gus Speth, Chairman, President's Council on
Environmental Quality (CEQ), 29 June, 1980

Seventy to 90 percent of all cancers are caused by environmental influences and are hence theoretically preventable.

CEQ, 1978

It is now apparent that a major potential threat to the life and health of every single American exists in the pervasive presence of poisonous chemicals in the environment. These toxic substances, many of which cause cancer, birth defects, nerve and brain damage, and gene mutations, are so prevalent in our daily lives that they are simply impossible to avoid. Deadly synthetic chemicals are now present in our food, air, water, and even our own bodies—including mothers' milk—where they remain and accumulate.

By the time many of the most dangerous pesticides were banned or restricted as powerful cancer-causing agents, they had contaminated virtually every American and most of our food supply. Dieldrin was being found in the flesh of 99.5 percent of all human tissue samples tested, as well as in 96 percent of all meat, fish and poultry. BHC had been detected in 99 percent of all Americans tested, and heptachlor in 95 percent, as well as in 70 percent of meat, poultry, fish and dairy products. DDT and PCB's were turning up in almost all human tissue samples, fresh water fish, meat and dairy products.

Lethal Future

Now that we know that almost every American carries detectable traces of several generally banned carcinogens, we must await the inevitable effects. How long can our bodies continue to accumulate such lethal poisons before succumbing to cancer? What will be the effects upon our genes, upon future generations? The answer, of course, is that we do not know, because never before in human history have such deadly substances existed, much less entered and lodged in our bodies.

Cancers usually take 20 to 30 years to appear after a person has been exposed to a carcinogen, and government studies are now detecting a regular increase in the cancer rate. Here is thus the first harvest of disease following the seeds sown in the 1950's and '60's, when chemicals first began to proliferate throughout the environment.

But the worst appears to lie ahead. Each year, some one thousand new chemicals are introduced to pollute our air, water and food. Most cancers—the estimates run between 60 and 90 percent—are attributed to environmental factors, including the widespread use since World War II of toxic chemicals. A 1978 report issued by the President's Council on Environmental Quality (CEQ) unequivocally states that "most researchers agree that 70 to 90 percent of all cancers are caused by environmental influences and are hence theoretically preventable."

The Current Cancer Epidemic

With exposure to toxic chemicals beginning at the moment of conception and continuing throughout life, one in four Americans now contracts cancer. This means that some 60 million Americans now living can expect to get the disease. Two-thirds of them will die of it, which comes to more than 400,000 deaths a year— over a thousand a day! To put that number in perspective, consider that fewer Americans died in the battles of World War II plus the Korean and Vietnamese conflicts combined. Each year, cancer kills about 8 times more Americans than do automobile accidents. . . .

Environmentally-Induced Cancer

The scientific community generally agrees that the majority of human cancers are environmentally induced. Estimates by the World Health Organization and the National Cancer Institute concur that between 60 and 90 percent of all human cancers are environmental in origin, and that approximately 90 percent of all human cancers are chemical in origin.

Karl Grossman, *The Poison Conspiracy*, 1983.

In order to determine scientifically the effects of toxic chemicals on our health, CEQ in 1977 formed a research team of 18 federal agencies called the Toxic Substances Strategy Committee (TSSC). After three years of study, the committee in 1980 issued a report clearly demonstrating that perhaps millions of Americans are killed or disabled by carcinogenic synthetic chemicals. TSSC confirmed that cancer incidence rates were on the increase— "about 10 percent between 1970 and 1976"—while this period saw all other causes of death decline. It pointed out that "Cancer is the only major cause of death that rose continuously from 1900 to 1978. Recent figures show that both incidence (new cases) and mortality (deaths) rates are increasing.

A Clear Report

The report stated clearly that almost all cancers are caused by substances present in the environment:

> It is generally believed that most cancer cases, possibly 90 percent, are related to at least one environmental factor—that is, external non-genetic factors like air pollution, smoking, chemical and other contaminants in the workplace, and dietary components.

In announcing the findings, Gus Speth, Chairman of CEQ, emphasized that "man-made toxic chemicals are a significant source of death and disease in the United States today." And it is no coincidence, CEQ member Dr. Robert Harris pointed out, that the production of chemicals greatly increased between 1950 and 1960, and the dramatic increase in the cancer rate showed up 20 to 25 years later, "the lag time one might expect."

The Worst Is Yet To Come

As Dr. Joseph Highland, Chairman of the Environmental Defense Fund's Toxic Chemicals Program, testified before a Congressional committee, "Through our current inaction, we have jeopardized our futures," and the worst is yet to come:

> As cigarette consumption rose, so did lung cancer rates, but only after a characteristic "lag time" or "latent period" of approximately 30 years. The lung cancer incidence we see today clearly reflects the smoking hazards of 30 years ago. Consequently, if a pattern similar to that of smoking occurs in that a 30-year lag time exists between exposure to these chemicals and the manifestation of disease, the effects of general exposure may not be seen until the mid-1980's.

On 27 August 1980, the Surgeon General of the United States, Julius Richmond, released an assessment of the threat to public health caused by toxic chemicals. Just as the Surgeon General's 1964 report was instrumental in convincing the public of the hazards of cigarette smoking, this 1980 report was equally forthright in declaring that the threat posed by hazardous chemicals is severe:

> . . . it is clear that it is a major and growing public health problem. We believe that toxic chemicals are adding to the disease burden of the United States in a significant, although as yet ill-defined way. In addition, we believe that this problem will become more manifest in the years ahead . . . We believe that the magnitude of the public health risk associated with toxic chemicals currently is increasing and will continue to do so until we are successful in identifying chemicals which are highly toxic and controlling the introduction of these chemicals into our environment.

The Surgeon General also reported that while "full implementation of recent environmental control legislation" could reduce the public exposure to such chemicals, nevertheless "through this decade we will have to confront a series of environmental emergencies and, therefore, are developing strategies to respond to their public health implications."

A Worldwide Problem

An accompanying report prepared by the Library of Congress makes it clear that this problem is not confined to the U.S., but is of worldwide dimensions:

> In the case of chemicals such as some of the pesticides (aldrin, dieldrin, DDT, etc.), PBB's and PCB's . . . these are so long-lasting and so pervasive in the environment that virtually the entire human population of the Nation, and indeed the world, carries some body burden of one or several of them . . . a significant proportion of the world's population, perhaps all of it, is exposed to the cumulative if unknown effects of a plethora of man-made pollutants from a number of diverse and often distant sources.

A more recent study on cancer is even more ominous. A June 1981 report by the National Cancer Institute states that the average American now stands almost a one in three chance of contracting cancer: "The cumulative incidence rate for all races, both sexes, all areas combined . . . , which can be interpreted as the probability of developing cancer from birth to age 74, is approximately 31 percent." . . .

Chemicals Are To Blame

Among the people most heavily-hit by cancer and other so-called environmental diseases—maladies caused by poisons put into the environment—are those who live near toxic waste dumps, people who live near factories where toxins are spewed out into the air, land and water, workers in industries where poisons are prevalent, and farmers and farmworkers heavily involved with chemical pesticides, herbicides and fertilizers.

Karl Grossman, *The Poison Conspiracy*, 1983.

Today, we are being exposed to more toxic chemicals than we were yesterday, and there will be even more tomorrow. The production of new, untested chemicals is a fabulously profitable "growth" industry. It has overwhelmed the government regulatory agencies, as well as our bodies' defense mechanisms.

The manufacture of synthetic organic (petroleum-based) chemicals in the U.S. has grown from less than a billion total pounds in 1941 for all such chemicals, to 172 billion pounds in 1978 for just the 50 major ones. In that same year, world trade in these chemicals rose by 18 percent. Production of the top 50 inorganic chemicals totalled 350 billion pounds—almost 100 pounds for each person on earth! . . .

These chemicals are, for the most part, substances that human cells have never before come into contact with in the entire history of human evolution, and with which our bodies do not know how to cope—to expel or digest—when we are exposed to them.

Scientists have long contended that there is no "safe" level of exposure to carcinogens. Since many carcinogens are stored and build up in our bodily tissues, especially the fat, repeated "insignificant" exposures over a period of time can accumulate to levels sufficient to trigger the process that causes cancer and other ailments. . . .

The Impending Tragedy

This, then, is the foremost health and environmental crisis of our times. It is perhaps, as EPA has described it, the most serious such problem our country has ever faced: the pervasive presence of dozens upon dozens of toxic chemicals which, at minute doses, cause cancer and/or birth defects in laboratory animals, and which presumably will affect many humans in a similar way. These toxins have been so widely distributed throughout our environment and food chain that most Americans carry detectable residues of them in their bodies. Even if all toxic chemicals were immediately banned, their effects would continue to show up for 20 or 30 years or more, and the environment would remain saturated with many of them for decades to come, in some cases for centuries. Philip Shabecoff, who has covered the environment for *The New York Times* for a decade and is not given to overstatement, says that "unless we can find a way to solve this toxic chemicals problem, our future is going to be very much in doubt."

If any one or a combination of these poisons has a serious health impact on only a small percent of the humans exposed—and it would be astonishing if *many* of these chemicals did not cause such effects—this will have implications for the health of tens of millions of Americans, as well as for unborn generations. In the long run, what may be at stake—and we will not know for sure until it is too late—is the very integrity of the human race.

When the final answers are in, we may well have sealed the fate of a generation of Americans—and perhaps of future ones as well. What we know so far indicates that only the magnitude of the impending tragedy, not whether there will be one, remains to be seen.

"There is no . . . evidence [of] . . . an overall increase in the incidence of cancer related to high levels of pollutants."

Toxic Wastes Are Not Causing a Cancer Epidemic

Elizabeth Whelan

Dr. Elizabeth Whelan is the executive director of the American Council on Science and Health and the author of twelve books on health issues, including *Toxic Terror,* from which this viewpoint is taken. Dr. Whelan believes that the warnings about cancer caused by toxic chemicals have been exaggerated. She argues that Americans are healthier than they have ever been, and that they would rather assume the slight risks of cancer than give up the advanced technology they enjoy.

As you read, consider the following questions:

1. What distinction does the author draw between the *rate* of cancer and the *number* of cases? How is this distinction important to her conclusion that cancer is not an epidemic?
2. Both Mr. Regenstein and Dr. Whelan quote scientists and statistics to reinforce their arguments. Are some statistics more convincing than others? Why or why not?

Elizabeth Whelan, *Toxic Terror.* Ottawa, IL: Jameson Books, 1985. Reprinted by permission.

189

Like most other Americans, I get a good deal of my information about health and the environment from books, magazines, newspapers, and the electronic media. And what I have seen, heard, and read in the past three years has led me to believe that when it comes to discussions of health and the environment, the word *news* is synonymous with *bad news.*

Daily we are subject to anxiety-producing reports about the "poisons" in our environment, the threat of premature death, human misery, defective children, or no children at all, caused by our careless use of technology. We are warned that calamity is on our doorstep, fresh out of a sinister test tube, and that we face an impending epidemic of disease and death. Human existence itself seems to be jeopardized, our ecology ruined, with nothing left for us to leave to the generations to come. And why is all this happening? The message is clear; our disrespect for nature and the environment, and our thoughtless, unharnessed use of modern-day chemicals have spelled doomsday and ecological catastrophe for our country, and perhaps the world.

Crying Wolf

I am aware of the fact that the bad-news/end-of-world scenario is not unique to our times. In 1962, Bertrand Russell told us that nuclear war was inevitable in the next few months. Dr. Paul Ehrlich's 1968 book, *The Population Bomb,* predicted that "the battle to feed all of humanity is over. . . . In the 1970s the world will undergo famines; hundreds of millions of people are going to starve to death in spite of any crash program embarked upon now." Early in the 1970s Jacques Cousteau opined that the oceans would be dead by the end of the century. *Life* reported in 1970 that by 1980 people would have to wear gas masks because of pollution, and that in the early 1980s people by the thousands would be killed in U.S. cities because of smog inversions. We were warned by many sources that rivers would reach the poisoning point in the early 1980s because of nuclear power plants. But the fact that pessimism has reigned in the past does not make the bad news any easier to accept today.

Dioxin, we read (in stories with subtitles like "Dioxin: In Search of a Killer"), is the "most toxic chemical known to man," capable of causing instant death in minute amounts, responsible for cancer and birth defects in laboratory animals, and threatening the life and health of residents of Love Canal in upstate New York; of Times Beach, Missouri; Newark, New Jersey; Midland, Michigan, and who knows where else.

Limits for acceptable residue limits of ethylene dibromide (EDB), a pesticide used on a number of agricultural commodities for some forty years, were recently set by the Environmental Protection Agency. Although the guidelines ensure that the risk of cancer from EDB to consumers is at worst negligible, hysterical claims to the contrary have been made by activist groups and politicians. The EDB situation exemplifies how self-serving individuals and organizations can twist public health issues for political motives.

Women on the West Coast of the United States have repeatedly charged that the widespread use of herbicides, particularly, 2,4,5-T, has caused reproductive failures, including low sperm count, miscarriage, and birth defects. Vietnam War veterans assert that all their symptoms and diseases were initiated by their exposure to the defoliating chemicals of Agent Orange in Southeast Asia.

Zero-Risk Impossible

If, suddenly, we reversed the whole nineteenth century and didn't have chemicals . . . we would still have very significant cancer risks and chronic disease risks from naturally occurring toxicants that are in our water, are in our food, are in our air. It will never be possible to make the risk zero.

Dr. Vernon N. Hour, *Chemecology,* April 1984.

Citizen groups have organized to interrupt the development of nuclear energy in this country, pointing always to their concern about the potential cancer-causing effects of low-level radiation, and solemnly noting the "tragedy" at Three Mile Island. We are told that we should not drink the water or breathe the air because it is poisoned with the "fallout of affluence," and advised to avoid living in a heavily industrialized state like New Jersey (if we must visit it, we are admonished to hold our breath).

The popular wisdom here can be summarized as follows:

1. America is being poisoned by chemicals and radioactivity.

2. Our country's health has never been worse, and is threatening to deteriorate even further.

3. Big business is responsible for the environmental nightmare and cares not at all about what it is doing, concerned only with its short-term profit margin.

4. Little people (like you and me) are the victims of this corporate greed and toxic crime.

5. This current and future wave of disease and death is the ultimate price we pay for technology and the "good life."

6. New and complex chemicals are poisons and must be either eliminated or highly regulated. The death-dealing technology must be stopped *at any cost.* . . .

Doomsayers' Style

Although the message of environmental gloom and doom comes from different sources, it does seem to have a consistent literary style. In discussing environmental issues, words are carefully chosen to convey horror and fear of the unknown. One of the most commonly used analogies is that of a time bomb, a technique that effectively introduces the concept of devastation occurring, outside our control, at an unknown time and place. A 1979 PBS TV network report was entitled "Defusing Cancer's Time Bomb." Regenstein, in a *New York Times* piece based on *America the Poisoned,* speaks of "silent time bombs ticking away." Grossman in *The Poison Conspiracy* writes of a "mammoth field of time bombs [which have] been planted, their full impact yet to come." Douglas Costle, a former Environmental Protection Agency administrator, used the same approach when he stated, "We didn't understand that every barrel stuck into the ground was a ticking time bomb primed to go off."

An analysis of the selection of words in the *Time* cover story, "The Poisoning of America," is revealing in that it confirms the authors' commitment to the concept of real environmental horror. In talking of chemicals, the article refers to "alchemists," whose "concoctions" "ooze," "seep," "brew," and "haunt" while "festering" and "fouling" in "Dantesque" horror.

The bad-news claims of the doomsayers are not only general and far reaching in their scope, but also quite specific about the devastating impact that technology is having on the health of America.

Growing Cancer Risk

Those attempting to rivet our attention on environmental dangers warn us of the potential risk of cancer from the environmental exposure to toxic chemicals. . . .

The Poison Conspiracy tells us that "it is evident that cancer's general increase is closely parallel to the deterioration of the nation's environment. A graph of industrial activities known to be major contributors to toxic pollution follows a concurrent rising trend of cancer mortality." . . .

Public opinion polls seem to indicate that American consumers are listening carefully to . . . these discussions of an "epidemic." A recent poll noted that 62 percent of the general public thought that "cancer in our society is increasing." . . .

No Epidemic

An analysis of United States cancer incidence (number of new cases) data and cancer death rates over the past few decades indicates clearly that the answer to this question is *no.*

In order to be able to make a valid comparison of cancer rates over time in this country, one must first keep in mind that it is the *rate* of cancer, not the *number* of cases, which is critical to the evaluation of a trend. Obviously there are more cancer deaths and cases in 1984 than there were in 1900, but our population base has more than doubled as well. Second, the age distribution of the U.S. population over time has shifted, with our society aging significantly in the last few decades. Because a larger portion of the 1983 population is over age sixty-five than was the case twenty, forty, or sixty years ago, and older people are more likely to develop cancer, it is necessary to "age adjust" cancer rates to establish a meaningful trend. Third, we have to recognize that cancer is the name for many diseases, each of which could have different causes and origins. So we must, in discussing cancer rates, make note of the types of cancer that are occurring with greater or lesser frequency.

Causes of Cancer Deaths

Factor or class of factors	Percent of all cancer deaths	
	Best estimate	Range of acceptable estimates
Tobacco	30	25-40
Alcohol	3	2-4
Diet	35	10-70
Food additives	<1	−5-2
Reproductive and sexual behavior	7	1-13
Occupation	4	2-8
Pollution	2	<1-5
Industrial products	<1	<1-2
Medicines and medical procedures	1	0.5-3
Geophysical factors	3	2-4
Infection	10?	1-?
Unknown	?	?

Elizabeth Whelan, *Toxic Terror*, 1985.

Fourth, when comparing epidemiological studies we must take care to ensure that data collection methods have been constant over time. In general, this has been true with one major exception which involves a comparison of data collected in two recent studies: (a) the National Cancer Institute's *Third National Cancer Survey*, 1969-1971 (TNCS), and (b) Cancer Surveillance Epidemiology and End Results (SEER) program, an ongoing study of cancer incidence which began in 1971.

Combination of data from these studies was the basis for the conclusion of Dr. Epstein and the Council on Environmental Quality that cancer incidence has increased in recent years. Pooling the data from these two dissimilar studies, however, gives an erroneous impression of trends in cancer incidence. According to a 1981 review of the TNCS and SEER reports which appeared in the *Journal of Fundamental and Applied Toxicology*, the studies "cover discontinuous time periods and nonidentical geographic populations. . . . They may not, as they were, be pooled for time trend analysis." . . .

A Clearer Picture

Taking into account age adjustment and the type of cancer, and comparing data from similar surveys over time, the national cancer data on incidence and mortality show the following about the U.S. cancer picture:

1. There is no general epidemic of cancer; that is, no sudden dramatic rise in cancer incidence or mortality, as a whole, over the past forty years.
2. The most important absolute increases in cancer incidence and mortality during this time period have been cancer of the lung, known to be caused largely by cigarette smoking.
3. The most important absolute decreases have occurred in cancer of the stomach and cervix. Cancer of the liver has also shown a steady decline.
4. Other than the above, there seem to be no significant changes in the incidence of other forms of cancer over the past fifty years.

A number of distinguished scientists and scientific organizations have evaluated the "cancer epidemic claim" and concluded as follows:

> There is no definite epidemiological evidence that the United States has experienced an overall increase in the incidence of cancer related to high levels of pollutants or contaminants in the environment.
>
> American Medical Association

> Examination of the trends in American mortality from cancer over the last decade provides no reason to suppose that any major new hazards were introduced in the preceding decades, other than the well-recognized hazard of cigarette smoking . . .
>
> Sir Richard Doll and Richard Peto

> Despite the popular conception that the United States is suffering from an "epidemic" of cancer, the scientific evidence collected to date does not support this view. With the exception of lung cancer, age adjusted cancer death rates for most other forms of cancer have decreased or remained constant for the past 50 years . . .
>
> American Council on Science and Health

There is no epidemic. The age corrected incidences of only two forms of cancer have altered significantly in our lifetimes. Bronchiogenic carcinoma due to cigarette smoking has risen sharply and the incidence of primary gastric carcinoma has declined dramatically for entirely unknown reasons. These two have more or less offset each other, and the age corrected incidence rate for the total of all forms of cancer has remained approximately constant for a half century.

Dr. Philip Handler, former
president, National Academy
of Sciences . . .

Environmental Panic

The standard cry of the environmental movement of recent years seems to be, "There is no time. The ship is sinking and the appointment of research teams to study the matter will not prevent her from going down."

The sense of urgency and the resulting panic are enhanced by the introduction of fear of the unknown: we might not have data now that indicate that it causes cancer, but just in case . . . We are left paralyzed by anxiety, because the unknown is actually scarier than the real thing, given the ability of our imagination to run wild.

As Donald R. Stephenson, an executive with Dow Canada, noted in *Vital Speeches,* "A threat of disaster can create more alarm than an actual catastrophe. It lends itself to speculation of the most sensational and irresponsible kind. That makes an impending disaster potentially more disastrous to an organization than an actual disaster that happens and is soon over with."

Carson's Fable

Rachel Carson in *Silent Spring* proved to be a master of stirring up fears of the unknown, anxieties about what might characterize our future. Her book begins with what she calls a "Fable for Tomorrow":

All life seemed to live in harmony with its surroundings. . . . But then a strange blight crept over the area and everything seemed to change. Some evil spell had settled on the community, mysterious maladies swept the flocks of chickens. . . . There had been several sudden and unexplained deaths, not only among adults but even among children, who would be stricken suddenly while at play and die within a few hours.

Of course, in the context of Carson's book, all this bad news is caused by pesticides. Oh, and also, all of this horror hasn't yet happened. Still she pseudo-innocently informs us as we shiver in fright, "But it might happen in the future." In using this "it might happen" approach, Carson set an example that alarmists are today following. Interestingly, in books like *America the Poisoned* and *Who's Poisoning America,* the qualifiers "could," "apparently," "seemingly," "possibly" appear frequently, as if the authors *knew* that the problems they were addressing were only hypothetical.

Indeed, in the long run, instilling fear of unknown disaster is by far the most effective route environmentalists have taken in capturing the interest of journalists and consumers alike. Veteran Canadian broadcaster Gordon Sinclair once said that four elements make news: love, money, conquest, and disaster. One might add to that list—the fear or threat of disaster. Or, as a *Time* cover story put it, "The most sinister side of the chemical waste threat may be the very uncertainty of its ultimate impact."

Chicken Little

Modern-day environmentalism is thus suffering from what might be called the Chicken Little phenomenon. Chicken Little was hit by a falling acorn, and interpreted this to mean the sky was falling. She panicked her little neighborhood for a good time, but happily a cooler head prevailed and the community lived happily ever after. Right now, the United States needs some cooler heads to enter the dialogue, until now dominated by Chicken Little environmentalists and their spurious premises and questionable techniques.

> *"Ocean dumping of industrial wastes should be stopped as soon as possible."*

The Ocean Should Not Be Used To Dump Toxic Wastes

Timothy Kao and Joseph M. Bishop

To avoid dumping toxic wastes near populated areas, many disposal companies have developed procedures for dumping in the ocean. In the following viewpoint Timothy Kao and Joseph M. Bishop describe the ecological harm toxic wastes cause to the ocean and urge that this dumping be ceased immediately. Dr. Kao is chairman of the Department of Civil Engineering at The Catholic University of America in Washington, DC. Dr. Bishop, a lecturer at the same university, is the author of a book on marine pollution called *Applied Oceanography.*

As you read, consider the following questions:

1. Drs. Kao and Bishop state that oil spills have increased public awareness of pollution in the ocean, but that toxic wastes are a more serious threat. Why is this so?
2. What measures do the authors advocate to reduce toxic wastes in the ocean?
3. The authors acknowledge the increasing costs of landfill dumping. Do they propose any other alternatives to dumping in the ocean?

Timothy Kao and Joseph M. Bishop, "Coastal Ocean Toxic Waste Pollution: Where Are We and Where Do We Go?" reprinted from *USA Today,* July 1985. Copyright 1985, by The Society for the Advancement of Education.

The world's coastal oceans are fragile and sensitive environments. In them are hidden enormous resources of all kinds—biological, chemical, and mineral. Each expanse of these waters has its own characteristics, having derived its uniqueness from the geomorphology and evolutionary processes that had gone to work well before the dawn of human existence. Along the east coast of the Americas, the coastal waters sit on a wide and gently sloping continental shelf that extends over 100 kilometers offshore to the shelf-edge. The depth of the water is only 200 meters at the shelf-edge, from whence it deepens rapidly to 5,000 meters toward the Abyssal Plain. By contrast, along the west coast, the water descends rapidly to great depths only a few kilometers offshore. . . .

Oil Spills

While environmentalists and some engineers have been concerned for decades with the protection of the coastal waters, the world was awakened to the reality of coastal pollution in March, 1967, by the sinking of the supertanker *Torrey Canyon* off the shore of southwestern England near Land's End, spilling 118,000 tons of Kuwaiti oil. Closer to home, a major blowout of an oil well occurred in January, 1969, at Santa Barbara, Calif., with immediate local ecological consequences. In that accident, 10,000,000,000 gallons of crude spilled out in the first 100 days. This dramatic event and the realization by the U.S. public of the enormously high level of industrial pollution in both the atmosphere and our natural waters led Congress to enact the National Environmental Policy Act of 1969 to reverse or ameliorate the dangers to our environment.

Subsequent to that, Congress passed the 1972 Federal Water Pollution Control Act Amendments (FWPCA), setting as a national goal to make "all waters of the United States" safe for shellfish, fish, wildlife, and people by 1983. The regulatory instrument to achieve this goal requires anyone who discharges wastes into public waters to obtain a permit containing limitations and monitoring requirements for the discharge. Progress was made in improving our water quality. However, major oil spills continued to occur. The *Argo Merchant* spill in December, 1976, off Cape Cod made it necessary to reexamine our oil spill response strategy. Active response resulting in a mechanical clean-up of the spill was not feasible due to the storminess of the region. Use of detergents or other chemicals were not attempted due to additional toxic effects on the ecology of the nearby George's Bank fishing grounds. . . .

A More Serious Problem

While major oil spills are highly visible and force their attention on the public conscience, the dumping of toxic wastes, on the other hand, is an insidious and potentially more serious problem. Although the focus of toxic waste has always been on landfills and ground water contamination, 8,000,000 tons of these wastes are still being dumped yearly in the coastal waters.

What are toxic pollutants? Principally, these are chemicals such as chlorinated hydrocarbons, benzenes, trichlorethylene, tuolene, solvents, and organic chemicals; pesticides and herbicides; polychlorinated biphynols (PCB's); and dioxin, as well as fibrous asbestos and heavy metals including antimony, arsenic, cadmium, chromium, copper, mercury, etc. Some of these are powerful carcinogens and mutagens. A major problem is that many of these toxic pollutants are nonbiodegradable. They persist for long periods in the environment, and small amounts of these pollutants can be dangerous. A concentration of one ppb (parts per billion) is usually about the limit of detectability with the most sophisticated scientific instrument. Yet, even at concentrations as low as one-tenth ppb, chlorophenol produces an unpleasant taste in fish and, at one-fifth ppb, DDT produces 100% mortality of shrimp in bioassay tests.

© Cantone/Rothco

What is worse is that the toxic pollutant moves up and concentrates in the marine food chain. At the base of the marine food chain is the phytoplankton, which may act as a primary concentrator of a pollutant. These are ingested by zoo-plankton, which in turn feed the crustaceans and fish. Concomitantly, the pollutant gets progressively more concentrated until it reaches lethal levels for land-based species including humans. It has been documented that many species of birds have died from feeding on marine animals contaminated with DDT.

South of Cape Cod, outside Hudson Bay, is a corner of the near-shore Atlantic which, "left to itself, would be a garden of oceanic life." This is the New York Bight, which is perhaps the most abused of our coastal oceans. It is indeed the repository of waste of the megapoli that have grown on its neighboring shores. Ocean dumping has taken place for years in the Bight. In the early 1970's, the situation had worsened, leading government officials to start the Marine Ecosystems Analysis (MESA) project to develop baseline geological, physical, chemical, and ecological information characteristics of this region. The results of the project indicated a significant amount of contamination to shellfish and the bottom-dwelling flora and fauna in the study region.

Ocean Dumping

The dangers of ocean dumping have also led to international agreements such as the 1972 London Ocean Dumping Convention. Under the Convention, no dumping is to be allowed without a permit; hazardous substances require special permits. At the national level, the Marine Protection Research and Sanctuaries Act implements the London Ocean Dumping Convention. In 1977, Congress amended the FWPCA by passing the Clean Water Act. This law directed EPA to focus its attention on controlling toxic pollutants. In the late 1970's, the Council of Environmental Quality (CEQ) investigated the problem in the U.S. and recommended a comprehensive policy on the ocean dumping of wastes. The CEQ report defined three major categories of dumped material, making the following recommendations:

Dredged material. Ocean dumping of polluted dredged spoils should be phased out as soon as alternatives can be found. In the interim, dumping should be done in a manner that will minimize ecological damage. The policy of the Army Corps of Engineers of dredging highly polluted areas only when absolutely necessary should be continued; even then, navigational benefits should be weighed carefully against ecological costs.

Sewage sludge. Ocean dumping of sewage sludge should be stopped as soon as possible, and no new sources allowed. In cases in which substantial facilities or significant commitments exist, continued dumping may be necessary until alternatives can be developed and implemented, although continued dumping should be considered only an interim measure.

Industrial waste. Ocean dumping of industrial wastes should be stopped as soon as possible. Ocean dumping of toxic wastes should be terminated immediately, except in those cases in which the alternative offers more harm to the environment.

Escalating Costs

A ban of ocean dumping at a number of sites in the inner New York Bight was subsequently imposed. However, the cost of land disposal of toxic waste is escalating. For example, a survey made by Carmen Guarino, past president of the Water Pollution Control Federation, found that the cost of land disposal of sludge in 1982 reached $30 per year per customer, compared to 50 cents per year per customer by ocean dumpings in 1970. In the meantime, Federal funds are not available to meet the estimated $110-$130,000,000,000 needed for the nation's cities to dispose of their waste. The pressure on ocean dumping is therefore expected to mount. . . .

No Life Without Water

The main role of the ocean is so obvious that nobody talks about it—and that is to sustain life. It does so not by providing food or minerals but by providing water. Without water there is no life.

In looking at the oceans I cannot say that one is more or less healthy than another, because differences are temporary. Water moves. That's why pollutants like DDT are found in the livers of penguins in the Antarctic, where there's no pollution. To show how water moves: In 90 years there will not be one drop of water in the Mediterranean that is there today. The pollutants in that sea will finally come to pollute the rest of the oceans. The same is true for the Caribbean, the North Sea, the Gulf of Finland and so on. While rivers and enclosed or semi-enclosed seas are in worse shape today than the open ocean, that may not be true in 10 or 20 years.

Jacques Cousteau, *U.S. News & World Report,* June 24, 1985.

The marine pollution problem will always be addressed as a trade-off between economic realities and the protection of the inherent values of the natural environment. We hope that the balance will tip towards the intrinsic and apparently intangible values given to us by our coastal oceans in order to make the world a better place for future generations.

"The ocean performs well as nature's trash basket."

The Ocean Can Be Used To Dump Toxic Wastes

Charles Osterberg

In the following viewpoint, Charles Osterberg advocates dumping hazardous wastes in the ocean rather than on land. He argues that the enormous oceans are far less likely to sustain damage from toxic wastes than are smaller and more fragile land and fresh water sites. Mr. Osterberg, an oceanographer with the Department of Energy, calls for new laws that will take advantage of "the least-used two-thirds of the earth's surface—the ocean."

As you read, consider the following questions:

1. Why does Mr. Osterberg believe Americans are so concerned about preserving the oceans? What does he think of this attitude?
2. What does he mean by "What this country needs is a Jacques Cousteau to protect the land and fresh water"?
3. What criticisms does the author make of the present dumping laws? What changes would he like to see in those laws?

Charles Osterberg, "Rubbish on the High Seas," Newsweek, October 7, 1985. Reprinted with the author's permission.

Americans love the ocean and want its waters kept pristine. Why something we spend little time with is so revered is a mystery. I suppose we've seen our air, land and fresh waters polluted by man's hand and wish to keep at least one part of God's earth, the ocean, as he created it, for our children's sake. Another reason might be the environmental pressures that push a willing Congress into passing tougher laws to guard the ocean.

An Affair of the Heart

At any rate, "Save our seas" is a popular cause, but it is an affair of the heart, not the brain, and we are sacrificing more to Father Neptune, god of the sea, than even the "saltiest" among us should want. For the special laws discriminating in favor of the ocean require the most toxic wastes of civilization to go on the land or into the air.

That is getting too close to home. We breathe the air and live on the land, which produces 98 percent of our food, all of our lumber, fuel and the fibers that clothe us. More scary yet, the land covers and protects the ground water and the rivers, streams and lakes; it contains the tiny proportion—less than 1 percent—of the liquid water in this world that is fresh, without which human life could not exist.

Toxic Impurities

Already our fresh waters contain toxic impurities picked up by their intimate contact with the land on which the wastes are legally put. Half of us drink from the ground water, often without pretreatment, yet only now have we begun to realize the danger from waste disposal. In a 1984 article in *Outdoor America*, Ed Hopkins, research director with the Clean Water Action Project, stated that the Environmental Protection Agency "has identified 15,000 'uncontrolled sites'—sites that are clearly contributing to contamination of water and air. Of these, at least 347 pose direct threats to drinking water supplies and could cause birth defects, cancer and other diseases." In 1983 the National Academy of Sciences reported that "the use of landfills should be minimized since constituents will very likely migrate over long periods [greater than 100 years] into ground water."

Yet over half of the planet is covered with sea water that is more than two miles deep, and 300 million cubic miles of sea water is unlimited when compared with the relatively few drops of priceless drinking water. Why should salty, barren sea water, deep in the mid-ocean and containing far less man-made contaminants than our drinking water, receive greater protection from the United States Congress? Why have they gone overboard on the ocean? What this country needs is a Jacques Cousteau to protect the land and fresh water.

Unfortunately, our laws regard the ocean as a single entity; they fail to recognize that shallow coastal waters are more valuable and more vulnerable than the deep, empty ocean and they protect the two alike. How foolish. The Chesapeake Bay, with only 18 cubic miles of brackish water, produces more food for man than millions of cubic miles of ocean water deeper than two miles. Like the land and fresh water, the Chesapeake Bay must be protected, but the deep ocean, so isolated and devoid of food for mankind, needs no such care. Our seafood comes from only 2 to 3 percent of the ocean's waters, from the top mile of sea water, mostly along the edges of continents.

Although it is an inefficient producer of human food, the ocean performs well as nature's trash basket. It is self-cleansing and can cope with pollution. Gravity carries clouds of particles downward, sweeping many contaminants out of the waters onto the bottom, where return to man is minimal. The ocean has a carrying capacity—an ability to absorb and dilute contaminants with little harm to flora or fauna, or man. Mother Nature knew what she was doing, and we should take advantage of her expertise.

No Damage to Fisheries

Pollution and most other man-induced changes of the environment have had little or no measurable effect on large-scale marine fisheries. Some local effects have been severe, but they have been limited to small areas—individual bays and harbors, for instance. The Mediterranean Sea is a case in point—pollution in many coastal areas is a serious problem. But fisheries have increased nearly 50 percent during the most recent 10 years, at a rate of over 4 percent per year.

Julian L. Simon and Herman Kahn, *The Resourceful Earth,* 1984.

Do I exaggerate when I say the laws favor the ocean? When the Navy proposed a study to see whether old, retired nuclear subs (minus their reactors and fuel) should be sunk in the deep ocean or put on land, Congress passed a two-year moratorium that effectively removed the ocean option. Despite strong scientific evidence to the contrary, the Navy bowed to Congress and, at great additional expense, chose the land. And why not? To put the submarines in the ocean, the Environmental Protection Agency would have to select a disposal site and issue an environmental-impact statement before it could grant the Navy a permit—and both houses of Congress would have to approve within 90 days.

In other words, forget sea disposal. U.S. law makes it easier to put the subs on farmland in Indiana, in Central Park as a monument or even far inland in the desert, which is where some environmental groups want them stored.

No, everything shouldn't be thrown into the sea. But our laws should permit those materials that are found to be more innocuous in sea water than on the land to go there. At the very least, the law should encourage intelligent choices instead of outright bans on disposal in the least-used two-thirds of the earth's surface—the ocean.

Recognizing Statements That Are Provable

From various sources of information we are constantly confronted with statements and generalizations about social and moral problems. In order to think clearly about these problems, it is useful to be able to make a basic distinction between statements for which evidence can be found and other statements which cannot be verified or proved because evidence is not available or the issue is too controversial.

Readers should constantly be aware that magazines, newspapers, and other sources often contain statements of a controversial or questionable nature. The following activity is designed to allow experimentation with statements that are provable and those that are not.

Most of the following statements are taken from the viewpoints in this chapter. Consider each statement carefully. *Mark P for any statement you believe is provable. Mark U for any statement you feel is unprovable because of the lack of evidence. Mark C for statements you think are too controversial to be proved to everyone's satisfaction.*

If you are doing this activity as a member of a class or group, compare your answers with those of other class or group members. Be able to defend your answers. You may discover that others will come to different conclusions than you. Listening to the reasons others present for their answers may give you valuable insights in recognizing statements that are provable.

If you are reading this book alone, ask others if they agree with your answers. You too will find this interaction valuable.

P = provable
U = unprovable
C = too controversial

1. Chemicals are poisoning America.

2. Millions of Americans are drinking water contaminated with toxic substances.

3. The people who think the US is being poisoned are overreacting.

4. If companies producing chemicals acted responsibly, human casualties would be avoided.

5. Laws will protect people and the environment from the chemical corporations.

6. The 1980 recession hurt the chemical industry.

7. Chemical wastes infected Love Canal.

8. The only way to save our environment is to abolish all chemical manufacture.

9. Tests determine whether or not a substance causes cancer.

10. The jobs and money that the chemical industry earns easily outweigh the dangers of its products.

11. Stricter Congressional controls will eliminate the dangers of hazardous waste.

12. An American Medical Association study says that herbicides cause miscarriages, reproductive failure, and birth defects.

13. The media contributes to the idea that environmental and health disasters are impending.

14. Government studies show that BHC has been detected in 99 percent of the population.

15. The American Cancer Society says that Americans have a 33.3 percent chance of contracting cancer.

16. The President's Council on Environmental Quality states that 70 to 90 percent of all cancers are environmentally influenced and hence, preventable.

Periodical Bibliography

The following list of periodical articles deals with the subject matter of this chapter.

Bruce N. Ames — "Cancer Scares Over Trivia," *Los Angeles Times*, May 15, 1986.

Michael H. Brown — "The National Swill: Poisoning Old Man River," *Science Digest*, June 1986.

Stuart Diamond — "U.S. Names 403 Toxic Chemicals That Pose Risk in Plant Accidents," *The New York Times*, November 18, 1985.

Michael Dowling — "Defining and Classifying Hazardous Wastes," *Environment*, April 1985.

Anne White Garland and Mary Sinclair — "New Ways to Tackle Toxic Wastes," *Ms.*, May 1985.

Robert W. Haseltine — "Economics vs. Ecology: Problems with Solutions to Pollution," *USA Today*, January 1986.

Ed Magnuson — "A Problem That Cannot Be Buried," *Time*, October 14, 1985.

Steven J. Marcus — "New Ways at Hand for Toxic Disposal," *The New York Times*, August 9, 1983.

Reader's Digest — "Our Toxic-Waste Time Bomb," March 1986.

Lewis Regenstein — "The Poisoning of America: How Deadly Chemicals Are Destroying Our Country," *USA Today*, September 1983.

William Ruckelshaus — "Not in My Backyard," *The Washington Times*, February 3, 1986.

Philip Shabecoff — "The Chemical Lobby's 'Turnaround,'" *The New York Times*, November 21, 1983.

Larry B. Stammer — "Toxic Waste—Are Seas the Answer?" *Los Angeles Times*, June 20, 1985.

U.S. News & World Report — "'We Face a Catastrophe' If the Oceans Are Not Cleaned Up," June 24, 1985.

P.J. Wingate — "Toxic Substances: How Much Is Too Much?" *The Wall Street Journal*, August 6, 1985.

Langdon Winner — "Risk: Another Name for Danger," *Science for the People*, May/June 1986.

How Harmful Is Acid Rain?

**THE
ENVIRONMENTAL
CRISIS**

"The burning of fossil fuels has released [sulfur and nitrogen oxides] into the air in quantities that dwarf nature's own output."

The Acid Rain Phenomenon Is Man-Made

Roy Gould

Roy Gould has a Ph.D. in biophysics from Harvard and lectures widely on the subject of acid rain. In 1983, he completed a three year scientific review and policy analysis of acid rain while a research fellow at the Harvard University School of Public Health. The following viewpoint is excerpted from his book *Going Sour*, an in-depth account of the science and politics of the acid rain controversy. In it, Dr. Gould contends that the burning of fossil fuels upsets the balance of nature in the environment. He states that there is a direct relationship between sulfur emissions in the atmosphere, their return to earth, and the acid rain phenomenon.

As you read, consider the following questions:

1. Why are biological sources an insignificant cause of acid rain, in the opinion of the author?
2. Why does the author believe that the amount of sulfur emissions that goes up equals what comes down?
3. What man-made phenomena does the author cite as the source of nitrogen oxides?

Roy Gould, *Going Sour: Science and Politics of Acid Rain.* Cambridge, MA: Birkhauser Boston, Inc., 1985. Reprinted with permission.

"If there is life and death in the air, we must believe the same of rain. . . ."

R.A. Smith, 1872

"Right as rain" and "pure as the driven snow" are expressions from a bygone era. Now the storms that sweep across eastern North America carry an acid rain—a rain gone sour. Tainted by pollution from the burning of fossil fuels, the rain is no longer "a kind physician." . . .

Acid rain has emerged as the most important and controversial environmental problem of the decade. It is the first global-scale problem to be caused by burning fossil fuels, and it marks a serious turning point in our brief history on the planet. Unlike the toxic wastes at Love Canal or the radioactive hazards at Three Mile Island, the substances that cause acid rain—sulfur and nitrogen oxides—are found throughout nature and are in fact part of nature's essential plan. But the burning of fossil fuels has released these substances into the air in quantities that dwarf nature's own output, and that for the first time have upset the balance of nature on a planetary scale. . . .

Rain holds a mirror to the environment. From the chemical content of rain we can infer much about the quality of the air in which it formed. . . .

Polluted and Unpolluted Rain

Even unpolluted rain can contain both acids and bases. For example, carbon dioxide naturally present in air dissolves in rain to form carbonic acid (H_2CO_3), the weak acid responsible for the fizz in soda pop. If there were no other substances in rain, CO_2 would lower the acidity from neutral (pH 7.0) to weakly acidic (pH 5.6). Unpolluted rain also contains small amounts of acid sulfate and acid nitrate that are produced in the stratosphere. These acids would further lower the natural pH of rain to about 5.4. Several alkaline substances partly neutralize the acidity in rain: *Ammonia*, which is naturally present in the air, dissolves in rain to form ammonium salts. *Soil dust* containing alkaline minerals such as limestone (calcium carbonate) and dolomite (magnesium carbonate) can dissolve in rain and raise its pH. *Fly ash* from coal combustion contains calcium and magnesium oxides, which also are alkaline. The pH of rain therefore reflects the competing influence of several different substances.

By far the major constituents of rain in eastern North America are acid sulfate and acid nitrate. . . . These acids come overwhelmingly from man-made pollution. . . . Rainfall in upstate New York contains twice as much acidity, sulfate, and nitrate as rain from S. Carolina, and nearly ten times as much of these pollutants as rain from Oregon. . . .

Eastern N. America and W. Europe: The most acidic precipitation in the world falls on eastern North America and western Europe. Precipitation in these areas averages 60 to 100 micro-equivalents acid per liter, corresponding to pH 4.0 to 4.3. This is 10 to 30 times as acidic as unpolluted precipitation. . . . Weak organic acids and small amounts of hydrochloric acid (HCL) are found in precipitation but do not contribute significantly to its acidity.

Western U.S.: West of the Mississippi, precipitation is generally neutral or alkaline, due to suspended soil dust containing alkaline carbonates. . . . In Pasadena and other parts of Southern California, rain is as acidic as pH 3.9, and individual fogs have reached as low as pH 1.7. Two-thirds or more of this acidity is acid nitrate, caused by NO_x emissions from automobiles.

Eastern Hemisphere: In Japan, the pH of rain in industrial areas is often between 3.0 and 4.0. In urban areas in China, rain is as acidic as pH 2.25, due primarily to nitric acid, apparently from the burning of local coal which is low in sulfur but high in nitrogen.

Trees and Mountains Do Not Pollute

Campaigning for President in 1980, Ronald Reagan hazarded a guess that the Mount St. Helens volcano spewed more polluting sulfur dioxide into the atmosphere than America's automobiles and industrial sources did. He was wrong. But he has persisted in thinking that nature, not man, is the main cause of damaging acid rain, which is made up of both sulfur dioxide and nitrogen oxides from industrial sources. . . .

For some years scientists and environmentally oriented politicians have pointed to the damage to lakes, wildlife and forests caused by emissions of power plants, smelters and automobiles that are carried by the wind and returned to earth in acidic rain, snow, fog or even dust. The problem is especially severe in the Northeast and in Canada. . . .

It is time to acknowledge that trees and mountains don't cause the bulk of pollution; people do. And people in Congress should start to protect Americans—and Canadians—from acid rain.

Los Angeles Times, January 10, 1986.

Remote Areas: In Antarctica and Greenland, the average concentration of sulfate in precipitation was less than 2 micro-equivalents/liter. In Poker Flat, Alaska; Venezuela; Samoa; Katherine, Australia; and Amsterdam I., S. Indian Ocean, the average concentration of sulfate in precipitation was 7.1, 2.7, 1.5, 5.5, and 8.8 microequivalents/liter, respectively; and the average nitrate concentration was 1.9, 2.6, 0.2, 4.3, and 1.7 microequivalents/liter. . . . Moderately acidic rain in some remote areas of the globe may be due to local biological sources of sulfur, or to long-range transport of man-made pollutants. . . .

Precipitation in the eastern U.S. contains some of the highest levels of acid in the world—10 to 30 time the "base-line" level of acid sulfate and acid nitrate from pristine regions.

Chemistry of Acid Formation

Acid rain in the eastern U.S. is caused almost entirely by man-made emissions of sulfur and nitrogen oxides from the burning of fossil fuels. This conclusion is based on two lines of evidence: an understanding of the chemical reactions that sulfur and nitrogen oxides undergo in the atmosphere; and a quantitative tally, or "budget," of how much sulfur and nitrogen is emitted from various sources and how much returns to earth.

The overall chemistry leading to the formation of acid rain has been known since at least the middle of the 19th century. When a fuel is burned, sulfur and nitrogen in the fuel combine with oxygen in the air to form sulfur and nitrogen oxides. (The sulfur oxides are chiefly sulfur dioxides, SO_2, and lesser amounts of sulfur trioxide, SO_3. The nitrogen oxides are a mixture of nitric oxide, NO, and nitrogen dioxide, NO_2. The nitrogen oxides are abbreviated NO_x, where "x" stands for 1 or 2.) In contact with air, SO_2 and NO_x are completely oxidized to form acid sulfate and acid nitrate, respectively. The overall reactions consume oxygen and water:

$$SO_2 + \frac{1}{2}O_2 + H_2O \longrightarrow 2H^+ + SO_4^=$$
$$NO + NO_2 + O_2 + H_2O \longrightarrow 2H^+ + 2NO_3^-$$

These reactions take place spontaneously, and are "driven" by the fact that the end-products, sulfate and nitrate, are chemically very stable. (The world's oceans, for example, are filled with sulfate and nitrate of ancient origin.) From the chemist's viewpoint, acidity is a *byproduct* of the complete oxidation of sulfur and nitrogen.

Just as water can find its way downhill by many different pathways, so there are many chemical pathways by which SO_2 and NO_x are converted to acid in the atmosphere. The major pathways do not involve oxygen directly, but instead involve more powerful oxidizing agents, including hydroxyl radical, hydrogen peroxide, and ozone, which are ubiquitous in the atmosphere. . . .

The relative importance of the above pathways will depend on many factors, including the ratio of NO_x to hydrocarbons in the air, the availability of sunlight, the humidity, and the presence of other pollutants. Overall, the conversion of SO_2 to acid is complete within several hours to several days, while NO_x is probably converted to acid within hours.

More than 95% of the sulfur emitted in the eastern U.S. comes from man-made sources, while less than 5% comes from natural sources, which include decaying vegetation, volcanoes, and sea spray. The following is an inventory of the sources of sulfur oxides.

Man-made sources: The burning of coal and oil accounted for virtually all the sulfur oxides emitted from man-made sources in the eastern U.S., about 30.6 million tonnes (calculated as sulfate) in 1980. (Emissions are estimated from the sulfur content of each type of fuel and the amount of fuel consumed.) Electric utilities contributed 71% of the total SO_2, with the majority of emissions coming from coal-fired power plants. The remainder came chiefly from industrial, commercial and residential combustion; transportation; smelters; and industrial processes. An additional 2.1 million tonnes entered the U.S. from Canada, principally emissions from metal smelters; and 1.2 million tonnes entered the region from the western U.S.

Greatest Source Is Man-Made Emissions

In the United States natural emissions of sulfur and nitrogen compounds are relatively insignificant contributors to acid rain. It has been estimated that in the eastern United States natural emissions of sulfur compounds are approximately three percent as large as man-made emissions. In the west they are probably somewhat larger, but still much less than 25 percent of man-made sulfur emissions. Even a major natural disaster such as the volcanic eruptions of Mount St. Helens emits relatively little sulfur compared to human activities. . . .

Clearly, man-made emissions of sulfur and nitrogen compounds contribute far more to acid rain in the United States than natural sources. They are emitted in much larger quantities and from a variety of widely distributed sources.

Drew Lewis and William Davis, "Joint Report of the Special Envoys on Acid Rain," January 1986.

Coal-fired power plants dominate the emission of SO_2 because much of the coal burned in the eastern U.S. is high in sulfur (greater than 3% by weight). Although there are thousands of individual sources of SO_2, just the top 20 coal-fired powerplants emit 20-25% of all SO_2 in the eastern U.S. These 20 plants account for an even larger fraction of acid sulfate in rain, because their sulfur is emitted from very tall smokestacks. (Emissions from tall stacks remain aloft longer and have more time to be oxidized to acid then to emissions from stacks of lesser height.) The 20 largest plants emit an amount of sulfur comparable to the sulfur that falls in all the acid precipitation on all states east of the Mississippi combined. The largest coal-fired plants have been the focus of efforts to control acid rain.

In Canada, metal smelters are the largest emitters of SO_2, accounting for 45% of that nations SO_2 emissions. (During the smelting process, metal ores containing sulfur are roasted at high temperature, and the sulfur is driven off as SO_2.) The giant metal smelter at Sudbury, Ontario, owned by the International Nickel Company, is the largest single emitter of SO_2 in North America.

Electric utilities contribute only 16% of Canada's sulfur emissions, because Canada relies heavily on hydropower and nuclear power rather than on fossil fuel combustion. Canada emits more SO_2 per capita than does the U.S., but comparisons are misleading because of the very different sources of SO_2 in the two countries. . . .

Natural Sources Total 5 Percent

Biological sources are an insignificant cause of acid rain. . . . They account for less than 5% of total sulfur emissions in the region. The sulfur is emitted at ground level and returns to earth relatively close to its source. Furthermore, biological sulfur emissions are part of the natural sulfur cycle and do not represent a net addition of sulfur to the environment: Sulfur that is oxidized to acid sulfate is reduced again by microbial action upon returning to earth—a process that *removes* acidity from the environment. Microorganisms of course cannot distinguish between naturally-derived and man-made acid sulfate, but the *amount* of man-made acid sulfate deposited exceeds the capacity of microorganisms in many soils to assimilate it. . . .

Can the sources of sulfur emissions . . . account for all the sulfur observed to be deposited? That is, does "what goes up" equal "what comes down"? The answer is yes. . . . Virtually all of the sulfur returns to earth within several hours to several days. About one quarter of the sulfur emitted in the eastern U.S. returns to earth in precipitation within the region. Another quarter of the sulfur settles on the region when it isn't raining ("dry deposition"), in the form of unreacted SO_2 and acid sulfate particles. Roughly another quarter of the sulfur is carried by the wind to Canada. The remainder is carried out over the Atlantic Ocean, where it contributes to acid rain as far away as Bermuda.

Amount of sulfur in precipitation: Virtually all the sulfur deposited in precipitation is in the form of acid sulfate. (Typically, less than 5% of the sulfur is dissolved SO_2, and this remnant is rapidly oxidized to acid after falling to earth.) The amount of acid sulfate deposited annually by precipitation in the eastern U.S. totaled 7.3 million tonnes in 1980.

The annual amount of sulfur deposited is relatively uniform from state to state (every state is within a factor of 2 of the average), in contrast to the wide variation in sulfur emissions among states.

This uniformity is due to the large-scale transport and mixing of sulfur in the atmosphere.

Amount of "dry deposition": Both SO_2 and acid sulfate also return to earth when it isn't raining, a process called "dry deposition." Although public attention has focused on acid rain, dry deposition in some localities contributes as much acidity as acid rain. . . .

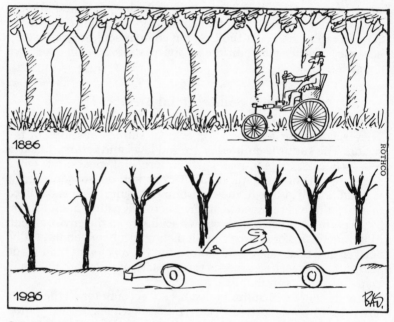

1886

1986

ROTHCO

© Bas/Rothco

Using empirical parameters, it is estimated that 9.9 million tonnes of sulfur (calculated as sulfate) are dry deposited on the eastern U.S. annually.

Amount of sulfur carried outside the eastern U.S.: The amount of sulfur carried by wind to Canada can be estimated knowing the average level of sulfur in the air, and the average northerly wind speed. It is determined to be 6.0 million tonnes of sulfur (calculated as sulfate) per year, about two to three times more than the amount of sulfur transported from Canada to the U.S.

The amount of sulfur carried over the Atlantic is determined in the same way, using the average westerly component of the wind, and is estimated to be 11.7 million tonnes per year. (An independent estimate can be made using rainfall data from over the Atlantic, and is consistent with the above estimate.)

Total amount of sulfur deposited: The four pathways described

216

above deposit a total of 34.9 million tonnes of sulfur (calculated as sulfate) per year.

The total amount of sulfur deposited agrees well with the total amount of sulfur emitted. In fact, the agreement is better than one might expect considering the moderate uncertainties in some of the terms. This agreement indicates that we have not overlooked a major source of sulfur. *We conclude that man-made sulfur emissions are the chief cause of acid sulfate in rain in the eastern U.S. and that these emissions are also responsible for dry deposition of acid sulfate.*

Sources and Fates of Nitrogen Oxides

More than 90% of the NO_x emitted in eastern North America comes from man-made sources. Fossil fuel combustion emitted 15.5 million tonnes of nitrogen (calculated as nitrate) per year in 1980. Part of this was derived from the nitrogen in the fuel. For example, coal can contain more than 1% nitrogen by weight. In addition, any flame or high-temperature combustion allows nitrogen and oxygen in air to combine, producing additional NO_x. Approximately 56% of NO_x emissions came from "stationary sources," i.e., from smokestacks on power plants and industrial and residential boilers. The remaining 44% came from "mobile sources," including motor vehicles, planes, and trains.

Natural sources of NO_x include forest fires, lightning, microbial processes in soils and, to a lesser extent, oxidation of ammonia and input from the stratosphere. These natural sources accounted for a total of 1.8 million tonnes of nitrogen (calculated as nitrate) per year.

Approximately 6.6 million tonnes is deposited annually in eastern North America as acid nitrate in rain and snow. Another 4.4 to 8.8 million tonnes is dry deposited. The remainder is carried outside the region.

In summary, man-made emissions are by far the greatest source of SO_2 and NO_x in eastern North America, and are the chief cause of acid rain in the region.

"Individuals better informed about the realities of acid rain are increasingly skeptical about the role fossil fuel emissions might have in the ecological conditions in distant regions."

Man-Made Emissions Are Not the Primary Cause of Acid Rain

Alan W. Katzenstein

Alan W. Katzenstein is a consultant in technical analysis and communication on a wide range of public affairs and consumer matters. A graduate of Massachusetts Institute of Technology, he has been involved in researching and clarifying the acid rain issue as a consultant to Edison Electric Institute since 1980. In the following viewpoint, Mr. Katzenstein suggests that fossil fuel emissions are not the primary cause of acid rain. He states that a better awareness of the natural acidity in our environment is emerging and will provide a better understanding of the phenomenon of acidic rain.

As you read, consider the following questions:

1. What factors beyond emissions from burning fuels does the author include in his definition of acid rain?
2. Why does the author state that it is misleading to say that rain "contains" sulfuric or nitric acids?
3. Why does the author believe that pH 5.6 for "clean" rain is not a realistic expectation?

Alan W. Katzenstein, *An Updated Perspective on Acid Rain.* Washington, DC: Edison Electric Institute, 1981. Reprinted with permission of Edison Electric Institute, 1111 19th Street NW, Washington, DC 20036.

The fact that most rain is acidic has been known for many years. British chemist Robert Angus Smith first used the term "acid rain" in 1872, but the acidity of rain did not become a matter of concern until the late 1960s, when Swedish scientists claimed sulfur dioxide emissions from Great Britain had adverse effects in Sweden. Some Norwegians soon joined in the allegations that industrial emissions were causing problems for fish, vegetation, and human health.

By the early 1970s, problems were reported in the United States, allegedly associated with the acidity of precipitation. Two U.S. researchers, analyzing data from studies made in the 1950s, 1960s, and 1970s, concluded that rainfall in the eastern United States had been growing increasingly acidic from one decade to the next and the areas of increased acidity were expanding. The acid changes were attributed to the large amounts of sulfur and nitrogen oxides emitted from heavily industrialized regions in the Midwest.

Research Uncovering New Facts

Research related to acid rain has expanded markedly in recent years, and technical publications carry frequent reports of research and assessments of the information available about acid rain. These reports have provided data or explanations that alter the earlier pictures of damage or threat of damage of sensitive ecosystems.

• Where popular reports mentioned that the acidity of rain had increased since the 1960s, the evidence now available shows no long-term increase in the acidity of rain, at least in the northeastern section of the United States, which has been the area of major concern.

• Earlier popular writing tended to hold pH 5.6 as the degree of acidity to be expected in unpolluted rain. (pH is the chemists' scale for expressing acidity.) Today, most atmospheric chemists concur that pH 5.6 is not a meaningful figure for the acidity of "clean" rain and that natural sources may well account for acidities much greater than that.

• Popular articles still point to acid rain as the source of acidification of mountain lakes and streams, particularly in New York's Adirondack mountains. There is increasing awareness, however, of the role of soil chemistry, pointing to the organic layer of decaying matter on the forest floor as the major source of acidity reaching those mountain lakes and streams.

• Acid rain has been widely held to be the cause of damage, or at least the major threat of damage, to crops and trees. Today, reviews of the evidence conclude that the popular impressions do not stand up under scientific scrutiny. Although the possibility of damage cannot be ruled out, the fears have not been supported by the evidence.

• Widespread stories of disappearing fish and "dead" lakes in the

Adirondacks are now seen in a more realistic light. Public records and published literature show that fishermen were complaining about the disappearance of trout more than half a century ago. Factors other than the rain and other than acidity are involved in the changes in the aquatic ecosystems in the Adirondacks.

In light of the evidence that has developed, the Hudson Institute, long noted for policy analysis and forecasting, recently identified an "emerging scientific backlash" on acid rain, as concerned scientists increasingly challenge unsupported assertions about acid rain in popular writing. New realities and new perspectives are developing where scientific research has supplied the facts.

The Answers Lie Underground

Upon reviewing literature from around the world on the effects of acidic deposition and related natural phenomena, I firmly believe that the answers to aquatic and terrestrial ecosystem acidification questions lie underground, that they are far more complex than a simple explanation in terms of atmospheric deposition acidity, and involve the singular influences of soil microbes and natural chemical and physical characteristics of soils as well as the interactions of atmospheric components with microbes and natural soil and water features. The quantity and chemical nature of atmospheric deposition alone, particularly wet deposition, cannot account for all the effects attributed to it. There is no doubt that certain levels of acidity have adverse effects on fish populations, microbes, higher plants, and materials, but to date, the definitive link between atmospheric deposition acidity *per se* and acidification of our natural ecosystems has yet to be demonstrated to may satisfaction.

T. Craig Weidensaul, testimony before the Subcommittee on Health and the Environment, Cleveland, Ohio, February 17, 1984.

With information now available to explain changes that have occurred, there remains little basis for expecting that further reductions in the emission of sulfur dioxide from fossil fuel combustion will lower significantly the amount of acidity reaching sensitive ecosystems or confer perceptible benefits to lakes and fish or to forests and trees.

Acid Rain Defined

Most rain is naturally acidic. Not long ago, it was widely thought that pH 5.6 was the level of acidity to be expected for "natural" or unpolluted rain. Values lower than pH 5.6 were said to represent contamination resulting from human activity. . . .

Few, if any, informed chemists today consider pH 5.6 to be a realistic definition of acidity for unpolluted precipitation. It is recognized increasingly that no single value can be set to cover the acidity that arises from the natural sources alone. In fact, acidities vary from time to time and from place to place.

When "acid rain" refers to an environmental issue, the concerns are focused on acidity that is said to originate at distant sources, i.e., from across state boundaries or even across international boundaries. Some kinds of environmental effects have been associated with acidity or chemical impacts from local sources such as nearby smelters, oil refineries, chemical plants, and heavy vehicular traffic, but in most of these cases, rain is not involved and certainly not the emissions from burning fuels several hundred or more miles away from the area of concern. . . .

Acid-Neutralizing Chemicals

The raindrop is a complex chemical broth—much more than simply condensed water vapor plus absorbed carbon dioxide.

Dozens of chemical substances can be found in rain, but only those which ionize in solution affect the hydrogen ion concentration—that is, the acidity of the liquid. Eight of these sufficed to measure rain acidity. Three are known as "anions" and carry negative ion charges: sulfate (SO_4^{2-}), nitrate (NO_3^-), and chloride ($Cl-$). Five are known as "cations" and carry positive ion charges: calcium (CA^{2+}), magnesium (Mg^{2+}), ammonium (NH_4+), sodium ($Na+$), and potassium ($K+$).

When the concentrations of the eight ions have been determined, the net balance between positive and negative ions is counted as microequivalents of hydrogen ions ($H+$), whose concentration in the solution defines its acidity. . . .

Natural Sources and Human Activity

Sulfates and nitrates come from both natural sources and human activity. Bacteria in the soil and in surface waters produce volatile sulfur compounds. . . .

Nitrogen compounds are produced by decaying organic matter on the ground and by bacterial activity in the soil, particularly soils that have been heavily fertilized. . . .

Sodium and chloride come primarily from the salt in sea spray that is swept into the air and eventually to high altitudes to be carried long distances. Calcium, magnesium, and potassium are mainly from fine dust particles wind-blown from the surface soils.

Once these and other compounds dissolve in moisture, they lose their individual chemical identity. The net balance of ions determines the acidity of the solution, with hydrogen ions assumed to complete the balance between the anions and cations. . . .

Sulfate Not Primary Factor

Sulfate is only one of the eight ions that are generally determined in calculating the acidity of rain. Is it really the primary determinant of precipitation acidity? Where the data are sufficient, analysis shows that not only is sulfate *not* the primary determinant, it is less strongly related to variations in acidity than some of the other components. . . .

This new insight may help reduce the impression that it is sulfur from fossil fuel combustion that is chiefly responsible for variations in the acidity of rain. . . .

Is PH 5.6 a Realistic Value?

What has been found in reality? The best approach is to look at the rain in places where it is least exposed to the products of industrial activity and fossil fuel combustion. The scientific literature, covering observations from many researchers in many parts of the world, shows rainfall varies widely in acidity, with most of the reported values being well below pH 5.6—that is, more acidic.

• In the forest areas of Brazil at the headlands of the Amazon River, an area remote from civilization, the monthly average of 100 rain events in the 1960s ranged from pH 4.3 to pH 5.2, with the median value of pH 4.6 and one reading as low as pH 3.6.

• In the Venezuelan region of the Amazon basin in 1979, 23 rain events averaged pH 4.65.

Major Uncertainties About Acid Rain

Acid rain is a serious problem. . . . But, . . . there are major uncertainties remaining about acid rain. . . .

Evidence to date supports the view that we are not facing an ecological emergency that requires corrective action at once. There appears to be sufficient time to acquire more scientific knowledge.

Lee M. Thomas, *The New York Times*, October 2, 1985.

• The rainfall from two hurricanes in September 1979, sampled at six stations from Virginia to upstate New York, averaged pH 4.5, with one reading as low as pH 3.6. Much of the weather came directly from the Atlantic Ocean and was quite unlikely to have been affected by emissions from industrial activity.

• On the island of Hawaii, remote from all industrial activity, the weighted average of precipitation over a four-year period was pH 5.3, with a minimum value of pH 3.8. During a three-year period, the rainfall at a sea level station averaged pH 5.2, while at a station at 11,000 feet elevation, the rain averaged pH 4.2.

• On the South Seas island of Pago Pago, the average pH has been reported as 5.7 with a low reading of pH 4.3.

• In heavy thunderstorm activity at the start of the monsoon season in the remote northern territory of Australia, the rain has averaged between pH 3.4 and 4.0.

- The Global Precipitation Network reported the following range of readings:

Indian Ocean	pH 3.98 - 5.26
Alaska	pH 4.54 - 5.50
Australia	pH 4.0 - 5.0
Bermuda	pH 3.5 - 6.0

Rainfall in remote regions of the world is generally less than pH 5.6. While there are exceptional readings of below pH 4 and above pH 6, the average values tend to fall in the range of pH 4.5-5.5. . . .

The early impression that pH 5.6 is the "natural" acid level of unpolluted rain is now acknowledged as inconsistent with the realities of atmospheric chemistry which explain the acidity of rain recorded in remote places around the globe. The composition of rain varies from time to time and from place to place, and, as noted earlier, no single value or set of values can adequately define the acidity that can occur from natural causes. . . .

Research Is Expanding Knowledge

The *issue* of acid rain remains troublesome and controversial to many people, organizations, and governments, but the *phenomenon* of acid rain and its relationship to our environment has become better understood as research has brought to light new facts and new relationships.

With expanded knowledge, it is now understood that the alleged link between the sulfur dioxide from fossil fuel combustion and the loss of fish in Adirondack lakes or damage to Vermont forests is far weaker than had been recognized only a short time ago. Research has corrected misconceptions and changed perceptions of natural phenomena and the picture becomes clearer with each addition to the scientific literature. . . .

As studies have produced new facts and insights and confirmed earlier ones, there has been increasing awareness in many places that many of the widely held beliefs were not supported by the facts. . . .

What form the "backlash" will take is not predictable, but there can be no doubt that individuals better informed about the realities of acid rain are increasingly skeptical about the role fossil fuel emissions might have in the ecological conditions in distant regions. The expanded knowledge of what is actually occurring in lakes and forests will help point to realistic solutions. . . . As the search for answers continues, the focus of this debate almost certainly will shift from the rain to natural sources of acidity, both in the air and on the ground, and will shift also to factors other than acidity to explain ecological changes that have occurred.

"No existing powerplant has ever installed [a scrubber] specifically to combat acid rain . . . [and] in the absence of technology-forcing federal legislation few will be installed in the future."

Existing Technology Can Control Acid Rain

Steven J. Marcus

Steven J. Marcus is the managing editor of the magazine *High Technology*. An engineer with a longtime interest in environmental issues, he wrote his Ph.D. thesis on air-pollution control. In the following viewpoint, Mr. Marcus contends that the technology to control acid rain does exist and is available. He believes that legislation to force emission reductions would eliminate the problem of acid rain and provide the incentive for improved technologies.

As you read, consider the following questions:

1. What are some of the drawbacks of stack scrubbers, according to the author?
2. What are some other types of technologies that the author describes as being effective in controlling sulfur emissions?
3. What does Mr. Marcus believe are some arguments that foreign governments can give to persuade the United States to clean up the air?

Steven J. Marcus, "Acid Rain: Technologies Exist To Flush the Problem Away," *Audubon*, March 1984. Reprinted with the author's permission.

News about efforts to control acid rain has been short on progress, long on conflict and frustration. . . .

The Technologies Are Available

Yet most experts agree that solutions exist. Technologies are now commercially available to coal-burning powerplants and other large sources of air pollution, the experts say, that could literally flush the acid rain problem away. There are drawbacks: Stack scrubbers are expensive and often produce large quantities of solid waste; a switch to low-sulfur coal would be politically difficult. In fact, there is likely to be little incentive for industry to move unless Congress acts to force emission reductions.

If the . . . push for national acid rain legislation is successful, however, business analysts see a coming boom in the nation's depressed air-pollution-control industry. Scrubber manufacturers such as Combustion Engineering, General Electric, Babcock & Wilcox, and Research-Cottrell could wind up competing for billions of dollars in new business. And work could be accelerated on new, low-polluting combustion technologies that are now provoking great excitement in the engineering community but would not otherwise be expected on line before the end of the century.

Acid rain is caused primarily by sulfur dioxide in the air derived from the burning of fossil fuels; sulfur in the fuel is oxidized and discharged to the atmosphere, where it combines with water vapor to form sulfuric acid and eventually returns to Earth as acid precipitation. The key to improving the rain, therefore, is to divert the sulfur before, during, or after combustion. Since coal-burning powerplants east of the Mississippi emit more than two-thirds of the country's sulfur dioxide, these are generally considered the principal targets for control.

Efforts To Establish Regulations

Environmentalists have been working for years to get regulations in effect to reduce sulfur dioxide emissions, which totaled 22.5 million tons in EPA's most recent inventory. Lawmakers in Washington now appear convinced that reductions should be made, but conflict has arisen over how drastic and prescriptive they should be. The Waxman-Sikorski bill . . . requires a phased reduction of sulfur dioxide emissions across the country by eight million tons and specifically mandates the installation of scrubbers at the nation's fifty largest coal-burning powerplants. That step alone would eliminate 6.5 million tons. The scrubbers' capital costs would largely come from a trust fund raised by a user's fee on non-nuclear electricity that would average about 75 cents per household per month.

Some acid rain bills are even more extensive and specific. Senator John Glenn, for instance, has called for a trust fund to subsidize the scrubbers' capital costs and 50 percent of their operating costs. But others would let the utilities choose their own pollution-abatement methods. The bill sponsored by George Mitchell, which many consider the major bill in the Senate calls for greater reduction—ten million tons—but allows flexibility: In many cases, a utility could merely change its fuel.

No Excuse for Delaying Action

The delay in acting [to reduce emissions], however explained, can hardly be excused. Devices called "scrubbers" could remove 90 percent of sulfur dioxides from stack gases. A process called "coal washing" could achieve about 25 percent of the needed reductions. Low-sulfur coal, other technologies and conservation to decrease demand for electricity could do the rest.

The cure for acid rain, therefore, is probably at hand even though the job can't be done cheaply or quickly. The overriding need, however, is to get started on it. For even if the necessary legislative or executive action were taken today, five years or more would pass before the foul load of pollutants in the atmosphere would begin to decline. . . .

Nobody can say what another decade or more of acid rain would do to the Eastern forests and waters of the U.S. and Canada; in any case, those years of pollution can't be redeemed.

Tom Wicker, *The New York Times*, April 27, 1984.

Switching from coal with a high sulfur content (more than three percent) to low-sulfur (less than one percent) would appear to be the simplest available solution. But the use of low-sulfur coal is costlier and bitterly opposed wherever high-sulfur coal is mined—including Ohio and Indiana, the states that contribute the greatest quantities of sulfur dioxide. Cleaning the coal prior to combustion is another option, but chemical bonding limits the removal of sulfur in this manner to only about 20 percent.

The remaining option at present is flue-gas desulfurization, in which chemicals such as limestone, together with water, are injected into the stack to react with the sulfur in the boiler's exhaust gases and then carry it away. The efficiency of the process is good, often with 90 percent of the sulfur diverted from release to the atmosphere.

Scrubbers Work

The price tag for scrubbers is daunting to most utilities. Ian Thomson, senior consultant at Environmental Research & Technology, Inc., a pollution-control engineering firm, estimates that in a typical powerplant the scrubber accounts for at least 10 percent of the capital cost and 20 percent of the operating cost. Sidney

Orem, executive director of the Industrial Gas Cleaning Institute, a trade association for manufacturers of air-pollution-control systems, acknowledges that a scrubber costs at least $30 million.

"There is no question that we will have to pay for scrubbers, but the fact is that they work," says Joanna Underwood, executive director of Inform, a New York-based environmental group that recently completed a study of the technology at powerplants around the country.

"In the near term," says ERT's Ian Thomson, "nothing will compete with scrubbers." But he notes that no existing powerplant has ever installed one specifically to combat acid rain—they have been used mostly where sulfur dioxide posed a severe local problem in its own right—and he suggests that in the absence of technology-forcing federal legislation few will be installed in the future.

Legislation Would Force Clean-Up Procedures

But any legislation that emerges from Congress is likely to stipulate at least some scrubbing. "There is uniform agreement," says Leslie Dach, National Audubon Society's associate director for energy and environment in Washington, "That the Waxman-Sikorski bill will be the vehicle for acid rain legislation." . . .

In the long run, however, the technological options with the greatest promise involve new ways to burn coal. The two leading alternatives are fluidized-bed combustion, in which fine particles of coal mixed with limestone react to remove the sulfur from the coal as it burns, and coal gasification, which eliminates the sulfur before the fuel is burned, as the solid is converted to gas.

Fluidized-bed combustion, the more advanced of the two, has attributes that go well beyond its ability to reduce emissions of sulfur dioxide at rates equivalent to those of scrubbers. The fluidized-bed boiler operates at lower temperatures than conventional coal boilers and thus emits less nitrogen oxides, pollutants that also contribute to acid rain. But the real carrot, says Richard Balzhiser, senior vice-president of the utility industry's Electric Power Research Institute, is that a fluidized-bed unit, unlike most boilers, promises great fuel flexibility. It accommodates low-quality coal as well as a variety of combustible solid wastes.

Problems with the "first-generation" technology—such as incomplete fuel combustion, lower-than-anticipated sulfur removal, a tendency to clog up, and sheer size—have inspired fluidized-bed combustion's second generation. . . .

Fluidized-bed combustion (its first generation at least) is now deemed commercial by most engineers for moderate-sized industrial uses only. But though no fluidized-bed boilers are yet in commercial operation for electric utilities, the major source of the acid rain problem, Gordon Baty, Wormser's president, waxes confident: "Fluidized beds today are where aviation was in 1925. Post-Wright

Brothers but pre-DC-3. We're en route to developing what has been shown to be practical into good, solid commercial products." ...

Motivated by Acid Rain Damage

In addition, progress both for industrial and utility application is being reported in Europe. In Germany, for example, Minister of Research and Technology Heinz Riesenhuber cites a demonstration plant in the Weser Valley powered by fluidized-bed technology that has been generating 129 megawatts of electricity and another at Völklingen that will soon be producing 200 megawatts. "We are motivated," says Riesenhuber, "by the damage acid rain has done to our trees." Scientists are now reporting that 25 to 30 percent of the trees in Germany have been adversely affected by acid rain, he says, "which to us is close to catastrophe." ...

© Liederman/Rothco

But if any foreign government is to influence American policy on acid rain, it will likely be Canada. Alex Manson, program manager in Canada's Environmental Protection Service, says that his government is committed to reducing the country's sulfur-dioxide emissions by 25 percent and that it has proposed to increase reductions to 50 percent if the United States cooperates by enforcing reductions of its own. In the meantime, he says, neither country can achieve little by itself, because the pollutants travel large distances and respect no borders.

"Political pressure should not force this country to implement a particular scientific theory before there exists sufficient scientific evidence."

Technology To Control Acid Rain Needs More Investigation

Michael L. Hardy

Michael L. Hardy is senior environmental counsel to the Cleveland Electric Illuminating Company [CEI]. The following viewpoint is excerpted from his presentation to Congress before the Subcommittee on Health and Environment. In it, Mr. Hardy argues that science has not yet determined the cause of acid rain nor how effective various methods to control it might be. He states that forced implementation of technologies to control acid rain is too costly and will not be justified until the benefits can be assured.

As you read, consider the following questions:

1. What is the fundamental question the author believes must be addressed before passing any more acid rain legislation?
2. What does the author say can be a problem with forcing companies to install scrubbers?
3. What assurances does the author want science to provide?

Michael L. Hardy, in testimony before the Subcommittee on Health and the Environment in Cleveland, Ohio on February 17, 1984.

Editor's note: Mr. Hardy testified on February 17, 1984 in Cleveland, Ohio before the congressional hearings on H.R. 3400, a bill to amend the clean air act to control certain sources of sulfur dioxides and nitrogen oxides to reduce acid deposition and for other purposes.

CEI is a privately owned electric utility serving 640,000 residential customers in an area of 1,700 square miles in northeastern Ohio. CEI services one of the most densely industrial areas of the country. . . .

CEI is proud of its record in the area of environmental control. Over the last 10 years, CEI has spent one half billion dollars on environmental improvements. . . .CEI is especially proud of its record in the area of air pollution control. CEI has spent approximately $320 million in capital costs alone for air pollution controls since 1973.

The effectiveness of these expenditures can be seen in the fact that CEI's coal burning plants today emit approximately 200,000 tons *less* SO_2 annually than they emitted in 1973. This translates into an enviable 36.7% reduction from 1973 levels. Part of this SO_2 reduction was achieved by shifting generation away from older plants in the Cleveland area to the scrubber-equipped Bruce Mansfield plant on the Ohio River. Currently, SO_2 emissions from all of CEI's plants are below the emission rates specified by the Ohio State Implementation Plant (SIP). . . .

The Premature Nature of H.R. 3400

There is a serious and fundamental question which must be addressed. . . . This Subcommittee must first confront the fundamental scientific question of whether there exists a need for acid rain controls at all. . . . CEI does not believe that there exists sufficient scientific understanding of the acid rain phenomenon to rush headlong into any control program at this time. . . .

There is currently underway, in this country and others, a massive scientific undertaking to determine the causes of acidification and to document its effects beyond the current levels of speculation. . . . Enactment of H.R. 3400 or any other acid rain bill at this time would make meaningless the scientific work which is being undertaken now and which is scheduled for the future.

Recent scientific evidence indicates that we need not rush to judgment on this issue. At the beginning of this decade there were reports of a rapid drop in the pH levels of rainfall and waterbodies. However, recent research had made it clear that the pH levels in the allegedly affected areas are becoming less acidic, not more. In June, 1982, the New York Department of Environmental Conservation released data which indicated that between the periods 1975-1978 and 1980-1981 the number of lakes listed as "critical" (pH below 5.0) decreased significantly while the number of lakes listed as "satisfactory" (pH over 6.0) increased by a very large

230

percentage. This trend has been confirmed in a series of recent reports issued by the United States Geological Survey. These reports indicated that the pH level of rainfall in the Northeast has been improving in recent years. This data and that of other studies demonstrate that there is sufficient time for the scientific inquiry to continue before this country must decide if a costly and uncertain control program is needed at all. . . .

The Defects of H.R. 3400

CEI believes that H.R. 3400 contains serious defects and inequities which make it an inappropriate vehicle for acid rain control even if its underlying scientific theory is sound. . . . H.R. 3400 would require the 50 plants emitting the largest amounts of SO_2 in 1980 to be retrofitted with scrubbers by 1990. . . .

The cost of retrofitting scrubbers on existing coal fired power plants is significantly greater than the cost of installing scrubbers on new plants. This differential is based upon the size, age and space constraints involved in each retrofit. . . .

Decisions Need Adequate Scientific Base

In the summer and fall of 1983, the U.S. government carried out a thorough review of the current status of acid rain knowledge and the options available for its management. From that review, the United States concluded that, although it was clear that acid rain was a serious concern, . . . it lacked the information needed to make a prudent decision on the need for or design of additional emissions controls.

This policy was not a decision either for or against additional controls, but instead a choice to defer such a decision until a more adequate scientific and technical base was established. It is not U.S. policy to wait for definitive answers on all major acid rain uncertainties before making a decision to act. Decisions on acid rain, like other environmental decisions, will always have to be made in the face of some scientific uncertainty. The United States is committed to act to control acid rain once it is reasonably certain that that action will achieve its intended results, and those results will justify the social and economic costs entailed.

Drew Lewis and William Davis, "Joint Report of the Special Envoys on Acid Rain," January 1986.

In 1979, a study prepared by Acurex/Jaca for U.S. EPA concluded that it was not cost-effective to retrofit scrubbers on all units . . . due to the space constraints. . . .

Retrofitting is precluded where the boilers are nearing retirement (age limited) or where the boiler is too small to economically employ scrubber technology (size limited). . . . The constraints involved in . . . these plants would make the construction of scrubbers very difficult and very expensive. . . .

Despite the various constraints involved, construction of scrubbers at these sites would not be impossible in the sense that, with enough money, a scrubber could be built to overcome the constraints of any location. . . .

Additional Problem—Scrubber Sludge

One additional environmental problem will result after the scrubbers are placed upon these plants—sludge disposal. . . . Scrubbers produce huge amounts of sludge. CEI estimates that, while H.R. 3400 would reduce CEI's SO_2 emissions by an additional 200,000 tons per year, the scrubbers mandated by H.R. 3400 would generate 1.5 million tons of sludge per year at the CEI plants alone. In other words, for every ton of SO_2 which H.R. 3400 would reduce, 7-½ tons of sludge would be generated.

This sludge cannot be dumped into Lake Erie. It must be transported by truck to a disposal site. . . . The disposal of scrubber sludge is a problem which this Subcommittee must confront before it concludes that scrubbers are the answer to the acid rain issue.

CEI believes that enactment of H.R. 3400 at this time fails to account for alternative explanations of the acid rain phenomenon. The scientific study underway has already revealed several alternative theories as to the causation of the effects commonly ascribed to acid rain. For example, it appears that the disappearance of fish from many Adirondack lakes may have as much to do with the fish stocking practices of the State of New York as it does with emissions of any sort. This Subcommittee has already heard the testimony of Dr. [William] Brown of the Hudson Institute who indicated that forests may produce up to 1000 times more acid on an annual basis than that received from rainfall. . . . Political pressure should not force this country to implement a particular scientific theory before there exists sufficient scientific evidence. . . .

CEI is not opposed to investing in environmental projects when there is a reasonable assurance of benefit. The Sikorski-Waxman bill does not offer that assurance, only the assurance of higher electric bills, problems with sludge disposal, the waste of a huge scientific effort and the aborted birth of promising new, clean generating technologies. Political pressure should not make decisions of science.

"Direct and indirect effects [of acid rain] threaten . . . the integrity of whole ecosystems on which society depends."

Acid Rain Is a Global Threat

Sandra Postel

Sandra Postel is a senior researcher with Worldwatch Institute. She has studied geology and political science at Wittenberg University and resource economics and policy at Duke University. In the following viewpoint, Ms. Postel states that environmental scientists, documenting a rapid decline of the forests, attribute the damage to the effects of acid rain. She believes that enough proof exists to serve as a warning of the potential economic and ecological consequences of acid rain.

As you read, consider the following questions:

1. What is the odd twist of fate that the author refers to, and how does she see this as being a threat to the future of humanity?
2. What, according to the author, are some of the economic and ecological costs of forest death?
3. What does the author believe will be the consequence of waiting for irrefutable scientific "proof" of the effects of acid rain damage?

Sandra Postel, "Air Pollution, Acid Rain, and the Future of Forests," published in the March 1984 *Worldwatch Paper 58*. Reprinted with permission.

Three hundred million years ago, when much of Europe and North America basked in a moist tropical climate, forests of fast-growing trees spread across vast areas of swampy lowlands. Giant "scale-trees" bearing little resemblance to the trees of today stood with stately cordaites, the forerunners of modern-day conifers. After these trees died, the brackish water in which they grew protected them from decay. Time and the increased pressure of sediment helped transform the trees and surrounding vegetation into solid masses of carbon, which now comprise the extensive coal fields of the British Isles, the U.S. Appalachians, the Ruhr Basin of West Germany and Belgium, the Saar-Lorraine Basin of West Germany and France, and the Donets Basin of the Soviet Union.

Damage Is Well Documented

In an odd twist of fate, humanity's use of the fossilized remains of these arboreal giants now threatens the health and productivity of their modern-day descendants. Over the past decade, scientists have amassed considerable evidence that air pollutants from the combustion of fossil fuels, both oil and coal, and the smelting of metallic ores are undermining sensitive forests and soils. Damage to trees from gaseous sulfur dioxide and ozone is well documented. Recently, acid deposition, more commonly called acid rain, has emerged as a growing threat to forests in sensitive regions. . . .

Air pollutants and acids generated by industrial activities are now entering forests at an unprecedented scale and rate. . . . Many forests in Europe and North America now receive as much as 30 times more acidity than they would if rain and snow were falling through a pristine atmosphere. Ozone levels in many rural areas of Europe and North America are now regularly in the range known to damage trees. Despite air quality improvements made during the seventies, the average concentration of sulfur dioxide in many areas is high enough to diminish tree growth.

A comprehensive look at worldwide forest damage reveals multiple pollutants—including acid-forming sulfates and nitrates, gaseous sulfur dioxide, ozone, and heavy metals—that acting alone or together place forests under severe stress. Needles and leaves yellow and drop prematurely from branches, tree crowns progressively thin, and, ultimately, trees die. Even trees that show no visible sign of damage may be declining in growth and productivity. Moreover, acid rain's tendency to leach nutrients from sensitive soils may undermine the health and productivity of forests long into the future. Taken together, these direct and indirect effects threaten not only future wood supplies but the integrity of whole ecosystems on which society depends.

North Americans must travel to isolated mountain peaks in the eastern United States to see the kind of massive tree disease and death now spreading throughout central Europe. The loss of West

Germany's woodlands is now a potent political and emotional issue among that nation's citizenry. "Waldsterben"—literally forest death—is now a household word. A survey in the summer of 1983 showed that West Germans were more concerned about the fate of their forests than about the Pershing missiles to be placed on their land later that year. Environmental scientists in Poland and Czechoslovakia warn that forests may become wastelands if plans for increased burning of their high-sulfur coal go unchecked. . . .

Signs of Destruction Unfold

In just a few years, forest damage has spread with frightening rapidity through portions of central Europe. Trees covering between 3.5 and 4 million hectares—an area roughly half the size

Jeff Danziger, *The Guardian* Newsweekly. Reprinted with permission.

of Austria—now show signs of injury linked to air pollutants. (1 hectare = 2.47 acres.) No nation has better documented the destruction occurring within its borders than West Germany, where forests cover 7.4 million hectares—roughly a third of the nation's land area. Following an extensive survey in 1982, the Federal Minister of Food, Agriculture and Forestry estimated forest damage at 562,000 hectares—8 percent of West Germany's forests. Just a year later, in the fall of 1983, a second survey found damage on over 2.5 million hectares, 34 percent of the nation's forests. Some of this increase resulted from a more thorough investigation the second year, but nonetheless, the damage has spread markedly. Visible injury typically takes the form of yellowing and early loss of needles, deformed shoots, deteriorating roots, a progressive thinning of tree crowns, and, in its severest stages, tree death. The symptoms appear on trees of various ages and in forests of both single and mixed species.

In the heavily wooded West German states of Bavaria and Baden Württemberg, home of the famed Black Forest, trees covering nearly half the forested area are damaged. Nationwide, three-quarters of the fir trees are affected, up from 60 percent a year ago. Damage to spruce, the most important species for the forest products industry, has risen from 9 percent to 41 percent, and a similar increase is evident with pine. These three conifer species, which together compose two-thirds of West Germany's forests, are the most severely struck. But damage has also been found among hardwood species such as beech and oak. Since most trees in the advanced stages of decline are removed from the forest, more have been affected than even these alarming survey results indicate. Dr. Georg Krause of the Land Institute for Pollution Control in Essen recently stated that "hardly anyone in Germany denies the great danger to forest ecosystems."

Severe Damage

In neighboring Czechoslovakia, forest damage covers an estimated half million hectares. Trees on some 200,000 hectares are believed to be severely damaged, and those on 40,000 hectares in the Erz Mountains reportedly have died. Dead and dying trees are plainly visible northeast of Prague in the Krokonose National Park, which has 34,000 hectares of forest, mostly populated with spruce. Not only are the spruce dying, they reportedly stopped regenerating in the park's mineral soils several years ago. Further north in Poland, another half million hectares of forest are affected. Forest researchers in Katowice, near Krakow, say that fir trees are dead or dying on nearly 180,000 hectares and that spruce trees in areas around Rybnik and Czestochowa, also in the industrialized southern region, are completely gone. Environmental scientists warn that by 1990 as many as 3 million hectares of forest may be lost if Poland proceeds with its present industrialization plans calling for increased burning of the nation's high-sulfur brown coals. . . .

Although forest destruction of the magnitude occurring in central Europe is not visible in North America, trees are suffering from air pollutants there as well. In the United States, forest damage is most evident in the Appalachian mountain ranges of the east and in the Sierra Nevada of California. Field and laboratory studies have documented not only tree disease and death, but sustained declines in growth as well. . . .

Changes in Forest Damage in West Germany, 1982 to 1983

Species	Area Showing Damage		Portion of Forest Affected	
	1982	1983	1982	1983
	(thousands of hectares)		(percent)	
Spruce	270	1,194	9	41
Fir	100	134	60	76
Pine	90	636	5	43
Beech	50	332	4	26
Oak	20	91	4	15
Others	32	158	4	17
Total	562	2,545	8	34

Source: Der Bundesminister Für Ernährung, Landwirtschaft und Forsten, "Neuartige Waldschäden in der Bundesrepublik Deutschland," Bonn, October 1983.

Detailed documentation of red spruce decline has come from research on Camels Hump in the Green Mountains of Vermont. There, with the benefit of two detailed tree inventories spanning the period 1965-79, researchers have found that seedling production, tree density, and basal area have declined by about half. In 1979, over half the spruce on Camels Hump were dead. A 1982 survey of spruce throughout the Appalachians has led researchers to conclude that spruce are declining over a wide area in a variety of forests. So far, no such decline is evident in commercially valuable spruce stands found at lower elevations in northern New England and Canada. Yet in light of the large wood volume declines on Camels Hump since 1965, botanist Hubert Vogelmann of the University of Vermont warns that "if such losses in only a few years are representative of a general decline in forest productivity, the economic consequences for the lumber industry will be staggering." . . .

Tree disease and death have unfolded in central Europe and limited areas of the United States at an alarming pace, and as yet show no signs of abating. The ultimate severity and extent of this damage is a looming question. As forests not yet showing injury remain exposed to acid deposition and high pollutant concentrations for longer periods of time, the damage may well spread. Moreover, if growth declines are occurring unnoticed, air pollutants may be quietly undermining the productivity of large areas of temperate forests. . . .

Counting the Economic Costs

West Germany's spruce and fir forests are typically managed in even-aged stands with trees harvested at 80-130 years of age. Although damage first appeared on older trees, spruce and fir of all ages are now affected. Foresters expect the death of the younger trees to significantly disrupt the wood market. In the summer of 1983, when forest damage was still placed at 8 percent, the reported value of the trees that had been lost was about $1.2 billion. Spread equally over a ten-year period, these losses translate into about a 5 percent decline in annual timber production, worth about $200 million per year. With damage now covering a third of West Germany's forests, the value of this annual timber loss is bound to rise. A growing portion of the planned annual harvest consists of dying trees removed from the forest. Over the next few years, the harvest may reach three times the normal level, and the dumping of valuable wood on the market will undoubtedly depress timber prices. Even under the optimistic assumption that the ongoing destruction ceases and that the damaged forests can be restored, future wood harvests will likely be reduced as a result of the present overcutting. Dr. H. Steinlin, Director of the Institut für Landespflege at Albert-Ludwigs University in Freiburg, expects that from the late nineties into the first quarter of the next century, West Germany will be less self-sufficient in timber. . . .

Global Ecological Costs

Although acid rain tends to be associated with the industrial world, it has now been measured in many developing countries as well. Large portions of Brazil, southern India, Southeast Asia, and eastern China are underlain by the type of soils most susceptible to acidification. Threatening levels of soil acidity have reportedly been measured in some of these areas. Trees are being planted in these and other developing regions to meet not only growing industrial wood demands, but critical needs for fuelwood and charcoal. The ambitious industrialization goals set by many of these countries—in which fossil fuels typically figure prominently—raise the possibility of acid deposition eventually countering some of the gains made from plantation forestry.

One special concern for Third World plantation forestry is the potential for acid rain to inhibit the functioning of soil microorganisms. These minute creatures appear to play key roles in successfully establishing tree plantations on degraded lands,

238

where much Third World tree planting is taking place. Nitrogen-fixing bacteria, for example, are behind the hardiness and partial nutrient self-sufficiency of legumes, a family of trees increasingly chosen for fuelwood plantations. These bacteria and other important microorganisms may not function as well under the altered soil conditions brought about by acidification. Devoting large areas to monoculture plantations of fast-growing trees appears necessary to lessen the Third World's growing fuelwood crisis. Yet unless soils are protected from increased acidification, vital wood supplies may diminish. . . .

A Worldwide Problem

The term *acid rain* was first coined in 1872 by Robert Angus Smith, an English chemist who used it to describe the increasingly acid precipitation that fell on the industrial city of Manchester. In fact, it is now generally agreed that acid rain is a product of the Industrial Revolution, for it stems largely from the burning of coal and oil.

In the intervening century, acid rain has been transformed from an environmental curiosity to perhaps the most pernicious global problem of the age. The specter of mass deforestation is real. But the forests of the industrial world are not the only victims. Entire lake regions are becoming sterile and devoid of life. Monuments that have withstood the erosion of centuries are being transformed into soft gypsum and may soon be washed away. Even human health could be at stake if acidified groundwater continues to leach out trace metals into the world's drinking supply.

Acid rain is a worldwide problem. It has been reported in Brazil, China and South Africa. And now the Arctic, one of the world's last great wilderness areas, has become a victim.

Nigel Sitwell, *Science Digest*, September 1984.

Collapse of Ecosystem Is Possible

The industrial world's forests are now subjects of an ecological experiment of unprecedented scale and untestable outcome. Where pollutants remain at relatively low levels, many forest systems will continue to absorb them without major damage to the soil, microorganisms, or trees. Yet as chronic stress increases, ecological theory predicts a staged decline that in extreme cases could end in complete ecosystem collapse. This has occurred around high emission sources such as the smelters at Sudbury, Ontario, and Copperhill, Tennessee. The forest decline spreading in central Europe could be the beginning of such a complete collapse on a much broader scale. Even if pollution remained at today's levels, forests and soils continually exposed to this degree of stress may in time lose their resistance. Moreover, long before the ecosystem ceases to function, other resources that depend on a well-functioning forest will be affected. Forest effects do not stop at the forest boundary, but ripple to groundwater, streams, and lakes which receive acids and metals that break from the forest cycle. Humanity's intimate connections to these forest systems ensures that it will not escape feeling the effects of their demise. . . .

Tragedy on a Grand Scale

What is now unfolding in the forests of industrial countries is a tragedy of the commons on a grand scale. Less polluted air would clearly benefit all nations, but most feel that acting to curb their own emissions, without guarantees that other nations will do likewise, will incur greater costs than it yields benefits. . . .

National leaders rarely make great political gains by attacking the problems of the next generation or the country next door. The lure of short-term economic benefits too often precludes measures geared toward sustaining natural systems over the long term. Moreover, some nations are unwilling to act without irrefutable scientific "proof" of acid rain and air pollution's damaging effects—proof that may require decades of additional research. Only as pollution of the common air space claims more victims will more nations recognize the severity of the threat that lies before them and take action. Yet at some point, when the consequences become irreversible, this late-course correction strategy will fail.

"There is no clear and unambiguous cause-and-effect relationship that makes [acid rain] undeniably guilty of any of the major accusations . . . leveled against it."

The Global Threat of Acid Rain Is Exaggerated

William M. Brown

William M. Brown is the director of energy and technological studies at the Hudson Institute in Indianapolis. He earned his BA, MA, and Ph.D. in physics at the University of California at Los Angeles. He was principal investigator of the Institute's report "The Great Acid Rain Mystery," from which this viewpoint is excerpted. Mr. Brown contends that scientists do not know what is causing the decline of the world's forests; they need to conduct extensive and long-term research to determine what is normal and abnormal. He argues that publicity by the media has contributed to the public perception that acid rain damages the environment and threatens the future of the forests.

As you read, consider the following questions:

1. In what ways, according to the author, has the media contributed to the mystery surrounding the phenomenon of acid rain?
2. What does the author believe are some of the faults with the scientific forestry research to date?
3. What does the author claim is the general consensus of the scientists and foresters regarding the German forests?

"The Great Acid Rain Mystery," by William M. Brown, published in 1986 by the Hudson Institute. Reprinted with permission.

In most good mystery stories, early suspicions and conclusions are often drawn from prejudice or more-or-less informed conjectures rather than solid facts. So has it been with acid rain, and the extent to which it has been labeled as the villain in the crimes of destroying lakes, rivers, trees, forests, crops, fish, buildings, monuments and human health.

There is also usually enough evidence in mysteries to make a case against one particular villain more plausible than against any other. While no single item of the accumulated evidence need be conclusive, the total must be convincing. Our investigation has found that the quality of the accusations against an "unsavory character," ACID RAIN, has ranged from reasonably convincing to far-fetched. In addition, some of the early evidence that seemed solid when originally presented has weakened over time as scientists sought to verify the data on which it was based.

Sensational News Is Interesting

The media, however, has seldom tried to temper the alarming hypotheses offered in the 1960s, and has given only scant attention to equally compelling evidence suggesting that acid rain, or acid precipitation (A-P), may be less lethal, or less villainous, than first thought. Clearly, sensational news is more interesting than bland news, and it is the business of the press to highlight the extremes rather than the mundane. However, public enlightenment requires that A-P reporting present a much more balanced coverage than heretofore.

This is not to suggest that the real villain is the media, or that acid rain is merely an innocent victim of bad press. The evidence doesn't point to either of these conclusions. What it does seem to indicate, however, is that acid rain—at most—has a mixed impact on the environment, some consequences being actually beneficial. What is conclusive is that there is no clear and unambiguous cause-and-effect relationship that makes A-P undeniably guilty of *any* of the major accusations which have been leveled against it. . . .

Publicity About Acid Rain and Forest Damage

Indeed, a major difficulty in research related to the effects of . . . pollutants on forests is that there are many potential contributors to the observed symptoms of forest damage, yet for none of them, singly or in combination with others, is there an obvious or non-controversial quantitative explanation of its impact.

In 1982 a widely publicized hypothesis, by botanist H. Vogelmann of the University of Vermont, claimed that acid rain probably was the responsible agent for a severe dieback among spruce trees on Camels Hump, a high mountain peak in Vermont. Vogelmann's hypothesis appeared shortly after an even more apocalyptic one of West German Professor B. Ulrich. In a presentation to an international conference in Stockholm, Ulrich suggested that acid rain was destined to destroy almost all of the forests in Europe and elsewhere—that is, wherever industrialization emissions were great enough to acidify rainfall. He claimed that the interaction of acid rain with soils would cause the decline and eventual dieback of the European forests over a period of several decades.

There Is No Environmental Crisis

It is interesting to go back and review clippings from the popular press dealing with the Clean Air Act. Prior to 1980, there is virtually no mention of acid rain. The issues which captured the public's attention were the effect of air pollution on human health, high pollution levels in urban areas, auto emissions, and protection of pristine areas in the West from degradation. Acid rain was not among those issues.

Even in the scientific literature, one can find only a few dozen papers related to acid rain which appear before 1980. In a sense, acid rain became an overnight sensation. With a name like "acid rain," this phenomenon was bound to attract widespread media coverage, rivet public attention, and consequently energize the people's representatives in Congress. . . .

Over the past several years, my company has devoted considerable resources to the scientific, economic and political issues of the acid rain debate. We have concluded several things:

There is no environmental crisis. We believe that a dispassionate review of the evidence clearly suggests that a large-scale emission reduction program is not warranted at this time.

Richard L. Kerch, testimony before the Subcommittee on Health and the Environment, Cleveland, Ohio, February 17, 1984.

The publicity following Ulrich's sensational presentation led to a strong political response in Europe, particularly in West Germany where the population has an unusually great attachment to its forests. Legislation mandating a reduction of sulfur dioxide emissions in West Germany was passed a few months later. The publicity spread rapidly to the United States where the image of forests being destroyed by acid rain was picked up and disseminated by professional environmental groups through articles in the press and in periodicals. Also, it became a topic for television news and even television specials.

Validity of Hypotheses Questioned

The extension of Ulrich's hypothesis to U.S. forests, combined with Vogelmann's hypothesis, created images that confirmed earlier impressions which the media and the public had received about the dangers of acid rain and made it relatively easy to accept those hypotheses as probable realities. However, since 1982, in both the U.S. and Europe the scientific community specializing in forests and soils has questioned the validity of the Ulrich/Vogelmann hypotheses and the evidence on which the hypotheses were based. Indeed, since 1982, nearly all such specialists have concluded that acid rain is *not* the primary suspect for the damage which has been observed or claimed—if, in fact, any unusual amount of forest damage is occurring at all. When it is recalled that trees in U.S. forests live, on average, about 100 years, then roughly one percent die each year, and perhaps five percent are in various stages of decline. That five percent implies that a careful inventory would *normally* find about 40 million acres of U.S. trees in various stages of decline.

Moreover, much of the damage in forests tends to be erratically distributed over space and time. The spruce budworm, the gypsy moth, or the Dutch Elm disease tends to create devastation over relatively large regions and usually occurs intermittently and unpredictably, as do other waves of pests and pathogens. Similarly, stresses from severe weather are also unpredictable. When they do occur they tend to be local or regional, rather than national or continental. As a consequence of the many potential stresses, symptoms of forest damage can exist in clumps or stands of trees, on mountain tops, in valleys, and/or in the plains. Indeed, in every wilderness dead or dying individual trees, or parts of trees, are a frequent sight to any hiker who cares to look.

The question of what amount and kinds of forest damage or forest mortality is *normal* in the U.S. and whether recent observations represent abnormal situations, has not yet been resolved. In fact, answering that question is especially difficult because forest science in the past has not been well supported. The data which would enable scientists to compare the past with the present, and determine if currently observable forest effects are abnormal, is grossly inadequate.

No Consensus

Even if it is assumed that some of the damage is abnormal, no consensus exists about how much of it, if any, is due to A-P. Indeed, we have found that the most prestigious scientific task forces, as well as most forest scientists, generally have concluded that A-P is unlikely to be the primary responsible agent, and that any unusual damage is much more likely to stem from combinations of natural stresses such as droughts, frosts, insects, and pathogens, · coupled with the impact of various air pollutants. Again, the state of knowledge is so poor that even such conclusions should be treated as informed conjectures, not facts. It will probably take several years for this situation to improve significantly. Still, at present we find that the best scientific knowledge about the impact of A-P on U.S. forests is incompatible with the public's perception.

Most scientists believe that in recent years some unusual stresses have been adversely affecting European forests. But there are a few in Europe who believe that whatever is occurring does not differ fundamentally from what has happened in the past. All seem to believe that in Central Europe the impact of persistent high concentrations of air pollutants on forests may be greater now than in prior decades, or perhaps than they ever have been. Most of Central Europe is also subject to frequent temperature inversions, during which the concentration of pollutants can reach levels much higher than the average, perhaps 10 times as much. These peak concentrations may have a disproportionately large impact on European forests. However, the data available is insufficient for a careful analysis of such effects.

Insufficient Evidence

The location, topography, and other characteristics of the high-elevation forests of eastern North America cause them to be receptors of high levels of acid deposition and airborne trace metals. We contend that no other major forested areas in the U.S. are subjected to such intensely acid cloud moisture, such heavy acid deposition, and such high rates of trace-metal deposition. The vulnerability of these forests to the pollutants has not been documented, but because of the spruce decline it is indeed reasonable to suspect vulnerability. In reviewing the data currently available, we find several possible pathways by which acid deposition could contribute to spruce mortality, but at this time none of these pathways are supported by convincing evidence. . . . We believe that the evidence regarding a triggering effect of drought is substantiated by our data and those of others, but we do not know whether drought is sufficient to cause the dieback and decline or whether an additional stress from pollution is involved. . . .

The prospects for ecosystem destabilization are difficult to assess in light of the available data.

Arthur H. Johnson and Thomas G. Siccama, *Environmental Science and Technology*, vol. 17, no. 7, 1983.

In West Germany a fear that abnormal forest damage has occurred and will continue to increase, perhaps rapidly, has led to an annual national inventory which attempts to measure the amount of tree damage, categorize it, and convey its nature and significance. However, in their haste to quantify the damage, the methods used in the last three years (1982, 1983, 1984) have changed so rapidly that no scientific basis exists for making accurate year-to-year comparisons. Nevertheless, the information published by the government indicates that total forest damage rose from 8 percent in 1982 to 34 percent in 1983, and then to 50 percent in 1984. That sequence, 8-34-50, has received an enormous amount of publicity and has left the impression both in Europe and in North America that a rapid acceleration of damage is occurring, and that before long all of the trees will be damaged or dead. Indeed, in Germany the phenomenon is called *Waldsterben*, which translates to forest death, or dieback.

The image of widespread, rapidly-growing damage since 1982 has been so dramatic that many scientific delegations were encouraged to examine and report on the European forest situation. The authors of this study also visited German forests to observe the Waldsterben phenomenon.

What We Found in the Forests

One of the surprises upon first entering a European forest (in our case, West Germany) was the sharp contrast between the experience and our expectations. We found (as have all others with whom we have since spoken) the forests of West Germany to be magnificent and apparently in a state of remarkable health and vigor. Indeed, without first obtaining careful instructions about what to look for, any evidence of trouble was hard to find. Nonetheless, the inventory data led the German government to claim that damage symptoms (needle loss, discoloration, etc.) are more prevalent than in prior years. How they arrived at that conclusion is quite clear; but its validity is questionable. Not only are their time-series statistics, namely the 8-34-50 sequence, scientifically meaningless, but the raw data on which it is based are not available to be examined—not by scientists, and not even by the federal government! Those data are closely held by the individual German States which have refused to share them; only statistical summaries have been released to the national government.

For European forests no scientists know beyond reasonable doubt (a) how to describe what is normal, (b) how much the environment has actually changed in recent years, and (c) whether a clear trend towards increasing damage exists. What can be stated with reasonable confidence is that the many scientists who have been exposed to the German data, discussed the situation with German experts, and visited those forests, have concluded that something unusual probably is happening and that a vigorous research effort should be conducted. Such an effort is now in progress.

During our trip we met no scientists or foresters familiar with the damage claims who believed that the German forests are doomed. That concept appears to be a highly imaginatory one which may have begun with Professor Ulrich and which, since then, may have been promoted by interests seeking or selling sensational publicity.

While reducing air pollutants clearly is a desirable goal with which no one would quarrel, solid evidence of pollution-induced damage on which control legislation might be based should be sound, scientific, and sufficient. Such evidence has not yet become available from scientific research on European or North American forests. . . .

The Myth Lives On

Forest damage can be readily found in both American and European forests, indeed in any forest. The central question is whether, or how much, the existing damage exceeds the normal amount that would be expected over long periods of time without the imposition of anthropogenic stresses. Unfortunately, the state of forestry science today does not permit that question to be answered because an operational definition of normality does not exist.

Furthermore, because of the recent rapid growth of public interest in the possible impact of acid precipitation and air pollutants on forests, an extraordinary amount of attention is being given to observing and quantifying the newly defined damage-symptom categories without much regard to what would be a normal range. The publicity derived from asserting that the more spectacular aspects of the existing damage symptoms stem from anthropogenic causes, such as acid rain, probably has led to the wisespread public perception that an unusual and major threat to North American and European forests has arisen and will worsen over time. Examples of such publicity about forest threats include Professor Vogelmann's acid-rain hypothesis about the vulnerability of red spruce trees at Camels Hump and Professor Ulrich's hypothesis about acid rain and dieback in Europe's forests. These relatively gloomy hypotheses appear to have been rejected by most forestry scientists, but they live on in the media and in the minds of citizens.

Distinguishing Primary from Secondary Sources

A critical thinker must always question sources of information. Historians, for example, usually distinguish between *primary sources* (a firsthand or eyewitness account from personal letters, documents, speeches, etc.) and *secondary sources* (a "second-hand" account usually based upon a "firsthand" account and possibly appearing in newspapers, encyclopedias, or other similar types of publications). The published notes of a chemist taking samples of acid rain is an example of a primary source. An article by a journalist based on those scientific notes is a secondary source.

It must be noted that interpretation and/or point of view also play a role when dealing with primary and secondary sources. For example, the journalist writing about acid rain will not only use statistics from the lab notes, but may also interpret them. The journalist may have been a vehement ecological activist who refused to acknowledge that any good could come from factories producing pollution that also produce a beneficial product.

This activity is designed to test your skill in evaluating sources of information. Pretend your teacher tells you to write a research report on why and how acid rain endangers the environment. You decide to include an equal number of primary and secondary sources. Listed below are a number of sources which may be useful in your research. Carefully evaluate each of them. Then, *place a P next to those descriptions you believe are primary sources.* Second, *rank the primary sources* assigning the number (1) to what appears to be the most objective and accurate primary source, the number (2) to the next most objective, and so on until the ranking is finished. *Repeat the entire procedure, this time placing an S next to those descriptions you feel would serve as secondary sources and then ranking them.*

If you are doing this activity as a member of a class or group, discuss and compare your evaluation with other members of the group. If you are reading this book alone you may want to ask others if they agree with your evaluation. Either way, you will find the interaction valuable.

1. A scientist's report from Western Europe about how acid rain has damaged the Black Forest.

2. Lab data taken by a biochemist on acid rain showing differing pH levels in different samples.

3. A historian in the year 2086, writing a history of acid rain using data gathered in 1986.

4. A US-Environmental Protection Agency report surveying the acidity of rain from the 1960s to the mid-1980s.

5. Viewpoint 2 in this chapter.

6. A documentary film on the manufacture of the pollution that causes acid rain.

7. A televised debate between a leading ecologist and the head of a large electrical utility.

8. A journalist writing about methods of controlling acid rain.

9. The complete record of the Congressional hearings on the proposed bill H.R. 3400.

10. Viewpoint 5 in this chapter.

11. A public television program based on William M. Brown's research on the decline of the world's forests.

12. A printed interview with a farmer who claims his crops have been ruined by acid rain.

13. A novel based on the life of an activist trying to stop emissions causing acid rain.

14. An editorial written by a columnist claiming that acid rain does not exist.

Periodical Bibliography

The following list of periodical articles deals with the subject matter of this chapter.

Betsy Ancker-Johnson	"Take Your Medicine and Swallow the Pill: Evidence Says Reduce SO_2 Emissions," *The Environmental Forum*, April 1983.
Robert H. Boyle and R. Alexander Boyle	"Acid Rain," *The Amicus Journal*, Winter 1983.
William M. Brown	"Maybe Acid Rain Isn't the Villain," *Fortune*, May 28, 1984.
Congressional Digest	"The Acid Rain Controversy: Pro & Con," February 1985.
David Graber	"Acid Rain: The Evidence Calls for Controls—Now," *Los Angeles Times*, March 31, 1985.
Arthur H. Johnson and Thomas G. Siccama	"Acid Deposition and Forest Decline," *Environmental Science and Technology*, vol. 17, no. 7, 1983.
Edwin Kiester Jr.	"A Deadly Spell Is Hovering Above the Black Forest," *Smithsonian*, November 1985.
Edward C. Krug and Charles R. Frink	"Acid Rain on Acid Soil: A New Perspective," *Science*, August 5, 1983.
John B. Oakes	"Acid Rain's Political Poison," *The New York Times*, April 8, 1985.
Michael Oppenheimer	"Acid Rain Falls and Falls," *The New York Times*, December 23, 1985.
Philip Shabecoff	"Acid Pollution May Be on the Rise," *The New York Times*, December 12, 1985.
Nigel Sitwell	"Our Trees Are Dying," *Science Digest*, September 1984.
John H. Sununu	"Acid Rain: Sharing the Cost," *Issues in Science and Technology*, Winter 1985.
Ronald A. Taylor	"Science Hot on the Trail of Answer to Acid Rain," *U.S. News & World Report*, January 14, 1985.
Albert C. Watson	"An International Storm Over Acid Rain," *The Christian Century*, May 7, 1986.

Organizations To Contact

The editors have compiled the following list of organizations which are concerned with the issues debated in this book. All of them have publications or information available for interested readers. The descriptions are derived from materials provided by the organizations themselves.

Contact your local public utility companies for free information concerning their operations.

Acid Precipitation Data Base (ACIDOC)
New York State Department of Environment
Conservation Division of Air Resources
50 Wolf Rd.
Albany, NY 12233
(518) 457-2823

ACIDOC is an international, bilingual (English/French) bibliography that covers all aspects related to acid rain. It inventories mainly periodicals, monographs, conference papers, theses, and reports, as well as official publications.

Acid Rain Foundation
1630 Blackhawk Hills
St. Paul, MN 55122
(612) 455-7719

The Acid Rain Foundation was incorporated to raise the level of public awareness about acid rain. It supports research and publishes a large number of educational materials.

Acid Rain Information Clearinghouse
Center for Environmental Information, Inc.
33 S. Washington St.
Rochester, NY 14608
(716) 546-3796

The Acid Rain Information Clearinghouse is a national resource center for both technical and general information on acid rain. It maintains a comprehensive reference library and publishes the monthly *Acid Precipitation Digest.* The Clearinghouse's services are available to any interested group or individual.

American Forestry Association (AFA)
1319 Eighteenth St. NW
Washington, DC 20036
(202) 467-5810

The American Forestry Association is dedicated to the protection and intelligent use of the nation's forests and related resources. The AFA sees public education as its main tool. It publishes the monthly *The American Forests*.

American Nuclear Energy Council
410 First St. SE
Washington, DC 20003
(202) 484-2670

The American Nuclear Energy Council supports the development of nuclear power as an energy source by coordinating and projecting the interests of the American nuclear industry to Congress and the Executive Branch, and relating congressional and executive actions to interested companies.

American Nuclear Society
555 N. Kensington Ave.
LaGrange Park, IL 60525
(312) 352-6611

The American Nuclear Society is a scientific, engineering, and education organization dedicated to the peaceful applications of nuclear science in a number of areas including energy, research, medicine, and industry. For the purpose of education, it publishes a number of books on nuclear issues.

Center for Environmental Education
624 Ninth St. NW
Washington, DC 20001
(202) 737-3600

The Center for Environmental Education, a marine conservation organization, works to protect whales, seals, sea turtles, and other endangered sea creatures from extinction.

Center for Environmental Information
33 S. Washington St.
Rochester, NY 14608
(716) 546-3796

The Center for Environmental Information is an unbiased organization which, through publications, educational programs, conferences, and its library, provides information about environmental issues.

Concerned Citizens for a Nuclear Breeder
PO Box 206
Ruffs Dale, PA 15679
(412) 722-5401

Concerned Citizens for a Nuclear Breeder maintains that in order to be independent of oil producing nations, America must keep the nuclear option open. It also compiles statistics and maintains a speaker's bureau. Its publications include the monthly *Newsclips* and a number of pamphlets.

The Conservation Foundation
1255 Twenty-third St. NW
Washington, DC 20037
(202) 293-4800

The Conservation Foundation is an environmental research organization which conducts interdisciplinary policy research on emerging issues in environmental and resource management. It is dedicated to improving the quality of the environment and to promoting wise use of the earth's resources. It publishes in-depth studies and the newsletter *Resolve.*

Critical Mass Energy Project
215 Pennsylvania Ave. SE
Washington, DC 20003
(202) 546-4996

The Critical Mass Energy Project has worked since 1974 to stop the growth of nuclear power, to make existing nuclear reactors less dangerous, and to promote safe and more efficient energy alternatives. The CMEP's approach to reaching these goals involves publicizing the problems associated with nuclear power, eliminating the need for future nuclear construction through efficient energy planning, and closing power plants presently under construction in the United States. The CMEP has assembled a considerable library of information on these subjects.

Department of the Interior
C St. NW
Washington, DC 20240
(202) 343-3171

The Department of the Interior, the nation's principal conservation agency, provides information about nationally owned public lands and natural resources.

Friends of the Earth
530 Seventh St. SE
Washington, DC 20003
(202) 543-4312

Friends of the Earth, founded in 1969, is a national and international environmental organization with twenty-four sister groups around the world. It is active in fighting for responsible energy development, sustainable agriculture, hydropower licensing reform, and many other international issues ranging from protection of rainforests to peace issues. It is committed to the preservation, restoration, and rational use of the ecosphere. It also publishes a newsmagazine, *Not Man Apart.*

The Health and Energy Institute
236 Massachusetts Ave. NE, #506
Washington, DC 20002
(202) 543-1070

The Health and Energy Institute is a research and education organization which advocates the preservation of a healthy environment, the wise use of energy resources and safe technologies, and the protection of human health and life. The Institute conducts research, produces reports and publications, organizes seminars and conferences, testifies before Congress and federal agencies, provides a speaker service, and maintains a small library.

The Nuclear Information and Resource Service
1616 P St. NW
Washington, DC 20036
(202) 328-0002

The Nuclear Information and Resource Service is a national organization working solely on nuclear power issues. It functions as an information clearinghouse about nuclear issues, assists citizens who want to take a more active part against nuclear power, monitors the state regulatory bodies and the nuclear industry, and provides the media with information and interpretations on nuclear issues. Its quarterly publication, *Groundswell,* is available to all members.

Nuclear Suppliers Association
c/o Baird Corporation
125 Middlesex Turnpike
Bedford, MA 01730
(617) 276-6204

The membership of the Nuclear Suppliers association is made up of companies involved in the manufacture or distribution of products and services for the nuclear industry. It serves to promote nuclear power and the interests of the industry.

People for Energy Progress
PO Box 777
Los Gatos, CA 95031
(408) 925-1967

People for Energy Progress advocates the development and implementation of an energy policy that permits continuing improvement of the standard of living of present and future generations. It does this through direct and active involvement in educational activities and public decision making. It is a non-partisan organization which works with, and promotes the development of, similar organizations.

Sierra Club
530 Bush St.
San Francisco, CA 94108
(415) 981-8634

Since 1892, the Sierra Club has been working to protect and conserve the natural resources of the Sierra Nevada, the United States, and the world. It publishes a weekly, the *National News Report*, a bimonthly, *Sierra*, and books and newsletters.

Southwest Research and Information Center
PO Box 4524
Albuquerque, NM 87106
(505) 262-1862

The Southwest Research and Information Center started with pollution issues in New Mexico and has worked since 1971 to identify sources of pollution and to find solutions to the problems facing that state. Among its national activities are providing information to a national network of people seeking to clean up uranium tailings, and coordinating a national effort for compensation of victims of radiation exposure from uranium mines. It publishes *The Workbook,* a quarterly environmental and social change journal.

STAPPA/ALAPCO
444 N. Capitol St. NW
Washington, DC 20001
(202) 624-7864

The State and Territorial Air Pollution Program Administrators (STAPPA) is the national association of state air quality officials in the fifty-four states and territories of the United States. The Association of Local Air Pollution Control Officials (ALAPCO) is the national association representing air pollution control officials in over 150 major metropolitan areas across the United States. The associations serve to encourage the exchange of information among air pollution control officials, to enhance communication among federal, state, and local regulatory agencies, and to promote good management of our air resources.

Union of Concerned Scientists
26 Church St.
Cambridge, MA 02238
(617) 547-5552

The Union of Concerned Scientists is an organization of scientists and other citizens concerned about the impact of advanced technology on society. It is a nationally respected advocate of arms control and safe energy. The UCS conducts independent research, sponsors and participates in conferences and panels, and testifies at congressional and regulatory hearings. The UCS publishes a quarterly newsletter, *Nucleus,* as well as books, reports, and briefing papers.

Bibliography of Books

F.E. Armbruster et al.   *A Perspective on Current Acid Rain Issues.* Croton-on-Hudson, NY: Hudson Institute, 1983.

Wildrid Bach   *Our Threatened Climate: Ways of Averting the CO_2 Problem.* Hingham, MA: Reidel, 1984.

Donald Barlett and James B. Steele   *Forevermore: Nuclear Waste in America.* New York: W.W. Norton & Company, 1985.

Michael C. Barth and James G. Titus, eds.   *Greenhouse Effect and Sea Level Rise: A Challenge for this Generation.* New York: Van Nostrand Reinhold Company, 1984.

John Berger   *Restoring the Earth: How Americans Are Working To Renew Our Damaged Environment.* New York: Alfred A. Knopf Inc., 1985.

Alan A. Block and Frank R. Scarpitti   *Poisoning for Profit: The Mafia and Toxic Waste in America.* New York: William Morrow and Company, 1985.

Michael Brown   *Laying Waste: The Poisoning of America by Toxic Chemicals.* New York: Pantheon Books, 1979.

D. Brunner, W. Miller and N. Stockholm   *Corporations and the Environment: How Should Decisions Be Made?* Stanford, CA: Committee on Corporate Responsibility, 1981.

Rachel Carson   *Silent Spring.* Boston: Houghton Mifflin Company, 1962.

Bernard Cohen   *Before It's Too Late: A Scientist's Case for Nuclear Energy.* New York: Da Capo Press, Inc., 1983.

Edith Efron   *The Apocalyptics: Cancer and the Big Lie.* New York: Simon and Schuster, 1984.

Larry Everest   *Behind the Poison Cloud: Union Carbide's Bhopal Massacre.* Chicago: Banner Press, 1983.

Karl Grossman   *The Poison Conspiracy.* Sag Harbor, NY: The Permanent Press, 1983.

W.H. Hartford   *Acid Rain—Some Dissenting Views.* Belmont, NC: Belmont Abbey College, 1980.

J.A. Heppenheimer — *The Man-Made Sun: The Quest for Fusion Power.* Boston: Little, Brown, and Company, 1984.

Jane H. Ives — *The Export of Hazard: Transnational Corporations and Environmental Control Issues.* San Francisco: Routledge & Kegan, Paul, 1986.

Petra Kelly — *Fighting for Hope.* Boston: South End Press, 1984.

James B. Lester and Anne O'M. Bowen, eds. — *The Politics of Hazardous Waste Management.* Durham, NC: Duke University Press, 1983.

Amory B. Lovins and L. Hunter Lovins — *Energy/War: Breaking the Nuclear Link.* San Francisco: Friends of the Earth, 1980.

Jon Luoma — *Troubled Skies, Troubled Waters: The Story of Acid Rain.* New York: Viking Press, 1984.

Samuel McCracken — *The War Against the Atom: The Overwhelming Case for Nuclear Power and Against the Groups and Individuals Who Continue To Fight It.* New York: Basic Books, Inc., 1982.

National Swedish Environment Protection Board — *Acidification: A Boundless Threat to Our Environment.* Solna, Sweden: Swedish Ministry of Agriculture, 1983.

Stanley M. Nealey et al. — *Public Opinion and Nuclear Energy.* Lexington, MA: D.C. Heath and Company, 1983.

Karl O. Ott and Bernard I. Spinred — *Nuclear Energy: A Sensible Alternative.* New York: Plenum Press, 1985.

Daniel Poneman — *Nuclear Power in the Developing World.* Boston: George Allen and Unwin, 1982.

Robert W. Poole Jr. — *Instead of Regulation: Alternatives to Federal Regulatory Agencies.* Lexington, MA: D.C. Heath and Company, 1982.

Jonathan Porritt — *Seeing Green: The Politics of Ecology Explained.* New York: Basil Blackwell, 1986.

Frank A. Record et al. — *Acid Rain Information Book.* Park Ridge, NJ: Noyes Data Corporation, 1982.

Walter A. Rosenbaum — *Environmental Politics and Policy.* Washington, DC: Congressional Quarterly Press, 1984.

Kirkpatrick Sale   *Dwellers in the Land: The Bioregional Vision.* San Francisco: Sierra Club Books, 1986.

Thomas C. Schelling, ed.   *Incentives for Environmental Protection.* Cambridge, MA: The MIT Press, 1983.

D. Scherer and T. Attig, eds.   *Ethics and the Environment.* Englewood Cliffs, NJ: Prentice-Hall, 1983.

Julian L. Simon and Herman Kahn   *The Resourceful Earth: A Response to Global 2000.* New York: Basil Blackwell, 1984.

Ian Smart, ed.   *World Nuclear Energy: Toward a Bargain of Confidence.* Baltimore: Johns Hopkins University Press, 1982.

Richard L. Stroup and John A. Baden   *Natural Resources: Bureaucratic Myths and Environmental Management.* Cambridge, MA: Ballinger Publishing Company, 1983.

Serge Taylor   *Making Bureaucrats Think: The Environmental Impact Statement Strategy of Administrative Reform.* Stanford, CA: Stanford University Press, 1984.

Carol Van Strum   *A Bitter Fog: Herbicides and Human Rights.* San Francisco: Sierra Club Books, 1983.

Gregory S. Wetstone and Armin Rosencranz   *Acid Rain in Europe and North America.* Washington, DC: Environmental Law Institute, 1983.

Joseph A. Yager   *International Cooperation in Nuclear Energy.* Washington, DC: The Brookings Institution, 1981.

Index

proves danger of nuclear
power, 163
Claybrook, Joan, 88
Clean Air Act (1963, 1970), 21,
37, 243
provisions of, 102-103, 107, 108
Club of Rome, 18, 27
Conrad, Paul, 18, 164
Council on Environmental
Quality, 31
Cousteau, Jacques, 190, 201
Cowen, Robert C., 177

Danziger, Jeff, 235
Davies, J. Clarence, 94
Davis, William, 214, 231
Delaney, James J., 175
Dobbins, 33
Doll, Richard, 194

Earth Day, 34, 37
The Economist, 155
Ehrlich, Paul, 27, 190
Englehart, Bob, 146
Engler, Robert, 77
the environment
corporate responsibility for
cleaning, 122-126
critical issues in, 20-23
economic incentive should
regulate, 98-99
government regulation of
agencies for, 91, 94-95
benefits to consumers of,
92-93
cost to consumers of, 30, 31
cost to industry of, 30-31,
103-104
failure of, 110-111, 113-114
history of, 101-103, 106-108
is ineffective, 99
is necessary, 88-96, 105-108,
125-126
is unnecessary, 97-104
opposition to, 89-90
by corporations, 91-92
public support for, 95-96
should be improved, 115-120
should be privatized, 109-114
successes of, 92, 107
economists' inability to
measure, 95

public ignorance of, 93-94
increased awareness of, 37
individual's responsibility for,
99-100
is in crisis, 16-23
myth of, 24-28
proportions of, 19
role of consumer in, 38-39,
61-65
role of industry in, 38-39,
55-60, 66-69
role of the US in, 17-18
see also acid rain; greenhouse
effect; nuclear power;
nuclear waste; pollution;
population explosion;
resources; toxic chemicals
environmental disasters
compared to highway
accidents, 71-72
corporate profit from, 56, 68
corporate responsibility for,
55-60, 66-69
extent of, 67
government regulations to
prevent, 72
risks are exaggerated, 70-72
see also Chernobyl accident;
Union Carbide: Bhopal
accident of
Environmental Protection Agency
(EPA)
and acid rain, 225
and air pollution, 102-103, 108
and the greenhouse effect, 41
and toxic chemicals, 56, 68, 89,
116
and water pollution, 102, 108
cost of, 31, 34, 62
creation of, 34, 101
review of pesticides, 60
environmentalists
goals of, 37, 38
have improved the
environment, 35-39
myth of, 29-34
Epstein, Samuel S., 174, 194

Feiffer, Jules, 68
Food and Agriculture
Organization (FAO), 22, 23
Friedman, Milton, 61, 63, 65